❦   A LIFE WELL LED   ❧

# A LIFE WELL LED
The Biography of Barbara Freire-Marreco Aitken
British Anthropologist

## Mary Ellen Blair

SUNSTONE
PRESS

SANTA FE

Sunstone books may be purchased for educational, business, or sales promotional use.
For information please write: Special Markets Department, Sunstone Press,
P.O. Box 2321, Santa Fe, New Mexico 87504-2321.

Cover: Barbara Freire-Marreco in 1910. Photograph cropped from Neg. No. 81918.
Book and cover design by Vicki Ahl        Printed on acid free paper
Typeface—Goudy Old Style

---

Library of Congress Cataloging-in-Publication Data

Blair, Mary Ellen.
  A life well led : the biography of Barbara Freire-Marreco Aitken, British anthropologist /
by Mary Ellen Blair.
      p. cm.
  Includes bibliographical references.
  ISBN 978-0-86534-496-9 (softcover : alk. paper)
  1.  Freire-Marreco, Barbara W. (Barbara Whitchurch), 1879-1967. 2.  Indianists--Great
Britain--Biography. 3.  Women Indianists--Great Britain--Biography. 4.  Anthropologists--
Great Britain--Biography. 5.  Women anthropologists--Great Britain--Biography. 6.  Indians
of North America--Southwest, New--Antiquities. I. Title.

E57.F74B53 2008
979.004'97--dc22
[B]
                                    2007049893

---

Published in

**WWW.SUNSTONEPRESS.COM**
SUNSTONE PRESS / POST OFFICE BOX 2321 / SANTA FE, NM 87504-2321 /USA
(505) 988-4418 / ORDERS ONLY (800) 243-5644 / FAX (505) 988-1025

Dedicated to Larry Blair, my late husband,
who inspired this publication and did much of the research with me.

# CONTENTS

Barbara Freire-Marreco in 1910. Photograph cropped from Neg. No. 81918.
Courtesy of the Palace of the Governors MNM/DCA.

# ❧ PREFACE ❧

Research on the history of Southwest American Indian art can take one to many places in the world, beyond the United States, including continental Europe and Great Britain, where there are rich fields to explore. Early European archaeologists, ethnologists and anthropologists who investigated and studied Native Americans from the middle of the nineteenth and in the early twentieth century, were often better trained and more experienced than their American counterparts, usually returning to their mother countries taking their knowledge, photographs, and specimens with them.

At that time, scientists, artists and fortune seekers from central Europe, Scandinavia and Britain began exporting "Indian" collections, as well as scientific papers describing their studies of Native American cultures, to deposit in overseas archives. In time, the export of some artifact collections became so extensive as to cause alarm that the United States might soon be drained of much of its historic treasures. As a result, legislation was eventually enacted to stifle this exodus.

Many of these collections have little documentation with field notes, and associated records are often difficult to locate, both in Europe and the United States. This situation was brought about primarily by World Wars I and II, with their accompanying destruction, looting and dislocation of both archives and antiquities.

Of great assistance to researchers investigating these collections as they existed in 1967 was Wilma R. Kaemlein's *An Inventory of Southwestern American Indian Specimens in European Museums* published by the Arizona State Museum, University of Arizona. This remarkable catalog provides rewarding assistance to those interested in exploring the writings and collections of those early foreigners who visited the Southwest United States. It was Kaemlein's work that aroused my curiosity about Barbara Freire-Marreco Aitken, leading to this publication.

Following Kaemlein's lead describing Tewa and Hopi-Tewa pottery held in the collection of Oxford University's Pitt Rivers Museum of Anthropology and Museum Ethnography, I discovered interesting Native American artifacts collected by Barbara Freire-Marreco between 1910 and 1913. How rewarding to find correspondence and documentation! The materials she collected and donated were unique for the early twentieth century. This provided bait for a researcher and lead to my desire to learn more about this British investigator.

Although she is mentioned in the anthropological and ethnological literature, her contributions have not been fully recognized and they are more voluminous than expected. Adding to my intrigue was the idea of a well-educated young English woman, brought up in proper Victorian fashion and enforced Church of England's doctrines of that time, taking off alone for the wilds of Indian country, U.S.A. in 1910!

It is the intention here to document Barbara Freire-Marreco Aitken's character and life and explore some of her investigations, emphasizing her adventures in the United States. Her correspondence that recorded facts as well as her reactions to Native people and their cultures is the focus.

Information gleaned from helpful and generous archivists and curators at the Pitt Rivers Museum revealed other sources at Oxford University. The Bodleian Library files and records, Lady Margaret Hall and Somerville College all provided information about her work and associates. This established a framework for investigation, leading to sources in the Smithsonian Institution and other museums, as well as universities in the United States.

Freire-Marreco's records of Native American life and her contribution to Indian welfare at the beginning of the last century deserve to be credited and given more recognition than previously documented. Had it not been for two World Wars, a happy and successful marriage to a husband with other interests, her contribution would probably have been far greater. Undoubtedly she was also held back by some discrimination against English women who attempted to make their way in academic circles.

This account of Freire-Marreco Aitken's life and American experiences, mostly in her words, is told through her notes, unedited writings, correspondence, legal records, collections and documented photographs as well as the recollections of those who knew this remarkable woman. Her words are left as she wrote them as much as possible and comments are made only when necessary for clarity and continuity. Information, now common knowledge to the student of Pueblo cultures, is included to credit her original work. The material selected, over a period of more than ten years, was judged to be of interest to most readers.

Visiting the homes in which she lived, finding correspondence and legal documents and investigating other archives, both in England and the United States, was rewarding and in turn led to my locating and interviewing people who remembered her. These included two elderly Tewas, one who lived atop First Mesa on the Hopi Reservation in Arizona and another at Santa Clara Pueblo in New Mexico. Residents in the village of Broughton, for years her home in Hampshire, were hospitable and informative, particularly her personal physician and a housekeeper/companion who both attended Barbara Aitken for the last thirty years of her life. Her nephew and godson, Anthony Marreco, provided much insight regarding her family life, personality and character. Undoubtedly a strong willed person, she was a caring, sympathetic, understanding, articulate and unobtrusive investigator, contributing to the knowledge and understanding of some Native American tribes.

One of Freire-Marreco's most impressive talents was her linguistic ability. The ease with which she could learn languages was demonstrated by her mastering enough Greek in six weeks to pass Oxford University's admission examination. Fluent in German, French, and Spanish, she also acquired a working knowledge of Russian as well as understanding some Oriental languages. Early in her American stay, she learned some Tewa language allowing her, as she lived with Native people, to understand much of what was being said, thus providing an opportunity to record what was going on around her without prying. Her extensive English vocabulary produced straightforward writing.

She translated Tewa into Spanish and then English, thus helping nine New Mexico pueblos clarify their government structures in order to seek help from the United States government in enforcing their already existing laws. She understood enough of the Yavapai language to assist some Arizona Native people with legal proceedings, concerning water rights, during a brief stay at Fort McDowell.

Fortunately, Barbara Freire-Marreco Aitken's hand writing is easily read. Fountain pens of the day were scratchy and leaky, but she refused to master the primitive and crude typewriters of the time. There are omissions where print has become illegible because the age of the document has taken a toll or when the information was irrelevant.

In documenting her writing, accuracy was of prime importance. Content determined sequence and continuity was judged to be more important than chronological order. Punctuation was changed only to clarify meaning and quotations are in italics. Phonetic Native languages are not recorded because there are many repetitions and few readers would understand or find them useful, but they are available in the original documents. British spelling has been Americanized. Further it should be noted that after Barbara Freire-Marreco's marriage in 1920, she signed her letters Barbara Aitken.

This is not meant to be a scientific dissertation. It is rather, a non-fiction adventure story of a life well led and under-documented.

# ❧ CREDITS ☙

This project could not have been completed without the generous and diligent assistance of many individuals and institutions. In alphabetical order many thanks are due:

Anthony Marreco
Arizona Historical Foundation, Tempe
Arizona Historical Society, Tucson
Bob Blair
Brooklyn Museum of Art
Broughton nr. Stockbridge, Hampshire, England town residents:
　　Mrs. Ethel Davis, Mrs. June Dawkins, Mrs. Joan Frampton,
　　Dr. and Mrs. Robert Parr, Mrs. Sugden, and Mrs. Joy Yates
Denver Art Museum, Douglas Library
Dozier, Marianne and Anya Dozier Enos
Guildford High School for Girls, Surrey
Harvard University: Tozzer Library and Peabody Museum of
　　Archaeology and Ethnology
Museum of New Mexico: Palace of the Governors, Fray Angelico
　　Chavez History Library, Photographic Archives and Laboratory
　　of Anthropology
New Mexico State Records Center and Archives, Santa Fe

Record Offices in England: General Register St. Catherine's House, London; Hampshire Record Office, Swiss Cottage Library, Hampstead; Surrey Record Office, Kingston upon Thames; and Winchester Hall of Records

School of Advanced Research, Santa Fe, originally School of American Archaeology

Smithsonian Institution: National Museum of Natural History, National Anthopological Archives, including the former Bureau of American Ethnology, and National Museum of the American Indian, Heye Foundation, Washington and NY

United States Department of the Interior, Bureau of the American Indian

University of Arizona, Arizona State Museum

University of California, Berkeley, Bancroft Library

University of Cambridge, Museum of Archaeology and Anthropology

University of Liverpool, Sidney Jones Library

University of New Mexico: Maxwell Museum of Anthropology, Zimmerman Library and Southwest Research Center, Albuquerque

University of Oxford: (Barnett House) Department of Social Policy and Social Work, Bodleian Library Department of Special Collections and WesternManuscripts, Lady Margaret Hall College, Pitt Rivers School of Anthropology and Museum Ethnography, and Somerville College

AND the Tewa and Hopi-Tewa people who verified photographs, reminisced about their forbears, recalling times past.

—Mary Ellen Blair

# ❧ PROLOGUE ❧

June 1910 in the New Mexico Territory. The young English woman stepped off the train at Lamy, sixteen miles southeast of the historic and fabled city of Santa Fe. She was entering another world. Gone was the soft English countryside of her childhood, behind her now the teeming cities of Philadelphia, Washington, D.C., and Chicago where she had been introduced to leading anthropologists, further preparing her for American fieldwork. As the Atcheson, Topeka and Santa Fe Railroad steamed from Chicago along the cornfields of Kansas and nearing the mountains of Colorado, the close, hilly Eastern countryside of oaks and maples yielded to sweeping vistas of the Rocky Mountains studded with aspen and pine. Her train ticket told only part of the story, only the last four days. Actually, she had come all the way from the hallowed halls of Lady Margaret Hall College at Oxford University. Her diploma read "anthropology" and her young career was being launched in the New Mexico Territory.

*There is so little time to write a decent letter,* she wrote her sponsor at Somerville College in Oxford a few days later from Santa Fe. *If anyone is kind enough to want to hear of me, perhaps you will show it to them too, asking them to excuse the roughness of it. Four days on the train and mountain air at the end does make you so sleepy.* (University of Oxford, Somerville College Library, Darbishire file, 26 June 1910. Hereafter cited as Somerville, Darbishire) Not to mention the high altitude, for Santa Fe was 7,000 feet high, higher than mile-high Denver. But the respite was not to last. A week after her arrival she would leave Santa Fe for a strenuous summer's work.

The roughest part was still ahead. Quitting Santa Fe for an excavation site in Indian lands, there came eighteen miles on the slow and jerky "Chile Line," a narrow-gauge railroad climbing the hills northwest of Santa Fe. After a dust-choking foray through juniper and chamisa-dotted countryside and nut-bearing pinon trees, the train arrived at the abandoned Buckman lumber camp on the edge of the Rio Grande. After crossing the river, the team of anthropologists assembled their goods and mounted horses. Climbing to the Pajarito Plateau by a primitive, rocky trail, they passed over the wooded mesa to the rim of Frijoles Canyon, one of five fingers of canyons whose rivers fed the Rio Grande.

Barbara Freire-Marreco must have questioned her commitment. Summer heat was building even at the Plateau's high altitude of 8,000 feet. She probably peered down to the canyon floor, where the next weeks would be spent at Edgar Lee Hewett's "Summer School" for archaeologists, attending lectures and performing excavations at Tyuoni, a large circular ruin in the mid-valley as well as exchanging ideas with fellow students and becoming acquainted with some local Native people. She would be exposed to different cultures, very unlike her own.

🌿 🌿 🌿

In 1910 the 20th century was new and fresh. Yet to come were the horrendous events of the Titanic's loss, the Great War, and the 1918 influenza epidemic. Innocence and optimism still bolstered the English spirit, comforted as it was by the social progress achieved in recent years toward the poor, the disadvantaged, the displaced peoples of the Empire.

Although Queen Victoria had departed the throne a scant nine years earlier, her heritage of cautious propriety lived on. So did the English spirit of adventure and curiosity about other cultures, other lands. The empire-building of Victorian England had transformed into a cultural exploration of prehistoric art, as discovered in the pyramids of Egypt, the archaeological digs in the Holy Land, and the scarcely known Indian villages of the American Southwest.

Perhaps it was the lure of distant lands untouched by cynical politics that had inspired and guided the conventional young British woman, trained in the English tradition, to journey beyond home boundaries in search of strange cultures. More likely, it was the opportunity to study social systems not yet intensely investigated by her peers.

Whatever the driving motivation, her survival both professional and personal, demanded high intelligence, curiosity and courage. Freire-Marreco's letters reveal the mind set of such a woman who pursued an unconventional life and left a legacy largely unwritten except in Pueblo memory.

# THE EARLY YEARS

Not far from London's Kew Gardens on December 11, 1879 Barbara Whitchurch Freire-Marreco was born. Queen Victoria reigned, still only two-thirds of the way through her 64-year tenure. Political and social changes were afoot, and 1879 was an auspicious year. Thomas Edison demonstrated the first practical incandescent light bulb, paving the way for the world's shift to cheap electric light. The Chicago Art Institute was founded and the first milk bottles appeared in Brooklyn, New York, ending the use of barrels and pitchers. In England, Thomas Lipton's grocery store chain made him a millionaire.

But the world was struggling with political turmoil, social unrest, and agricultural failures. Wars in Chile, Bolivia and Zululand destabilized the status quo. Britain had its worst wheat harvest of the century. Ireland's potato crop failed again, as it had in 1846, and India suffered a crop loss further ravaged by rats after a meager harvest. And far out in the American West, the last of the Southern bison herd was killed by U.S. hunters at Buffalo Springs, Texas.

Into this rapidly shifting world of the Industrial Revolution, the new baby arrived at 4 Park Villas West, on Queen's Road, Richmond. On the birth certificate, her father, Walter Freire-Marreco, listed his occupation as a public accountant. The family viewed the man as something of a tyrant, an impression that lived on in the recollections of his grandson Anthony

Marreco many years later. It appears young Barbara, apparently the favored child, turned this parental domination into a means of avoiding situations in which she did not wish to become involved, using her father's rules as excuses.

Most of the Freire-Marrecos were blond and blue eyed British subjects, but Barbara's paternal grandfather had been Portuguese, probably accounting for her uncharacteristic dark hair and eyes and aquiline nose. Freire was their original Portuguese surname; Marreco was added by the grandfather after a trip to Brazil at a time when it was popular there to add names of flowers and birds, Marreco being a type of duck.

Gertrude Blechynden Waggett, Barbara's mother, had married Walter Freire-Marreco that year of 1879. The Waggetts were locally regarded as a family of intellect. Gertrude's brother, Philip Waggett S.S.J.E., a member of the Society of St. John the Evangelist, a high teaching order of the Anglican Church akin to the Jesuits, was also known as an enthusiastic natural scientist. He served as an army chaplain during World War I, Military Governor of Jerusalem, and as vicar to the churches of St. Mary the Great in Cambridge and All Saints Church on Margaret Street in London during his career. No doubt this uncle, with whom Barbara had a close relationship, had a great influence on the intellectual and spiritual development of his niece.

Another illustrious relative was Marriott Whitchurch (honored in Barbara's middle name), a great uncle from her mother's family, a barrister, and evidently a gentleman of some means, from whom Barbara inherited a cherished Georgian sterling silver tea service. His wealth must have been important to his fellow brethren in London who had him moved from Bournmoth, when he was near death, back to London to insure their inheritance of some of his fortune.

Barbara's brother, Geoffrey Algernon, was the only sibling to grow to adulthood. An unidentified animosity developed between sister and brother that lasted for decades and was not resolved until in their later years a tearful hugging reunion took place.

A properly posed undated photograph of Walter and Gertrude Blechynden
Freire-Marreco, Barbara's parents. Graham's New Studio, Leamington, England.
Courtesy of Anthony Marreco.

Geoffrey married Hilda Gwendolyn Francis and they in turn
had a son, Anthony Blechynden Freire-Marreco, Barbara's nephew and
godson. One of the executors of his aunt's will, he inherited her house.
For simplicity Anthony dropped the Freire from the family name, was of
great help to this publication with family information and died in 2006. A
remarkable person in his own right, he served his country as a barrister at

the Nuremberg trials following World War II and was a moving force behind Amnesty International, a cause his Aunt Barbara heartily supported due to her interest in, and efforts to protect, the rights of subjugated people.

🦋 🦋 🦋

Young Barbara grew up at Potter's Croft on Albany Road, Horsell, in the town of Woking, located in Surrey to the southwest of London and much of her early correspondence bears the Albany Road heading. As it was then, Woking still is a commercial town on a main rail line, heavily bombed during World War II. In rebuilding the town, whole sections were reconfigured. Potter's Croft no longer exists, and Albany Street is gone.

Not much is known of Barbara's early childhood. From available records and her correspondence, it was clear the family was devoted to the Church of England as well as to intellectual pursuits. Her letters indicate she was a loving and considerate daughter. She had an inquisitive mind, and to her parents' credit they encouraged her intellectual curiosity at a time when it was not always highly valued in young women. At the tender age of seven she composed a poem.

*First Attempt*

*A stone lay on a road.*
*Inside it sat a toad.*
*He had been there for hundreds of years,*
*As he now lamented with tears.*

—Aitken, Barbara Whitchurch. *Verses, 1886 to 1953.*
Blair Collection. Hereafter cited as Aitken, *Verses*

Potter's Croft, Albany Road, Horsell, Woking, Surrey. The Freire-Marreco's attractive and spacious home where Barbara grew up. Sold in 1921, it was destroyed during World War II. Courtesy of Anthony Marreco.

In the last era of Victoria's reign when Barbara was growing up, English girls were expected to become submissive housewives and mothers, and their education stressed etiquette rather than substantial intellectual achievement. During her lifetime Barbara would have been considered a woman's liberation advocate for her radical departure from the conventional model of a compliant housewife. Yet throughout her life she remained devoted to the Anglican Church, and her last known publication is a tribute to Christian ways.

A movement toward feminine emancipation through education progressed slowly at the end of the nineteenth century. Previously, daughters of middle or upper class parents had been educated by domestic tutors and in exclusive private schools, called "Ladies' Academies." A pupil's daily round included sewing, singing, conversational French, drawing, and a lunch-time walk in an orderly line wearing the prescribed hats and gloves.

Undated photograph of young Barbara Freire-Marreco, already looking bright, quite serious and determined. G. T. Jones and Co., Kingston on Thames.
Courtesy of Anthony Marreco.

However, women's education in late Victorian times gradually began to change, and for the first time colleges for women were established. Secondary schools thus became needed to provide a sound academic background to prepare girls for university study. The Church Schools Company, established in 1883, was formed to meet these needs. Eventually there were seven institutions in this organization scattered throughout England, and one of the seven was the Guildford High School for Girls in Surrey established in 1888. The goal from its inception was *Christian kindness, toleration, academic integrity and generosity of mind and resources* as was stated in the publication **The First Hundred Years**, by Howard Bails, head of history at the school in 1988.

Guildford High School for Girls in Surrey where Barbara Freire-Marreco obtained her secondary education. Much has changed since it was established in 1883 to meet its growing needs, but the old gymnasium, used when she was a student, remains. 1987 photograph by L. Blair.

Guildford High School affirmed that Barbara Freire-Marreco had registered as its 204th pupil in September 1893. The fee of just over four guineas (less than fifty dollars) covered one semester. An article from the **Surrey Times** from the school files and undated described Prize Days. Among those present at one such Prize Day were Mr. and Mrs. Freire-Marreco, and their daughter was mentioned as distinguishing herself in several subjects in *the higher forms of French and the viva voce examination.* She also won *a second prize in upper Form V with a Cambridge certificate* given by the Church Schools Company as well as *honor certificates in Division II Drawing examination.* In Fourth Form she earned *first prizes for Shakespeare and Literature and Divinity.* It was evident to all that young Barbara was an excellent scholar of great promise and had a unique and interesting turn of mind. At the age of fifteen she wrote a poem for the Guildford High School Magazine.

*School-room Wit—<u>The Yacht and the Poet</u>*

*A poet sat upon a snow-white deck*
*Just as a gentle swell began to rise,*
*But little of the pitching did he reck*
*While in "fine frenzy" rolled his speaking eyes.*
*"How very fine a sailor's life must be*
*Far, far from babes that scream and doors that slam!*
*An ode is just occurring unto me.*
*I think I'll dedicate it <u>AD Nautam</u>."*
*The poet's friend remarked his dreamy state –*
*Stared—fidgeted awhile—and scratched his head,*
*And after holding with himself debate,*
*He cleared his bashful throat and mildly said: -*
*"Might it not be <u>Ad Nauseum</u>, don't you know?"*
*The poet took the hint—and went below!*

(ibid. 1894)

# PREPARATION FOR A CAREER

After graduation from High School, Barbara attended Lady Margaret Hall College, University of Oxford from 1902 to 1905. Her father's permission for her move to Oxford was initially difficult to obtain because of his conservative views, but after proving herself by learning enough Greek in six weeks to gain entrance, he succumbed to her wish to be resident at the University. Continuing her distinguished academic progress, she received the Sedgwick Latin prize in 1904 and a year later had completed the requirements for a diploma in Classics with honors in Greek and Latin.

While still in her formative years trying to determine a direction for her life, in 1905 she wrote a play titled *"Flowers in the Garden:" an Infant Operetta performed by School children at Bishopthorpe before the Archbishop of York*, (ibid. 1905) but what inspired this production is a mystery. It was probably considered appropriate theatrical material for young English children at the beginning of the twentieth century. Relating, in verse, a day in the life of a chorus of flowers who were visited by a butterfly, a bee, and a gardener and involving sun, rain, and seasons of the year—it was indeed a very flowery production!

An archway, typical of the architecture of Lady Margaret Hall, University of Oxford. Here Freire-Marreco completed her undergraduate work and started making lifelong professional relationships. 1989 photograph by J. Blair.

Her earliest correspondence was located at the University of Oxford's Bodleian Library. Dated 1906, it contained an exchange between Barbara Freire-Marreco and John Myres, who became her advisor and mentor. Sir John Linton Myres, 1869-1954, was a leading British archaeologist, anthropologist, ethnologist and historian of repute though not as well known in the United States as in his own country. Among many other accomplishments, he was Wykeham professor of Classics in Oxford.

He held a chair of Classical Literature at the University of Liverpool at one time, and served as a president of the Royal Anthropological Institute of Great Britain and Ireland, inaugurating the publication *Man* of that society. Contributing in both World Wars, he also inspired students with his generosity and kindness. He was one of the first mentors in anthropology and related subjects.

John Linton Myres, distinguished British archaeologist, historian, ethnologist and anthropologist, who more than any other promoted and influenced Freire-Marreco's career. Reproduced by permission of Barbara Williams, daughter of the photographer Walter Benington. Courtesy of University of Oxford, Bodleian Library, Room 132 Duke Humphreys Library, MS Myres 16.

Myres relationship with Freire-Marreco was formed when she was an undergraduate at Lady Margaret Hall, studying under his tutelage. He became interested in furthering her career, and though her early letters reveal her naivete, he saw a determined young woman with an eager mind that reached in many directions. More than any other he furthered her career.

❧ ❧ ❧

Prejudices against women in the academic world were widespread in the early 1900s, perhaps more in England than the United States. With few exceptions, teaching as a profession on an advanced level was seldom available to women. Freire-Marreco's education and abilities could have been wasted if not utilized, and there was little choice for ambitious women. She was interested in languages and cultures and the related sciences pointing the way to anthropology, pursuing other avenues only when she had a specific financial need. Funds were not available from her family after college so she needed to be subsidized. It was evident she sought a situation that would provide a means to meet her requirements. She looked to the most obvious and important connection she had in Oxford, Professor Myres.

The first letter found from Freire-Marreco to Myres was written shortly after she left Lady Margaret Hall and is a request to Myres for guidance. Always polite, as was her practice, there was first an apology for troubling him and then thanking him for past kindnesses. Of particular interest, it pointed to a professional direction she wished to pursue. She was aware of the availability of such a possibility and with courtesy asked for permission to give his name as a reference. *I want to apply for the Somerville College Research Fellowship; it is tenable for three years, the holder must pursue some line of study approved by the Council, and publish the results, if they desire it, at the end of her time. A scheme of work and the names of three persons willing to testify to the candidate's qualificatons must be sent in before May 7th. The line I wish to take up is European, the origin of Tragedy.*

Somerville College buildings, University of Oxford, one of the primary institutions where Freire-Marreco studied, received grants for international research, and maintained association with all of her professional life. 1989 photograph by J. Blair.

She then references Sir William Ridgeway, 1853-1926, a British Classical scholar of repute who was a Professor of Greek at University College, Cork, and Disney Professor of Archaeology at Cambridge University. His publications include those on early life in the Mediterranean area, thoroughbred horses and the origin of tragedy. *You will remember that Professor Ridgeway read a paper at the Hellenic Society in May 1904, maintaining the connection of tragedy with the cult of the dead. I should like to re-examine the classical evidence and look for more, but especially to carry the idea much further and try to establish a European history for the really dramatic part of Tragedy. As far as I am concerned, the idea is original.* (University of Oxford, Bodleian Library, Room 132 Duke Humphreys Library, Myres file, 30 Apr 1906. Hereafter cited as Bodleian, Myres)

William Ridgeway of the University of Cambridge. A classical scholar, professor
of Greek and archaelology, and an outstanding educator of his day, though very
conservative. Courtesy of Cambridge University Museum of Archaeology and Anthropology,
No. 54.

Unknowingly Freire-Marreco had blundered in her choice of subject and even more, by inadvertently setting up a conflict with a potentially dangerous academic giant. It appeared that Professor Ridgeway thought he was covering the subject adequately in his forthcoming publication. He also was a member of the Council that approved or eliminated candidates for Somerville College Fellowships, a fact that perhaps accounted for subsequent events concerning Freire-Marreco's fellowship application. He was opposed to granting degrees to women as well as the abolition of compulsory study of Greek.

On learning of her blunder, she wrote again to Myres, her advisor: *I fear that I have made a serious mistake in sending in my scheme.*

A little clarity came from Jane Ellen Harrison of Somerville College, Oxford who shared a letter she had received from Professor Ridgeway with Freire-Marreco, a letter that revealed his conviction on his theorem. Harrison, 1850-1928, who had a passion for all languages and lectured on Greek art primarily at the British Museum, was considered a liberated woman in Victorian times and was probably on the Selection Committee of the Research Fellowship.

*Miss Harrison*, said Freire-Marreco to Myres, *writes enclosing a letter from Professor Ridgeway to herself, in which he says that he has worked out the origin of Tragedy not merely for Greece but for the world; that it forms a substantial section of his forthcoming Volume II of Early Age of Greece; that it was the chief work he did last summer and autumn, and that but for family affairs he would have already published a full paper embodying the results of his investigations, which indeed he proposes to do shortly. He adds that he is naturally unwilling to see his ideas developed and published by an outsider.*

*Please be so very kind as to tell me what you think the proper thing for me to do. To withdraw my application for the fellowship explaining that I supposed that the line I meant to take was not covered by Professor Ridgeway, and that the ideas were original as far as I knew?*

Freire-Marreco suggested plans to continue independently with this study without interfering with Ridgeway's work, perhaps filling in details after his book was published. (ibid. 10 May 1906)

Myres replied: *Miss Harrison says it is quite clear that Professor Ridgeway wishes to reserve the matter for his own publication. As soon as his Volume II is out, which I believe will be this autumn, it will of course be open to you to pursue the subject further and you may supply many missing links. For a fellowship treatise I should think it might be wise to select another subject.* (ibid. 10 May 1906)

The speed of mail delivery in 1906 is impressive. In a letter bearing the same date, Myres obviously is quick to respond to Freire-Marreco's request on how to proceed, and indeed he gave her good advice. He very clearly explained how the system worked and advised her to give more detailed information on how she planned to use the fellowship regarding her request. Also interesting are his remarks about Ridgeway, intimating his opinion about a colleague without specifics. *Professor Ridgeway is indeed to be congratulated if he has really worked out the subject of tragedy; and his Volume II will be very different from Volume I if it closes any question which is open now. If you do not mind being content with the crumbs which fall from the Cambridge man's table, I should say by all means continue your researches both before, and still more after, he has had his fill. He can only take it as a compliment to his own work, that it has suggested useful work to other students of the subject.*

*As to the matter of offering this subject for the Somerville Fellowship, I think we must suppose that both Miss Harrison and Professor Ridgeway are judging the practice here by the Cambridge practice of awarding a Fellowship on the strength of a fellowship thesis or dissertation written out and sent in by the candidate as evidence of work already done.* Freire-Marreco had not done this.

*This is the more likely, as such dissertations are sometimes required to be printed without delay; and if this were the case in this instance there would obviously be a risk of your thesis being published before Professor Ridgeway's book was out; and this might conceivably take the wind out of his sails. But under the actual circumstances of the Somerville Fellowship, I do not see that there is any need to take any steps to alter your program. If you care to send a supplementary letter to Somerville to say that since making your former application you have learned that Professor Ridgeway has a work on the subject nearly ready, and that you will have to be guided by the nature of his results, as to the precise direction in which your own subsequent researches are directed, you will only be saying that it is obvious in any case what you would do; but it might possibly be considered an evidence of common sense and acquaintance with the lie of the land. It is not in the least necessary. Somerville probably has its own means of information about Professor Ridgeway's plans, if it thinks them worth consideration in the matter.*

*Meanwhile, I think if you are writing again to Miss Harrison you might explain incidentally what the nature of the Research Fellowship is; and it might smooth wounded feelings if you added that you would naturally prefer to await Professor Ridgeway's publication of his views in full before criticizing them.*

*I am very sorry that you have had this contretemps; but I do not think, as I say, that it affects your position in the least. Suppose Professor Ridgeway's explanation of tragedy is (to put it that way) only partly right.* (ibid. 10 May 1906)

The next two communications from Freire-Marreco to Myres acknowledged how very grateful she was for his advice. She was truly a woman of her convictions, and the letter revealed a dogged approach to serious situations, yet she also had the wisdom to listen to the voice of experience.

*I will do exactly as you advise: explain the situation briefly to Somerville and leave the matter to them, explain to Miss Harrison that this fellowship is a matter of faith and not of works, and await the publication of Volume II of Ridgeway's book.* (ibid. 11 May 1906)

She mentioned a letter from a Miss Lorimer, the secretary to the Fellowship Committee. Elizabeth Hilda Lockhart Lorimer, 1873-1954, a British scholar at Cambridge University, was also a tutor and author in Classical Archaeology. A Member of Council at Somerville College, Oxford, she published on Greek, Yugoslavian and Siberian archaeology. Subsequently she became Freire-Marreco's colleague and good friend. Evidently Lorimer lent her advice also.

Undated photograph of Elizabeth Hilda Lockhart Lorimer. As a member of the Somerville College Council she was on the committee that controlled grants to scholars for study and research. Courtesy of University of Oxford, Somerville College, Lorimer File, Thomas Photos No. 82083.

A few days later Freire-Marreco had not changed her mind. *Practically, I suppose it means that they cannot entertain the application, unless I try to come to a friendly understanding with Professor Ridgeway. Of course that would be far more comfortable for me too, and though I haven't very much hope, I think I must try it, for I don't want to give up altogether if it can be helped. . . . If you do not disapprove, I think of writing boldly to Professor Ridgeway (as well as to Miss Harrison) and asking him to give me an interview in Cambridge or in London before May the 28th. It would be quite a reasonable request under the circumstances, wouldn't it?* (ibid. 16 May 1906)

Promptly responding to the inquiry, two Myres letters bear the same date. The first one, sent to Freire-Marreco, contained an authoritative reply to her last request that obviously hoped to divert her from what Professor Ridgeway considered his territory and telling her not to intervene in the relationship between Somerville College and Ridgeway. With a little sarcastic humor he balanced the severity of his remarks. *Would you also see whether a good deal of your inquiry could not be made to center round the question of funerary games? It may be that the professor has treated this also in a world wide fashion. This is a kind of mute inglorious Olympic which used to go on under the name of church yard wrestling in the West, and so far as the collection of material goes, the one subject is I think as good as another. Neither Professor . . . who suggested these games, nor I, have any copyright on the suggestion!* (ibid. 18 May 1906)

The second letter from Myres went to an unknown recipient, presumably someone with the fellowship committee, wherein he stated Freire-Marreco's case on her behalf, not recommending the above-mentioned meeting and affirming that he had already suggested another subject of study to her. He proved himself to be a very good mentor indeed, by intervening and offering to help in any way he could to clear a tense and potentially damaging situation that had developed between the over-anxious Freire-Marreco versus Ridgeway and the Somerville College Committee.

The political undercurrents discouraged Freire-Marreco, who began to understand that it might be wise to abandon her original plan and try an alternate one in order to gain her objective. The following letter written to Myres shows she was learning a lesson about academic power and accommodation. *I was not hopeful of very much result from an interview with Professor Ridgeway—only I felt that Somerville College had a right to prescribe what they wished a candidate to do to satisfy them; and I thought it just possible that Professor Ridgeway was more placable in word than in letter.*

*All the communication so far has been through Miss Harrison. He has not been told yet that the Somerville College Fellowship is not awarded on the strength of a written thesis, or that I could publish nothing for two or three years.*

She remarked that Miss Harrison had already showed him the first rough scheme, and that she would be quite willing to show him the rest. *Of course I should be quite willing to show him the whole or any part of the improved scheme that you thought advisable. I enclose herewith a rough copy I have of it; I altered the form a little afterwards, but in substance it is what I sent in to Somerville . . . I might still keep part in mind; and if, when the book comes out, Somerville College might allow me to return to it.*

Later in the day she added a postscript stating she was receiving contradictory advice from her family, who were apparently caught up in the strategy of their daughter's career. Given her father's occupation as an accountant, not an academic calling, it is surprising that Freire-Marreco gave such credence to her parents' guidance as to her professional choices. Perhaps she was still relying on the dominating father theme to deflect the decision-making process away from herself. *May I supplement my letter of this morning by saying that my family press my doing everything possible to carry out the wishes of the Somerville Committee by attempting to interview Professor Ridgeway. They take it that the College does not wish to be involved in any personal difficulty with him, rather requiring the candidate to show a satisfactory state of things as a preliminary to their considering the application.*

*I must say that I see a good deal in this point of view. But you know much better what is advisable and proper in such a case, and indeed I should not wish to be so incredibly ungrateful as to do anything contrary to your opinion. I only add this in order that this view of the case may not be under represented.* (ibid. 19 May 1906)

Myres continued to exert pressure on the Council of Somerville College on Freire-Marreco's behalf, and told her strongly he felt it was the Council's responsibility to deal with Ridgeway, not hers. Nevertheless, fearing more difficulties might lay ahead, he urged her to give up her original scheme in order not to create a powerful enemy, and suggested that she submit an alternate program for further consideration.

After the academic conflicts among the players, not surprisingly Somerville College awarded the Fellowship to another candidate, a Miss Isaac, thereby solving a highly charged and difficult situation. To Somerville's credit, the choice of a woman did show its open mindedness. Indeed there were several women in high places at Oxford University.

Freire-Marreco felt disappointed, but not overwhelmingly so. As she told Myres: *As far as not getting the Fellowship goes, it is a very ordinary and reasonable disappointment; but I am truly sorry that there should be no result visible of all your extraordinarily kind efforts for me. At any rate they are not lost in the way of gratitude: I shall always think of them with the warmest feelings, and so will my people.*

*It is not likely that I can make any progress in the subject just now, for want of teachers and libraries, but I need not give up hoping for some chance in the future; and every day, evidence trickles in.* (ibid. 14 June 1906)

After the rejection, Barbara Freire-Marreco continued her studies for the next three years. She also lectured at the various Oxford colleges, probably to first year students, and was active in several organizations, especially the Royal Anthropological Institute of Great Britain and Ireland, where she was elected an Ordinary Fellow in 1907. She also belonged to the prestigious British Association for the Advancement of Science and the Folklore Society of Great Britain. Regrouping and strengthening her professional standing, Freire-Marreco was building a reputation in the anthropological community.

Undated photograph of Oxford University anthropology students and faculty during Freire-Marreco's tenure. Left to right back row: Wilson D. Wallis, Diamond Jenness and Marious Barbeau. Front row: Henry Balfour, Arthur Thompson and Robert R. Marret. Freire-Marreco developed a great respect for Marret in particular. Courtesy of University of Oxford, Pitt Rivers Museum, School of Anthropology and Museum Ethnography.

She made a singular contribution to The Anthropological Institute by editing publications and writing book reviews, at first under the supervision of John Myres. An early assignment, read as a tribute at an Anthropological Society meeting and then published in **Anthropological Essays, Oxford 1907**, was a "Biography of Edward Burnett Tylor from 1861 to 1907." Sir Edward Burnett Tylor, 1832-1917, was a British anthropology professor and keeper of the University Museum, Oxford. An active member of the Anthropological Society, he was instrumental in making the infant subject of anthropology an accepted science and was considered an expert in the origins of magic and religion as well as an exponent of animism.

This article evidently gained some recognition for Freire-Marreco, and the next year her contributions on a variety of topics began to appear in respected publications such as the University of London's **Sociological Review** and also in **Man**, of the Royal Anthropological Society of Great Britain and Ireland.

❦ ❦ ❦

In 1906 John Myres accepted a Chair of Classical Literature and History at the University of Liverpool. Freire-Marreco was pleased for him. *Please let me send very sincere congratulations: I have only just heard that you have accepted the Chair of Historical Geography at Liverpool. I hope it will turn out interesting and satisfactory in every way. Meanwhile it will be very poor sport to try to learn geography or anthropology or anything convincing at Oxford!*

*Thank you again very much for all your kindness at Oxford. I wish I had worked much harder, but I thought I had years ahead!* (ibid. 9 August 1906)

Myres and his family moved from Oxford to Liverpool. For the three years he held the Chair, taught Greek, and was Editor-in-Chief of the University publication **Annals of Archaeology and Anthropology**. Freire-Marreco probably missed seeing him, but as a result of their efforts, mainly through correspondence, their friendship and mutual respect grew. She continued to seek his council and he seemed happy to advise her regarding the direction in which she should proceed. Myres would prove especially helpful in guiding Freire-Marreco through these troubled waters.

The education systems of Great Britain and the United States differed significantly and still do. British forms had and have different requirements than American grades, and at the university level these organizations became even more diverse. The American university undergraduate took specified courses including required lectures, assignments and examinations to earn a certain number of credits for a degree. The British put more responsibility on the student who, under the guidance of a qualified tutor, "read" for a degree, as well as attending lectures on the subject, wrote a dissertation, and took an oral examination administered by a team of experts in the field, all this to qualify for even a Bachelor's degree!

Diplomas, not degrees, were awared to women and stated simply that the requirements for a degree had been met. Thus by the time she left Lady Margaret Hall, Freire-Marreco had taken the required courses for a diploma, but had not taken the examinations.

In one letter to her advisor Myres, she asks for guidance on a reading list and mentions Mary Ann Henley Rogers of Lady Margaret Hall College. Mary Ann Henley Rogers was a pioneer in women's education at Oxford and Secretary of the Association for the Education of Women, later named St. Anne's College. She and Freire-Marreco became colleagues and close friends, the loyal younger anthropologist donating a memorial gift to Lady Margaret Hall at the time of Rogers' death.

*Thank you very much also for the plans for my reading next term. Miss Rogers says that when you talked it over with her, you did not seem to suppose that I wanted to go in for the certificate or the diploma in June; but I think you told me before that it would be as well to try independent reading this term and leave special preparation for the diploma until after Christmas.*

Reading between the lines, it appears Myres indicated that her plans and goals were not yet well-defined, and yet he and Rogers, a professor of some stature, clearly discussed Barbara's future. Freire-Marreco's reading request to Myres continued: *My people have settled that I may go up next summer term as well as this term, and read at the British Museum next term. Meanwhile I must take the Law group this December, and I am reading for it now. I should like the four coachings you suggest with Mr. Marett and Dr. Farnell.*

Dr. Robert Randolph Marett of Oxford's Exeter College, 1866-1943, was a respected and published academician and authority on anthropological, archaeological and philosophical subjects; he also served as a president of the Royal Anthropological Institution. Dr. Lewis Richard Farnell, 1856-1934, who served as administrator and rector of Exeter College, Oxford, was a British classical scholar and lecturer in archaeology as well as a published author on Greek religion.

*Miss Rogers says you are good enough to promise to look over some written work at the end of term. Nothing could be a pleasanter duty than to colere Dr. Tylor if he will let me, and I know he makes himself very accessible. Thank you so much for the request.* (ibid. 9 September 1907)

By the next year Freire-Marreco had not yet determined how to proceed with her profession. Conditions at home demanded her time and she needed funding. She considered teaching, but accepted the necessity of being satisfied with a less-advanced level that offered nothing relating to anthropology or ethnology. She turned again to Myres, who was still at the University of Liverpool. *Thank you for asking my plans. It is difficult to make any, because of my mother's health. If she were fairly well and I could go away for a term at a time, I should think nothing so fortunate as a chance to learn at Liverpool. Perhaps Paris later on.*

*As to ways and means, it is possible that I might be eligible for the Gilchrist Fellowship (really a studentship) of 100 pounds for one year of postgraduate work. The difficulty about that has been that it has been limited to training with a definite professional object, and I was not able to say that I expected to make a profession of anthropology: it was not enough to say that I hope to write a book. The conditions may possibly be relaxed this year.*

Always in the forefront of Freire-Marreco's mind was the two-pronged need to earn money while pursuing a respected career. In many letters to Myres she evinced family ties that, whether a choice or a burden, constrained her choices.

*Do you think that the teaching of anthropology as an educational subject is likely to develop fast enough to provide subordinate teaching work for people like myself? At present, I suppose there is so little, that the important people who care to teach can take it all. I shall never be able to take school teaching, which means leaving home for too long, but if there were a chance of university work with short terms, it would be a good thing to train for it. I have no money to spend on learning, and must make my expenses as I go. I am entirely responsible for them now that my three years at Oxford are over.*

She decided, as a temporary measure, to consider giving lectures at a vacation course for elementary teachers during the summer of 1908, and made enquiries of the County Education Committee. Her goal was to earn enough to pay for the summer term in Oxford and the diploma examination. Ever mindful of her frequent requests to Myres, she first asks: *If my applications come to anything, may I ask you for a testimonial?*

She then adds self-deprecatingly, *I have troubled you with a great deal about my affairs, but it is better to be plain about them and show you the double difficulty in the way of making plans. I should not like you to think me either ungrateful or unambitious.* Once again revealing her family's' keen and often opinionated attitude toward their daughter's modern career—or is this a bit of British humor—she closes the letter by saying: *My mother begs me to make it clear that she is not mental. She does not feel much tempted, she says, by your kind offer of parts of West Africa, she thinks I am too dark-complected to last long there.* (ibid. 18 February 1908)

☙ ☙ ☙

Freire-Marreco was in Oxford off and on in 1907 and 1908, as some of her correspondence was so headed. Thanks to Myres, in 1908 she was employed temporarily in Liverpool as cataloger of an ethnographic collection in the Free Public Museum. Although Myres commented that her pay was low, she was nevertheless appreciative of the income. Minimal as it was even for that time, the meager amount she received enabled her the following summer to take the required examinations and obtain the coveted diploma. In June 1908, Barbara Freire-Marreco was awarded a Diploma in Anthropology with distinction from Oxford University, the first woman so honored.

University of Oxford's students to be awarded diplomas in anthropology in 1908. Left to right: F.H.S, Knowles, Henry Balfour, Barbara Freire-Marreco, and A. Hadley. What an accomplishment for an English gentlewoman in 1908! Courtesy of University of Oxford, Pitt Rivers School of Anthropology and Museum Ethnography.

*❀ ❀ ❀*

She lived at home for the next year and going to Oxford to attend meetings and lectures. She continued to write book reviews and edit for anthropological publications. Correspondence with Myres mainly concerned details related to these publications and is otherwise low-key, with periodic exchanges of reading material of mutual interest and flashes of humor. In one witty letter she takes anthropology into the realm of herpetology. *My Grandfather has just given me a quaint book,* **Myths and Legends of the Indians of British Guiana**, *by a missionary, all done into verse. Pray have you considered the regional differences in the speech of frogs? The Arawak* (an American Indian tribe located on the coast of British and Dutch Guiana) *frogs do not say Breekekkek Koax but Boro-okh, Boro-okh, Boro-oo and you will remember that in Borneo they say Fatak Batok.* (ibid. 10 December 1908)

*❀ ❀ ❀*

By the middle of 1909 Freire-Marreco's home situation had stabilized with the improvement in her mother's health and she felt free to leave for an extended period. It had been three years since she had been rejected for a Somerville Research Fellowship and she felt better prepared for another try. She shared her intentions in a brief note to Myres who, by then, had obviously gained respect for her, and she asked him for a reference. *Will you be so kind as to let me give your name again as a reference for the Somerville College Research Studentship? I shall not undervalue your kindness if you will take the trouble a second time. I am asking Mr. Hobhouse for a second reference, and I think Mr. Marett for the third?* (ibid. 1 May 1909)

The well-known British philosopher and journalist Leonard Trelawny Hobhouse, 1864-1929, published extensively, particularly in his special interests of ethnography and geography. Lecturing mainly at the University of London, he was the first professor of sociology when it was introduced as a study subject.

The ever-supportive Myres responded that he would be happy to recommend her again for the Fellowship and promised to do his best. He approved her new plans proposing to work for three years determining the nature, extent and genesis of the authority of kings and chiefs in uncivilized society, agreeing that a limited field should be chosen, such as South American or Central Asian kings and chiefs.

At this time Freire-Marreco's interest in authority had revealed itself for the first time, showing her move into a very different course of study from her first scholarship application that was to have focused on European origins of tragedy. The enforcement of laws by elected officials was now to become her consuming passion. Myres advised her to be certain to mention her earlier work with the Royal Anthropological Association.

Having recently returned from anthropological meetings in North America, Myres went on to write some thoughts on a lighter level, showing again their shared sense of humor: *I had a good time in the States and in Canada. We must discuss the political and social effects of galoshes and ice water.* In a funny reference to the ill-fated British liner ultimately sunk in wartime, he said: *The Lusitania vibrated so abominably, in the particular section in which I crossed that my Letters Persones are jumbled up into a cipher which I cannot decipher.*

Did he go too far, one wonders, in his teasing comment about American women and his perception of their desires: *Women have such a good time in the States that they scorn the idea of a vote: they would as soon have a bank account of the own. Those who don't have a good time I only heard of, as inaccessible and probably rare. So I don't think I shall waste my suffragette (or was it suffragist) lecture on the British Association.* (ibid. 12 May 1909)

Freire-Marreco applied again for the desired Fellowship, and the Selection Committee explored her worthiness. A request to Myres from Helen Darbishire, Secretary of the Selection Committee of the Somerville Research Fellowship, soon followed. Darbishire, 1881-1961, a British academician and an expert on Milton and Wadsworth, published extensively, tutored and lectured in English at the University of London as well as Somerville College. She served from 1931-1945 as principal of that institution and had a reputation for helping foreign students obtain an education in England. She had asked Myres opinion of Freire-Marreco's ability and what he thought of her proposed research project.

Helen Darbishire when she was Principal of Somerville College, University of Oxford. This pioneer woman educator helped young Barbara Freire-Marreco and others in furthering their educations. An unknown photographer took this picture sometime after Freire-Marreco obtained her fellowship. Courtesy of the University of Oxford, Somerville College, Darbishire file. Thomas Photos, Neg. No. 82087.

Myres reply to Darbishire was a glowing report of Freire-Marreco's abilities and accomplishments, and he recommended her highly. *Miss B. Freire-Marreco has done work under my supervision at intervals during the last five years, at first on archaeological subjects in the Mediterranean region, then on general questions on the influence of physical environments and on matters more closely connected with the subject she now offers. Last year, also, she undertook at my suggestion, a piece of difficult cataloguing work in the ethnographic collection of the Free Public Museum in Liverpool, which she carried out admirably under very difficult conditions. I mention this to show that she has not yet showed her special sociological study to eclipse her interest and her efficiency in other branches of anthropology. Miss Freire-Marreco is also engaged at present in reviewing for me some difficult sections of the British Association's* **Notes & Queries in Anthropology**, *in preparation for a fresh edition.*

Myres continued with observations of her scholarly attitude. *She is quite the ablest student in anthropology, that I have had; a good and very accurate scholar, with a marked gift of style. A rapid and most industrious worker, she is very quick and versatile; and a clear-headed and judicious critic of other people's work. She brings a remarkably fresh and ingenious imagination to bear on what she knows (which is already considerable), and has already made out some good points in the field of work which she proposes now. I have seen her programs of study: it is carefully thought out and shows that she starts well abreast on the principal of the subject. Her wide range of interests make it possible to see her work along fresh and very promising lines; and her recent analysis of the main problems and their interrelation is quite the most original piece of constructive criticism which I have received. I look forward confidently to considerable contributions to knowledge as the result of Miss Freire-Marreco's work in the next few years* (ibid. 25 May 1909)

This time the Fellowship application was successful and brought the desired results. Freire-Marreco gratefully communicated the good news to Myres and immediately outlined a project for her research endeavor. *I have the honor to report that at 6:45 last night I was appointed Somerville Research Fellow; which is very greatly due, I know, to the testimonial you were so kind as to give me; for which I remain, as ever, your attached and obliged pupil. I hope I shall give them satisfaction.*

She planned to ask for a leave of absence from London University, a current obligation, well in advance of her proposed field work project.

Exactly what her commitments were at that time is not known but she was considering, among other things, studying for a Doctorate in Science as an alternative. As Freire-Marreco pondered her professional choices, now greatly expanded, she told Myres she felt *almost sure* that Central Asia would be the preferred area to begin, rather than South America. *If I came up to Liverpool for one term to attend your geography lectures, should you have time to overlook my reading a little? I think that after working on Central Asia under supervision I should be better able to tackle South America alone. I suppose that I could register at the University for one term? Then I could stay at the Hostel, or else get lodgings nearer the University.* (ibid. 16 June 1909)

Myres promptly replied. *Very hearty congratulations on the news of your assignment to the Research Fellowship: it is a great delight to anyone to whom you have given so much help as you have to me. It is an added pleasure to think that there is a proposal that you do part of your work here: the principal hesitation that I have in falling in with the suggestion is that you will find very little literature here bearing upon Central Asia (which I quite agree is the best area to begin upon), but you cannot expect a seaport university to specialize in the anthropology of a region devoid of navigable rivers.* Almost as an afterthought, he suggested she could *quite well register at the University as a post-graduate student for a single term.* (ibid. 17 June 1909)

In good humor, Myres requested her help in finding a new assistant in Liverpool. This request, put forth in two different letters, revealed his feelings concerning what he considered the frivolous attitudes of many women assistants in the workplace as well as the trust he had in Barbara. *I may want another assistant in the autumn. If I do, it will be a lady that I should want: learned if possible; competent, to deal faithfully with the women students, as if they were human; to be a real Fellow of All Souls, but we can't hope for everything. Such paragons will of course scramble for the 150 pounds we should be likely to offer. You have seen the conditions here, and I should be glad if you would keep your eye open for a likely person, in case there is need.* (ibid. 20 June 1909) Freire-Marreco then alerted two of her associates of the job opportunity.

Anthropomorphizing ornithology next, Myres goes on hilariously about assistants: *Some are migratory, aggressive, and others (more or less feminine) are sedentary,* noting also that *the migratory types return after brief intervals to the seasonal habitat. (1) Why is this so? (2) If so, why does the Professor survive? (3) Is it the shortness of frocks, or their length of hair which prompts the return of the emigrant? (4) What is proper?*

*I am writing to your friend, as she has already written to me, to say: 1) that we have at present two vacancies, one of which we may fill by appointing a woman; 2) that nothing will be done till an appointment of a new Professor of Latin (for which see next Wednesday's newspapers); 3) that if she wishes to be considered as a candidate, will she say so.* (ibid. No day or month 1909)

Obviously Myres enjoyed his own joke. But on a far more profound note, this letter revealed a surprising new direction for Freire-Marreco, which she evidently had communicated to him. No longer was she planning on investigating the authority of kings and chiefs in South America or Central Asia as she had stated in her application. Now her aim had shifted, and she announced her intention of exploring Native North American culture in the United States. He replied with total support, immediately offering his counsel on the most helpful contacts to make in the United States. He communicated with Alice Cunningham Fletcher.

Fletcher, 1833?-1923, was a pioneer American ethnologist with strong ties to the Omaha tribe, who also had helped several other Native tribes settle land disputes and housing problems. Among her many contributions, she was associated with the Ethnological Department at the Peabody Museum, Harvard University, served as president of both the Anthropological Society of Washington, D.C. and the American Folk Lore Society, held office in the Archaeological Institute of America, and published for the Bureau of American Ethnology. It was evident to both Freire-Marreco and Myres that she could be of inestimable help to the fledgling anthropologist.

Myres advised Freire-Marreco: *As to your plans of field work, I quite agree; and you could not do better than make friends with her* (Fletcher) *and get her to take you up with her next time she goes among her beloved Omaha: her big book is nearly finished, but she will probably have another season with them. We know her well and she is charming, and most stimulating; and she*

Alice Cunningham Fletcher, the American ethnologist, properly attired for an old fashioned lady of the time, as she must have looked to Barbara Freire-Marreco. Under the black silk garb there was a respected woman of intellectual stature who made many contributions in a man's scientific world. Courtesy of the Palace of the Governors, MNM/DCA Neg. No. 9874.

*will be at Winnipeg* (for an anthropological meeting) *this August. Madame* (Myres' wife) *says I am to give you a pressing invitation to come and I may add that if you can, I think I could get a small subsidy out of the Association towards traveling expenses. In any event I will see what invitations there are next year in America.* (ibid. June 1909)

As usual, Freire-Marreco promptly replied. *Thank you again* (as *well as in a letter to Mrs. Myres yesterday) for your very kind idea of getting me an Association grant for Canada: I wish it were not impossible to go this year. I shall be most grateful for the introduction to Miss Fletcher, if you have the opportunity.* (ibid. 14 July 1909)

Myres reassured his young friend, telling her he was sorry that it was not possible for her to go to Canada, and adding that he would approach Fletcher and try to arrange something that would fit with her plans.

Freire-Marreco was convinced that field work first was the right direction to take and looked toward North America as her destination. Her attitude reflected the thinking of the time: British "on location" work was coming to the fore, and at the same time American anthropologists and ethnologists were experiencing an energetic growth. The leading anthropologists believed that collecting data in the field was the best way to test theoretical questions. While seeking advice from Myres about available opportunities, Freire-Marreco reaffirmed her solidarity:

*People have been telling me how wrong it would be to enjoy an anthropological scholarship without fieldwork, and I begin to believe it. What I think I want to do is to go and see some Northwest American societies still in working order, say Salish or Dene* (tribes from southern British Columbia and the United States). *If I were a year farther forward I should go now, and trust to find openings on the spot; but as it is, various reasons make it impracticable. But will you be so good as to keep it in mind when you are out there, and enquire, if you have time and opportunity, about what I could do? I want to join someone else's expedition, I think. Will there be one in 1910 or 1911? Whose? To what district? What will it cost to join? I have 120 pounds a year for three years, and I daresay I could devote 250 of it to the fieldwork, if necessary. Are there any Canadian funds from which I could get assistance?*

*If there will be no expeditions, I suppose I could go to a mission; but it would be unsatisfactory in comparison. Of course this scheme may prove out of the question, too difficult, too costly, or many other things. But if there is any sense in it I ought to make enquiries long beforehand, so as to work at the geography and languages of the right place before I leave England. I don't, indeed, wish to give you trouble about this, but if you will keep me in mind when you are seeing people in Canada, I shall be very grateful.* (ibid. 5 July 1909)

True to his word, Myres wrote to his associate and friend Alice Fletcher alerting her to what he hoped would be Freire-Marreco's field work destination and commending his student for her many capabilities. He said briefly that she wished to work with an American tribe, perhaps joining an expedition.

Fletcher wrote to Freire-Marreco who, in turn, reported to Helen Darbishire at Somerville College regarding her use of the Fellowship. *I had an answer this week from Miss Alice Fletcher (Omaha Sociology,), and you will see by her letter that she does not encourage my British-Columbia scheme. However, I think I will read on the American area all the same, the published material is so excellent.*

*I should like to come up to report myself some time this term.* (Somerville, Darbishire, 13 September 1909)

The reply from Darbishire was not found, nor was the one from Fletcher mentioned in the following response from Freire-Marreco to Darbishire. While she awaited her upcoming field work to develop, Freire-Marreco made good use of her time. She wrote again to Somerville College. *Many thanks for your letter received this morning. I shall be very glad to go before the Fellowship Committee when I come up. Of course I could come up earlier if they desired it, but I think it would be far better to have done a little work first: I could tell them so much more about my plans. If the dates I suggest Oct. 28th to Nov. 1st will suit, would you please ask not to arrange any interview for me until Friday night, the 29th, because lectures at the School of Economics may prevent my getting away before five or six o'clock Friday afternoon.*

*As to the plans for the three years: I propose to read, for the first three terms at least, at the London School of Economics, where Prof. Hobhouse, who has a seminar for research students, has promised to superintend my work; taking advantage at the same time of some of the lectures given there on Ethnology, Regional Geography, and the Method of Sociological Research. I shall register there as an Internal Student of the University of London at the beginning of Michaelmas Term, Oct. 1ˢᵗ. I pay a research fee of 3 pounds 30 for the year. With the approval of the Fellowship Committee I am registering myself as a candidate for the Doctorate of the University of London (D.Sc. in Economics) as a graduate of another university reading under the superintendence of a Professor in a recognized school of the University of London, (viz. Prof. L. T. Hobhouse).*

Freire-Marreco's candidacy for a doctorate seems an ambitious scheme, given that women were not granted degrees under the British system at this time, but if she achieved her goal she would be well qualified in the field of anthropology. She reported to Myres that the degree could be taken by research on a sociological subject, and that an ethnographical treatment of sociological material would be accepted. The piece of work she planned to prepare for publication under the conditions of the Fellowship could also be submitted as a thesis for the Doctorate. Two years attendance at a school of the University of London was required, but leave of absence to study elsewhere was frequently granted, clearly an important aspect for her, since she sought assurance that no difficulties would be likely to arise if she did so. The thesis could be presented in a flexible time frame, and not necessarily immediately after the two year's study.

*I shall very much appreciate the kindness of the Fellowship Committee, if they will leave it undecided for the present whether I am to reside in 1910-11 or 1911-12. I am told that I ought to manage some ethnographical work in the field, and I am in communication with Miss Fletcher (Washington, D.C.), who seems the likeliest person to advise me. I wanted to try British Columbia, but Miss Fletcher warns me that the climate and conditions are very severe for a European and doubts whether I should get sufficient results to balance the expenditure of strength. She is consulting other American anthropologists for me.* (ibid. 18 September 1909)

Another prominent British anthropologist stepped to the fore to assist Freire-Marreco. William Halse Rivers, 1865-1922, a psychologist and physiologist, was well known for his contribution to the development of British social anthropology. Lecturing primarily at St. John's College, Cambridge, he authored many books and served as President of the Royal Anthropological Institute. His analysis of kinship patterns and social organization of primitive societies influenced Freire-Marreco's work. However, his attempt to help bore no fruit because he offered her an introduction in Fiji and she rejected the idea of studying Polynesian society. The young woman increasingly had her eye on North America.

She wrote to Myres of her hopes to go abroad in 1910, leaving the last year of her fellowship to write up results in Oxford. As planned Freire-Marreco completed the fall term of study in 1909.

❦ ❦ ❦

America beckoned, but it is unclear whether her next post arose through John Myres efforts with Alice Fletcher or whether Fletcher acted on her own, but in any case the doyenne of anthropology contacted Dr. Edgar Hewett, who was working in New Mexico. It was a propitious connection. Hewett would prove to be the greatest contributor to the success of Freire-Marreco's American experiences.

Edgar Lee Hewett, 1865-1946, started his career as a superintendent of various schools and became a noted American anthropologist, archeologist and ethnologist. Though his research was international in scope, his particular interest was in the southwest United States and Central America. In 1905 he had been appointed director of the Institute of Archaeology's new American program as the first Director of the School of American Archeology in Santa Fe where he also held the post of Director of the Museum of New Mexico. Feeling great empathy for indigenous people, he taught that they were neither primitive nor inferior, an innovation at that time. He was influential in getting the U.S. Congress to pass the Preservation of American Antiquities Act in 1906 to check vandalism on archeological sites and halt the dispersion of autochthonous cultural and religious items. As one of the first U.S. student mentors, he encouraged women to enter the field of anthropology and related areas.

Left: Frederick W. Hodge when he was ethnologist in charge of the Bureau of American Ethnology, Smithsonian Institution. While visiting the School of American archaeology's camp in Frjoles Canyon he met Freire-Marreco leading to correspondence in succeeding years. He proved an invaluabale advisor for her. Right: Edgar L. Hewett was the first Director of the American School of Archaeology in Santa Fe. Here he organized the summer session at Frijoles Canyon and became Freire-Marreco's mentor during her stay in the southwest United States. Courtesy of the Palace of the Governors, MNM/DCA Neg. No. 7296.

The School of Archaeology, known later as the School of American Research and now is the School of Advanced research in Santa Fe, has no records of Freire-Marreco's correspondence from this time. The Angelico Chavez History Library, Museum of New Mexico, where most of the historical records from the area are housed, also has no record of their meeting; but contact had been made, as the following letter from Freire-Marreco to Hewett confirms. *May I take advantage of Miss Alice Fletcher's kind introduction to write to you about my plans for next year? Miss Fletcher has given me your message, offering to superintend my work, and to let me join your camp near Santa Fe* (School of American Archaeology's first summer session), *and I am most sincerely obliged to you. It will be a very great advantage to me.*

*I hope to come out at the end of June or the end of July next year, and to stay for about six months. What I want to do is to study the social structure of some of the Pueblos, and Miss Fletcher tells me that, though the main work of your School at Santa Fe is archaeological, there will be good opportunities for getting to know the Indians. If you can spare time to write to me, will you be so very kind as to tell me a few particulars about the prospect of work.*

*Where will your camp be next summer? What Pueblo will it be near, and which set of Indians shall we see most of? Do you expect any other women students? Do the Indians speak Spanish? How does one travel? By riding? On horses or mules? Shall I be enrolled as a member of your School? And what are the arrangements about fees, and about the expenses of the camp?*

She requested that Hewett consider admitting another young woman, an American, to the Summer School, who had been recommended by Alfred Haddon, a compatriot. Dr Alfred Court Haddon, 1855-1940, lectured in physical anthropology and ethnology at the University of Cambridge and helped make that University's Museum of Archeology and Ethnography a primary research center. He was a noted champion of women's rights and their education.

Continuing her letter to Hewett she wrote: *Dr.Haddon, whom I think you know as the Reader in Ethnology in the University of Cambridge, told me last week that he knew a young American lady who might like to share in my sociological work; and I think that he is writing to her about the plan. If she is willing to join, will you be willing to accept us both as members of your party? I think it would be a great advantage for me to have another worker interested in the same questions, and we should be able to go about together.*

*A Committee has been started in England this year to arrange exchanges of students between the United States and this country, and I am applying to them for help and information, as they may be able to get special steamship fares and so save something in traveling expenses. If the Committee wishes to make enquiries from you, as to your willingness to receive me at the School and so forth, will you be so very kind as to answer them? I feel that I must apologize for troubling you with correspondence for my benefit.*

*With many thanks for the kindness you have already shown.* (Palace of the Governors, Museum of New Mexico, Angelico Chavez History Library, Edgar L. Hewett file, 8 December 1909. Hereafter cited as Museum of New Mexico, Hewett)

To further Freire-Marreco's quest, the president of Somerville College, Dr. C. B. Heberden, wrote a letter of recommendation to Edgar Hewett. *I write on behalf of Somerville College in order to commend to you Miss Freire-Marreco, Fellow of the College, whom I understand you have kindly agreed to receive as a member of your School of Archaeology. She has been appointed to the Somerville Fellowship to pursue ethnographical research, the special subject of her study being "The Origin of the Kingship." In accordance with the advice of experts in Anthropology and especially that of Dr. Rivers, whose method she is studying, the College is anxious that she should undertake some field work in the course of the three years during which she holds the Fellowship, and I believe that the confidence which she will gain and the opportunities which she will have by joining one of your summer camps and by study in the Museum of Santa Fe will be of great value to her.*

*The College will be most grateful to you for any advice and assistance which you may be able to give to Miss Freire-Marreco. I need hardly say that she will be guided by any instructions which may be given to the students attending the camp.* (ibid. 3 May 1910)

Now at the beginning of her work in the field, Barbara Freire-

Marreco showed all the abilities to make a serious contribution to the relatively new sciences of anthropology and ethnology. As a second-generation member of these scientists, she possessed the intention and patience to work hard, as well as a talent for listening and learning diverse languages that would allow her to gather new information not previously recorded by anthropologists.

The opportunities were building. From 1909 to 1913 while a Somerville College Fellow, Freire-Marreco held the Mary Ewart Traveling Scholarship, which permitted her to make two trips to the United States to visit various museums and universities in a foreign country as well as live in endemic societies. The scholarship enabled and encouraged her to associate with, contribute to, and learn from American anthropologists, archaeologists and ethnologists. She was able to visit and live at some of the American Southwest pueblos and tribal reservations, mainly Santa Clara Pueblo in New Mexico and the Hopi/Tewa First Mesa in Arizona.

Leaving the familiar academic world of the British universities, she was ready to embrace new adventure that propelled her to new levels in her professional life: to investigate, cope with and accept the world of the pueblo Indian, which she ultimately came to love.

Her original fellowship proposal, *The Origin of Chiefs and Kingship in Uncivilized Society,* was to expand far beyond her expectations and change her basic premise, for she came to believe that Native Americans were not uncivilized at all. After spending her daily life in the pueblos and making professional and personal contacts, some lasting her lifetime, she concluded that their cultures were not inferior, simply different from the one she had known.

# AN AMERICAN ADVENTURE

Barbara Freire-Marreco sailed west across the Atlantic in June 1910, disembarking in Boston. Her first adventure in anthropological research in a location beyond Great Britain had begun. Introductions had been arranged through the efforts of colleagues at Somerville College, her mentor John Myres, and anthropologist Alice Fletcher in Washington, D.C., who in turn, arranged to connect Freire-Marreco with universities, museums, and government agencies across the United States concerned with Native American cultures. The purpose of these meetings with the luminaries of American anthropology lighted her path by informing the British-born woman in American ways of conducting field work to guide her during her stay. The itinerary from England to Santa Fe, New Mexico had been planned for Freire-Marreco to arrive in time to attend the American School of Archaeology's first summer session. Decisions for the remainder of her stay in the United States were fluid, made as opportunities unfolded. The best report of her journey from the East Coast to the Southwest, was written the next year to the Fellowship committee at Somerville College through Helen Darbishire.

*The arrangements for the journey were made by the Honorable Secretary to the International Interchange of Students who obtained concessions for me from the White Star Line and the Santa Fe-Atchison-Topeka Railroad Co., recommended hotels, gave some useful introduction and offered help of every sort.*

Arriving in Boston she started making calls on the professionals in her chosen field where she made candid and judgmental remarks. While visiting Harvard University she had encountered Frederick Ward Putnam, 1853-1915, an American anthropologist with a long career in scientific positions and author of more than 400 publications. Considered a keen observer of nature, he was Professor Emeritus at the University of California as well as Harvard. *I saw Professor Putnam for a few minutes— quite old, not very impressive to a stranger, evidently much revered and loved by the men there.*

She also mentioned meeting Alfred Marten Tozzer, 1876-1954, another American anthropologist at Harvard who specialized in Mayan culture and published extensively on that subject. He was credited as an inspiration to many students. *I had hours of talk with Mr. A.M. Tozzer, an assistant lecturer in anthropology there, about the present state of theory there and in England, and university teaching, and popularization. I have got some of their papers, but won't post them now, but keep everything to show you when I get home. They run a general elementary course in anthropology for undergraduates, and graduate courses in physical anthropology, archaeology, etc. General course looked rather old fashioned in syllabus, and certainly Mr. Tozzer's theories of religion are old-fashioned. But he is a fieldworker, and strong upon field methods, and very good and vigorous all round I should think. But the general impression of Harvard anthropology is that it is primarily archaeological, and that it centers round a man who is getting old.*

On to New York where Freire-Marreco envied the graduate students at Columbia University, whose faculty boasted the estimable Franz Boas. Franz Boas, 1858-1942, was called the "Father of Anthropology" in the U.S. Professor of physical anthropology and an expert on Native American languages, he was associated with the Bureau of American Ethnology, the American Folklore Society and was Curator of Anthropology at the Museum of Natural History when Freire-Marreco met him. An early mentor or student sponsor, he encouraged women in the study of anthropology.

*Dr. Boas has no cut-and-dried syllabuses, but my goodness, what a man! And it seems that he makes his men discuss large questions and do a lot of solid independent work. Very strong on environment: treats culture entirely on environmental lines. Rather estranged from the Museum, perhaps? Strong on psychology, but perhaps lays most emphasis on linguistics. He is a great man, I do believe; certainly his men think so. It was thought a great honor for me that he kept me talking for three quarters of an hour.* (Somerville, Darbishire, 26 June 1910)

She informed John Myres of her progress also: *I arrived in New York yesterday by the Fall River boat, and presented your letters of introduciton to Dr. Boas. He gave me quite a long interview, talking about the teaching of anthropology in this country, and then to Mr. Robinson, (an assistant at the Metropolitan Museum.) They both received me in the kindest way possible, and were very glad to hear news of you and Mrs. Myres. Mr. Robinson showed me some magnificencies of that magnifical place.*

*This morning I am going to the Natural History Museum before starting to Philadelphia.* (Bodleian, Myres, 15 June 1910) No other evidence exists of Freire-Marreco's visit to Philadelphia.

To return to her report to Somerville College: *I feel that my visits in the East have been rather expensive, but it has been most useful to me to meet American anthropologists and get some idea of the kind of work that they are doing. Incidentally, I have had a chance to tell them something about English work of the last few years, about which very little is known over here: In Harvard they know something of Dr. Rivers, in New York and Washington they seemed genuinely surprised to hear that there was any English method of field work. They judge English anthropology entirely by the old-fashioned "comparative" work.*

As the name implies, the comparative method meant studying by analyzing and classifying relationships. In order to verify a statement, a comparison to a number of different societies, including customs and ways of life that were influenced by their environment, should be made to establish authenticity. Ethnographic data obtained from explorers and travelers was to be organized into a sequence for evaluation. Popular in the nineteenth century, this approach was criticized as too inferential and unproven, really only conjecture.

Freire-Marreco seemed to feel she was truly in a strange land distant from the respected British anthropological traditions and lamented that she did not meet anyone familiar with Mr. Marett's theories and the vogue of "mana" and "wakonda" that was fodder for academic discussion in England. Mana concerned animistic spirits or a supernatural force in certain religions that believed the power for good or evil in objects and people could be transferred or inherited. Wakonda, a belief sometimes found among primitive people, saw a mysterious life power permeating all natural forms, such as stones or insects.

To Freire-Marreco, as with her British colleagues, these concepts were held in the highest importance. *It almost seems as if such American conceptions as wakonda had less effect on the general anthropological theory of religion in America than with us, possibly because here they care very little for Melanesian evidence, or for any evidence outside their own continent, and so they have failed to correlate wakonda with similar categories elsewhere. Luckily I have Mr. Marett's* **Threshold of Religion** *with me.*

Her observations of undergraduates everywhere and women's colleges in particular led her to believe they were less enlightened than those in the British system. *As to popularization, it seems there is not the same demand from teachers in connection with geography that we are getting in England. Of women, a fair number at Radcliffe and at Barnard College take the undergraduate anthropology lectures as an option in their mixed B.A. course, but practically none take the graduate work. And it is curious, from the Oxford point of view, to see that the professors and lecturers care nothing for undergraduate work. They look on them as schoolboys and girls. No undergraduate holds the position that a fourth-year man with us holds in the interest of his teachers. Their real pupils are the men (and women in some subjects) who are reading for M.A. and Ph.D.*

*At Wellesley, a self-contained women's college like Holloway, only more so—surprisingly like Holloway it seemed—they had no anthropological course, but a lot of sociology and psychology.* The Holloway College she mentioned was an institution for women at Egham and part of the University of London. At a later date it joined Bedford College to form the Royal Holloway and Bedford College.

Her most profitable visit in the East was in Washington, D.C. where she connected in person with the famed anthropologist Alice Cunningham Fletcher. *Miss Fletcher is really wonderful: nice old-fashioned lady, grey crinkled hair, black silk clothes, very correct manners and has done everything in the way of fieldwork with the Omaha, and then as the head of a government commission has allotted millions of acres of land to various tribes. Thanks to Mr. Myres introduction, she took me in hand most thoroughly; talked to me for four hours on anthropology in general, and field methods, and her own work; sometimes she was absolutely inspiring, with a high serious enthusiasm for the work: then she gave me a lot of practical advice about people and places here, and particularly about certain people I was not to get in with.*

*She knows NOTHING of recent English work, thinks Dr. Frazer is our all. I put before her respectfully all that I know about it, and she was awfully nice and interested. As she says herself, she may be old in years but she hasn't yet got rheumatism of the mind!*

Sir James George Frazer, 1854-1941, was certainly well-known and very inspiring to other scientists working in the field. A British lecturer at various Cambridge colleges and much published in classical studies and social anthropology, he held honorary degrees from Cambridge and Oxford Universities as well as some on the European continent. But as Freire-Marreco said, he was by no means the only important figure on the European scene.

As for other American figures, Miss Fletcher took Freire-Marreco on an introductory tour of the influential players in Washington. First they went to see Robert G. Valentine, 1879-1954, the Commissioner for Indian Affairs at the Bureau of Ethnology. It was evident Fletcher only had to ask for what she wanted. Valentine gave the young protegee an excellent comprehensive letter to all government agents and superintendents.

They then proceeded on to Frederick Webb Hodge, 1864-1956, the head of the Bureau of Ethnology. Hodge, (pictured with Edgar L. Hewett in the preceding section, p.57) an American ethnologist, explored and excavated pueblos in Arizona and New Mexico. His career spanned posts at the Museum of the American Indian, Heye Foundation, the Southwest

Museum, and was currently at the Bureau of American Ethnology, where he was responsible for the Smithsonian Institution's **Handbook of the American Indian**. Freire-Marreco's association with Hodge continued long after this first meeting.

*Hodge is an absolutely charming man, to whom Miss Fletcher made me repeat the whole tale about the Cambridge method and Mr. Marett. He talked also of Mr. Myres and of the Pitt Rivers. It does warm your heart to hear your friends praised in a foreign country! I promise you, I could have cried for pleasure.*

Next on the introductory tour was William Henry Holmes, whom Hodge knew as his predecessor at the Bureau of Ethnology, and went with personally to present Freire-Marreco. Holmes, 1846-1933, an American anthropologist and archaeologist, was also an artist with an eye for detail, a valuable asset prior to reliable photography. Associated with the Bureau of American Ethnology, he was also curator at both the National Museum and the National Gallery in Washington, as well as serving as President of the American Anthropology Association. *Very nice,* she wrote, *but I didn't like him so much, I don't know why; perhaps because he seemed worried and not enthusiastic about his job* (Somerville, Darbishire, 26 June 1910).

Among her many pointed observations she noted that neither Harvard nor Columbia offered any organized cooperation between geographical, anthropological and sociological teaching, and although Dr. Boas sent his men to geography and sociology lectures, those departments did not reciprocate very much. This letter, reflecting her British training and mind set, obviously was critical of American anthropologists, archeologists and ethnologists. And Americans claimed, with much truth, that their British counterparts rejected all work that wasn't British, particularly that of Americans. In the United States, British anthropologists were judged to have closed minds of limited range, and were perceived as confining their work almost entirely to kinship and social relationship subjects. In the light of these judgments, Freire-Marreco maintained a comparatively open mind and there is no more written criticism from her.

William H. Holmes at the time Freire-Marreco met him was curator of the
United States National Museum and chief ot the Bureau of American Ethnology,
Smithsonian Institution. Courtesy of the National Anthropological Archives, Smithsonian
Institution, No. 45-a-1.

As a final courtesy resulting from her East Coast visit, Alice Fletcher wrote to Edgar Hewett on behalf of Freire-Marreco to discuss her summer plans, and Hewett had also received the Somerville College's Council's letter. He met his new pupil when she arrived at Santa Fe and brought her to the School, and that very evening gave her a sort of tutorial interview.

# The Journey West

Arriving by train in Lamy, New Mexico, Freire-Marreco wrote to Helen Darbishire from St. Vincent's Sanitarium in Santa Fe.

El Ortiz Hotel, Lamy, New Mexico in 1912. This was the scene that greeted Barbara Freire-Marreco when she detrained from the nearest railway stop to Santa Fe, sixteen miles to the northwest. Courtesy of the Palace of the Governors, MNM/DCA Neg. No. 61669, Jesse Nusbaum photographer.

Patient's room in the Satitorium, St. Vincent's Hospital in 1911 where Freire-Marreco stayed upon arriving in Santa Fe. *All rooms were equipped with electric light, steam heat, electric call bell and running hot and cold water. Accomodations may be had with or without private bath, single or in suite.* Private rooms and suites ranged from $100 to $160 a month. Courtesy of the Palace of the Governors, MNM/DCA, SVH Photograph #0021 Neg. No. 61377, Jesse Nusbaum photographer.

Another SVH photograph, not pictured, is #0004 by D. R. Payne, Palace of the Governors, MNM/DCA bears the statement: *On Saturdays, the needy and poor gathered on the steps to receive food and clothing from the sisters. Because of the shortage of hotel rooms in town, overnight guests were accepted at the sanatorium, a practice which continued at the various hospital buildings until 1925.*

*I arrived yesterday at noon, leaving Washington on Wednesday evening, and delightful it is to get up into this cool mountain air. Railways here, tho less comfortable than their advertisements, seem to me much more comfortable than described which is not saying much, perhaps I am staying here for a few days, probably until Tuesday.*

*I think I have come to the right place: The Harvard people and Dr. Boas find fault with this association for calling itself a School of American Archaeology when, as they say, it has not the organization of a school; but it looks to me as if Dr. Hewett were the sort of man who constitutes a real school. He is ready to take responsibility and evidently means to provide real opportunities for work. The idea is, roughly, this: about the middle of this week I am to go to Santa Clara or San Juan (both Indian villages) to stay with people known to Dr. Hewett; there I am to stay five or six days and acclimatize, not ask too many questions but pay calls and try to make myself agreeable; about July 4ᵗʰ to join the camp at Rito de los Frijoles and begin work with the Indians there ( among them is a man who has been chief of his village and he might be induced to talk about the civil authority).*

Rito de los Frijoles, located in a canyon through which Bean Creek passes, is located not far from Santa Fe, a scant 20 miles as the crow flies. Now part of Bandelier National Monument, it was the location for Hewett's summer school. To get there in 1910 required an uncomfortable and rather dangerous journey. After a jerky eighteen plus miles on the "Chile Line," a narrow gauge railroad out of Santa Fe, passengers arrived at the abandoned Buckman lumber camp where the next step was to cross the Rio Grande. This passage was followed, on foot or horseback, by a climb to the Pajarito Plateau by way of a primitive and rocky trail, across the wooded plateau to the rim of Frijoles Canyon. The way to the bottom of the canyon was by a steep foot path, and all camp supplies had to be carried down this forbidding canyon trail.

Freire-Marreco's letter to Darbishire continued after she moved from Santa Fe to the camp in the canyon. *As soon as I have made enough friends, I can move to a pueblo—probably there will be no difficulty in finding one where I can rent a native room and have a girl to help me cook, and at the same time be in reach of white people (as stipulated by family). After some weeks, rejoin the school in camp or in town, and compare results with Mr. Harrington and Mr. Wilson, who are on the staff; then go back to the pueblo, and so on as long as the money lasts.*

The two figures she mentioned were both well-respected on the American scene. John Peabody Harrington, 1907-1961, American ethnologist, was reputed to have understood 100 Native American languages. He recorded accurate data about some of these languages as well as tribal ceremonies, material culture, music, land boundaries, geology, botany and folklore. When associated with the Bureau of American Ethnology, he was the Commissioner of the Bureau of Indian Affairs for the Interior Department and has been classified as the least social of his contemporary ethnologists. Meeting Freire-Marreco at the Summer Session of the School of American Archaeology, he became important in her professional life as they continued to work together and share information of mutual interest.

Not as important in Freire-Marreco's career, W.P. Wilson was an American archaeologist who, after his association with the School of American Archaeology, excavated under the auspices of Philadelphia's Commercial Museum. He did much to help Native people by arguing for their rights in Washington, D.C..

Also to Darbishire: *I hope you approve of all this—of course it will be modified from time to time. Supposing I find it necessary to get off to some out-of-the-way pueblo and there is no other white person there already. It might turn out that no good material could be found in the tame villages; and if a companion were absolutely necessary, it would be better to spend the money (nearly 40 pounds perhaps) on a competent collaborator than on a mere chaperon. I wish you would give me an opinion on this before long.*

*This is rather a rigmarole, isn't it? But there is so little time to write a decent letter. If anyone in Senior Common Room or in College is kind enough to want to hear of me, perhaps you will show it to them too, asking them to excuse the roughness of it. Four days in the train and mountain air at the end does make you so sleepy!* (ibid. Somerville, Darbishire, 26 June 1910) The Senior Common Room was reserved for resident tutors and other members of

Somervile College Staff, only about six in 1910.

That letter was written on the eve of her splendid summer experience at the summer school at Rito de los Frijoles. This experience would prove supremely important to Freire-Marreco's professional future, shaping as it did her focus and putting her in touch with several influential figures in the field of anthropology.

*John P. Harrington recording Indian speech patterns, Santa Fe, New Mexico, ca. 1912.* The ethnologist, who devoted his life to detailed and accurate information about Native Americans, and Freire-Marreco developed a cordial working relationship and published jointly, sharing many interests, mainly language and botany. Courtesy Palace of the Governors, MNM/DCA Neg. No.88417.

# ✌ Life in Camp

Freire-Marreco attended Hewett's summer study session from early July until the end of August 1910 with trips to nearby Rio Grande pueblos. An impressive group of Southwestern anthropologists crossed her path at the school, some as instructors and some fellow students who later left their marks in like fields. Among them were Donald Beauregard, Charles Lummis, Jesse Nusbaum and Neil Judd.

Donald Beauregard, 1881-1915, was an American artist who explored southwest Indian country with Neil Judd in places such as the Wetherill country and Rainbow Bridge in Arizona. He died at the age of 34 just after he started a mural for the Santa Fe Art Museum from sketches he had made in Europe.

Charles Fletcher Lummis, 1859-1928, a passionate and hot-tempered American archaeologist and author, lived at various southwest Pueblos for lengthy periods of time. Associated with the School of American Archaeology, he founded the Southwest Archaeological Society and the Southwest Museum in Los Angeles.

Jesse M. Nusbaum, 1887-1947, was an archaeologist who accompanied Hewett on an expedition to Quirigua, Guatemala in 1911 and later became a Director of the School of Archaeology.

Neil Merton Judd, 1887-1976, was a student assistant when Freire-Marreco attended the School of Archaeology's summer session. As an American anthropologist he concentrated his work in the southwest United States. He was associated with the Museum of New Mexico and later the Smithsonian Institution. Judd's Fall 1962 article in *El Palacio Magazine* describes the human and humorous side of life at the camp.

Those who attended the first summer session in 1910, under the auspices of the School of American Archaeology, in El Rito de los Frijoles, New Mexico. Identified standing left to right were: "W.W. Robbins, Donald Beauregard, J.P. Harrington, F.W. Hodge, Edgar L. Hewett, Neil Judd, Maude Woy, and Barbara F. Marreco Aitken; Seated left to Right: Sylvanus G. Morley, Kenneth Chapman, Percy Adams, Jesse L. Nusbaum, Gold?, and Julius Henderson." Here Barbara Freire-Marreco met American scientists, both faculty and fellow scholars, most of whom went on to make contributions in the fields of archaeology, anthropology and/or ethnology. Courtesy of the Palace of the Governors, MNM/DCA Neg. No. 81918.

*Excavations for the summer centered at Tyuoni, the great circular ruin in mid-valley, and two terraced dwellings at the base of the north cliff, the upper* terraces opening into individual cavate lodges. Beauregard and I occupied a suite of half a dozen such lodges or rooms, in Snake House, highest of all, thinking we would be safe from interruptions. But, to our surprise, when Charles F. Lummis and his son arrived to attend an annual meeting of the Council, they took up residence in a suite just around the corner from our retreat. At that time Lummis was convinced, along with Thomas A. Edison, that no man needed more than three hours sleep a night, so he built a small fire outside his cavate room at eleven o'clock and played his guitar until four when he retired, unmindful of the fact we working men had to be at a 7:00 o'clock breakfast and ready for work at 7:30. Not that we didn't appreciate Lummis' endless repertoire of old Spanish and cowboy songs; it was just that we needed more than three hours sleep.

The Director, never one to give free rein to young appetites, had driven a tight bargain in contracting meals for the summer camp. As I recall, each of us were allowed three thin pancakes and ham gravy for breakfast. We never did learn who got the ham. All we got was the gravy, and it was thin too. If those pancakes had been square-cut they could have served as cigarette papers.

Judd casually mentioned another visitor, Sylvanus Griswald Morley, 1883-1948, an American archaeologist and expert on Mayan culture, who later served as Director of the Museum of New Mexico. For at least part of the season Morley had the morning and I the afternoon shift. So distributed, time remained for individual study at the camp library. One morning Morley came running into camp to show an Indian idol that one of his Tewa crew had just uncovered. Not until later was it discovered that the idol had been carved from a piece of cottonwood and carefully aged with bacon grease and red ocher. But there was relatively little horse-play on the job; everyone was too busy. When the Director announced to our San Ildefonso Indian workmen that Harrington wanted to learn their language, he had several volunteers, each of whom thought it would be easier to sit in the shade of a cave room and talk Tewa than to work in the sun nine hours a day. But none lasted more than two days; after that they begged to be put back on the pick-and-shovel crew. Harrington was a Simon Legree; he was utterly relentless in pursuit of a new word.

*Rito de los Frijoles, New Mexico, summer session camp, study tent, 1910, School of American Archaeology.* Primitive perhaps, but what an enjoyable way to study! Jesse L. Nusbaum photograph. Courtesy of the Palace of the Governors, MNM/DCA Neg. No.81921.

The work week was intense, Judd recalled, but the weekends allowed time to explore the beauty and serenity of the area. *Sunday was the day for washing clothes; bathing in the ice-cold pool down canyon below the falls; and for walks to places of interest: the Ceremonial Cave; the Stone Lions of Cochiti; or the Painted Cave, some five or six miles south of Tyuoni. The rest of the week we worked nine hours daily. I recall seeing Juan Gonzales, San Ildefonso Indian and a graduate of Carlisle sitting in breech-cloth on the round of a ladder in Tyuoni, reading the funny page of the New York Times.*

*Another time, perhaps the day after the Jack Johnson-Jim Jeffries prize fight of July 4, 1910, an Easterner with great expectations, knowing there was a Harvard graduate in camp, stood silhouetted momentarily on the cliff 200 feet above Tyuoni, and gave the traditional Harvard 9. And I can still imagine his disappointment when he received in return, not the answering 9 but an impatient, "W ho won the fight?"*

In 1910 Frijoles Canyon was still far-away and wild. Judd remembered one moonlit night when a youthful huntsman in the party, proud of his .22 rifle, shot a bear in the vegetable garden. The next morning he discovered it hadn't been a bear at all—he had killed the host's black calf!

Freire-Marreco frequently described her camp activities, especially to her mentor, John Myres, back in England. In one of her first letters to him from the U.S. she asked him to excuse *the sort of paper that survives the end of camp.* She acknowledged receipt of his letter more than a fortnight earlier, explaining that she had been expecting on a daily basis to get a scheme from Harrington, who had made it back to camp only the previous week from Mojave country. She promised to send it on to Myres. *I hope it will not be much longer delayed, and meanwhile I write the letter to accompany it. . . . Mr. Hodge (Bureau of American Ethnology) is in camp with us now, and he is most willing that the scheme worked out for the Bureau should be made use of in any way for the diffusion of knowledge.*

*My doings have not been as picturesque as your report of them to Miss Rogers must have made them. I have had three short stays in Santa Clara pueblo, and a visit to Santo Domingo for a dance, and the rest of the time I have been in camp, working with Indians from Santa Clara and San Ildefonso. Since Mr. Harrington's arrival this has been very profitable. Mr. Harrington is an extraordinarily clever young man and knows it, very generous in sharing his material and his pet interpreter. Indeed a generous hospitality is characteristic of the School, and the great advantage of Mr. Hewett's guidance and introduction almost makes up for the extreme difficulty of the field. It is perhaps the worst in the world for a beginner; the people reserved and suspicious in the highest degree, and quite aware of what anthropological work and publication means.*

*You should see the Indian workmen here in camp, pouring over the Smithsonian Reports! You have your choice between the Rio Grande pueblos, Americanized, all the native life running just below the surface; and places like Santo Domingo, where the people are so resolute in resisting Americanization that information is obtained with very real danger to your native informant's life and not without danger, perhaps, to your own. If I had known the difficulty of the field I would never have come and yet the material, on native government particularly, is very rich, and the people so well worth knowing for their own sake. It is hard to think of them as material, they are too real.* Freire-Marreco's 1910-1914 Album 34 at Pitt Rivers Museum reveals growing and deep ties to her pueblo hosts.

She acknowledged, rather humorously, one reason her friendship was special. *At Santa Clara I have some friends, but I have got them by sinking the ethnologist in the polite visitor, doing endless needlework and advising on babies' health. Next thing I know I shall be teaching Sunday school! I go back there at the end of this week; and I have some faint hopes of making better progress: I happened to say to one of the Native officials that my grandfather owned a green parrot, and the effect was as if I had said that I was heir to a gold mine. I have written home for all the feathers that the bird can part with; and if anyone you know will send me some more (green Mexican parrot with long red and blue tail feathers, and feathers from the little ring round the back of the neck) I shall be most seriously grateful. They are essential for certain ceremonies and very hard to get since the Native trade with the South (Old Mexico) broke up. No doubt some enterprising firm will soon get wind of it and begin to supply parrots on a large scale; meanwhile, they are the thing to bring out.* (Bodleian, Myres, 31 August 1910)

Whether her Grandfather's parrot feathers were sent from England is not known, but Freire-Marreco successfully obtained them from another source, as affirmed in a letter she wrote to Frederick Hodge. *Thank you very much for sending me Mr. Baker's letter about the possibility of getting a Mexican parrot from Washington or from Tampico.* This probably was Frank Collins Baker, 1867-1942, an American zoologist who did field work in Mexico.

*Yesterday I had a letter from the National Museum saying that a parrot's skin was being sent to me. I think I will wait until the skin arrives before I send for a live bird, so as to be quite sure that it is of the desired sort. Meanwhile I will write to the dealer in Tampico to ask his prices.*

*I feel as if I were getting on slightly better here, but it is hard to say; it may be only the general affability of harvest time. At any rate I am sure that the parrot-skin will have an excellent effect; thank you very much indeed for getting it for me.* (Smithsonian Institution, National Anthropological Archives, Frederick W. Hodge papers, 24 Sept. 1910. Hereafter cited as National Archives, Hodge)

🕊 🕊 🕊

During study at the summer session, relations between Freire-Marreco and the Pueblo workmen were cordial. Her work in camp at Rito de los Frijoles seemed to have gone well even though the living conditions were primitive and archeology, not anthropology, was the planned focus. Whenever she visited any of the pueblos, she made it a point to join the women at their work or social groups, keeping silent and listening to their conversations endlessly as she came to understand their language. She was genuinely fond of the Native people she met and her observations were written privately so as not to offend. Her compassion showed in her care of the sick.

Only one letter was found that criticized her behavior; it was written to Hewett from Thomas S. Dozier, a trader and merchant from the nearby town of Espanola, and John Harrington's confidential informant. Educated and a Bureau of Indian Affairs employee, he was the father of the better-known Edward Dozier, a prominent Native researcher, educator and writer who later became Freire-Marreco's friend. The elder Dozier's letter was blunt. *Last Sunday a week, Miss F-Marreco requested me to lend her a couple of mss. referring to you. I readily complied but told her that I hoped no further use would be made of them than to read them. She left the pueblo last Saturday and failed to return the mss. I am at a loss to understand why this was done, & can hardly keep from expressing myself in a more distinct manner.*

*Will you be kind enough to see Miss Marreco & explain that in as much as she is a stranger to me, her holding these mss. for more than 10 days instead of a necessary two or three hours is unusual and I shall be pleased to have her to place them in your hands at once; you can return them to me at your convenience. Please favor me with your reply by return mail & oblige.* (Museum of New Mexico, Hewett, 16 Aug. 1910) The outcome of Dozier's criticism and request is not known. There was no further evidence of criticism of Freire-Marreco by the Rio Grande Pueblo people or fellow associates.

🦅 🦅 🦅

The year turned to late September, when the aspen trees in canyon country were turning gold, and Freire-Marreco witnessed the breaking down of the summer camp. Ever observant of the relationships between people, most especially the undercurrents and subtle tensions as the Indian culture rubbed up against the scientific one, she described the atmosphere to Myres. Among her concerns was the recurrence of malaria, an ongoing menace carried by the mosquitoes breeding in Bean Creek's stream-side pools.

*The archaeological work here is immensely interesting, and most necessary to explain the features of modern pueblo life. Just now we are seeing the tiresome side of camp life just preparing to break camp, the workmen rather cantankerous, two days of rain and cold, and two Indians down, or rather up and down, with malaria. By common consent sick-nursing is left to anthropologists, and very justly, considering the way we strain the Indians constantly with cross questioning. They all say they would sooner shovel on the ruins, so Mr. Harrington and I each have a patient. Mine has been pretty bad, and frightened about himself, "thought he may be going dead" and I sympathize with the feeling as I had a mild attack myself lately, so I have been pretty busy with a horse to feed and water, and a vain effort to reach Mr. Harrington's standard of ten hours investigation a day.*

*Future plans are, to stay round these pueblos until the end of November, and then possibly to make a little expedition to the Yavapai, who border on the Lower Colorado. They are said to be quite undignified and communicative.*

*I did not mean to run on at such a length, or rather I meant to write all this to Mrs. Myres, to whose kind and most welcome letter I enclose an answer. Does the Liverpool Museum want any pueblo pottery? I believe it can be got in winter for about 50, if it were a large vessel, and freight would be extra.* (Bodeian, Myres, 31 Aug. 1910) Though the currency is not specified, pottery sold for almost nothing in the early twentieth century compared to today's prices.

# ❦ Rio Grande Pueblos, New Mexico

At the end of the summer 1910 Freire-Marreco moved to Santa Clara Pueblo. A little curiosity toward her was exhibited by Margaret Tafoya, then a little girl of six. Tafoya went on to become a renowned potter who, years later, remembered that there was such a person in residence and *we didn't understand what she was doing.* (Personal conversation)

Some Indians did understand what Freire-Marreco's purpose was, but one important figure helped her immensely. Santiago Naranjo was one of the most famous Santa Clarans of his day. He was trusted by his people and served on their Council in different capacities, eventually becoming Pueblo Governor. He also was friendly to whites, and no doubt he knew and understood what the young anthropologist was attempting to do at the Pueblo. He became Freire-Marreco's guide, guard and political advisor. After a period of initial distrust, they came to a mutual understanding and she claimed that he was of great help in her work, even though at times she felt his information was contradictory. She accounted for this apparent contradiction at times as his attempt not to divulge ceremonial secrets. Native people were understandably sensitive to criticism and ridicule from white investigators. At a later date, a negative picture of Santiago was painted in Hall's **Enchanted Sand** pp.107, 108. Perhaps this writer had antagonized the Santa Clara people by prying.

*Santiago Naranjo in his house.* A Santa Clara Pueblo informant for Freire-Marreco and though she doubted some of his information, she appreciated his help. The article on the wall may be the one mentioned in a letter to Edward Dozier years later dated 19 May 1954 from Barbara Aitken. Courtesy of University of New Mexico, Maxwell Museum of Anthropology, W.W. Hill Collection No. 84.55.461.

Hall wrote: *When I first met him I had been impressed by his quiet dignity; it was the manner he always tried on white people and never failed to get away with it. On closer acquaintance I found that he was a dreadful humbug. But he was a born tactician. Though long past his prime, he still swayed the councils of the pueblo. He possessed all the qualities of a politician, the gift of gab and an artful way of playing off one party against another.*

    *Naturally avaricious, he saw in the white people a ready prey. Being a consummate actor, he played the old Indian chief for their benefit; told the most dreadful lies about his prowess and made up songs out of his head which he said were the long-forgotten music of his people.*

❧ ❧ ❧

August 12th is Santa Clara Pueblo Day, an annual celebration at the Pueblo in honor of their patron saint. The festivities consisted, and still do, of a Roman Catholic mass, a procession to place religious statues in a shaded ramada, ongoing prayers, Native dancing, feasting and endless hospitality in the form of food and drink. All are welcome. Priests attend feast days at Santa Clara and the other Rio Grande missions on their saints days, coming out for the day from the mother church at Santa Cruz near Espanola. Their priestly duties to the pueblos were to perform the sacraments and ceremonies of mass, marriages and baptisms.

On Santa Clara day 1910 Freire-Marreco was invited to the wedding of Marianita Chavarria to Herman Velarde. The Church-recorded date, clearly mistaken, of this marriage was February 22, 1909 because Freire-Marreco was not even in the United States at that time, and the photograph she took of the couple on their wedding day is well-labeled. Priests sometimes did not record events until months, even years after they occurred, entering a group at one time afterward when memory of the events had faded, accounting for some inconsistencies in church records.

Freire-Marreco confirmed an inaccuracy 42 years later, after reading an article about the Velarde's daughter, Pablita, by Dorothy Dunn titled "Painter of Pueblo Life" in **El Palacio Magazine** 1952. Pablita Velarde was a famous Santa Clara pioneer artist and author, who not only made a big contribution to the art world with her own paintings but also inspired many others. Many years afterward, Pablita shared a letter she received from Freire-Marreco, who by then had become Mrs. Robert Aitken.

Because her mother had died when she was three years old, Pablita had no recollection of her, and was most appreciative of this letter as well as the wedding photograph Freire-Marreco sent her. She reciprocated with a gift painting, but the painting's whereabouts is not known.

The letter from Barbara Aitken described specific memories of the wedding and also expressed her gratitude for the painting from Pablita.

*Naibi kwiyobithaedi* (Our Old Lady's Day)

*You are too generous. To have one of your beautiful paintings is more than I ever dreamed of. It will indeed be a treasure. And your affectionate letter gives me much pleasure.*

*But Santa Clara people are like that. They are not timid and suspicious like the people of other pueblos. I remember how San Ildefonso people said, "you have spent a great deal of money to come here, so you must be able to pay us high prices," whereas Santa Clara people said, "poor thing, she is far from her home and has spent much money, let us give her things for nothing."*

Pueblos always have a clean-up day in preparation for important events.*On the Day of the Kings when I came out with the other women to sweep the plaza the men kept saying, "Here, Saiya, here is some clean dirt for you!" I was very ignorant and innocent, and they all took such pains to keep me so! As for dear Santiago Naranjo and Filomena and Sophia (whom God have in His holy keeping) they were like father and mother and sister to me.*

*Your father and mother were married on Santa Clara Day 1910.* The text and photo of the Velardes is in Freire-Marreco's 1910-1911 Album 34 PR No. AL.34.18, Pitt Rivers Museum, University of Oxford. *I was staying with Jose Domingo Gutierrez and his wife. They were very good to me, and I should not have left them but for the alkaline water of the Winter Party's well which made me unwell, so Santiago had moved me to a little canvas house which Juan Naranjo had put up for some tourist. On the eve of the fiesta we had a cloud burst, part of the plaza was flooded, we had to rescue the ceiling cloths of the saint's booth* (the aforementioned ramada). *As Santiago and I stood on a sandhill outside the village, the arrows of lightning shone round our feet and the thunder shook the ground. About 6 o'clock it cleared; two processions met on the further side of a long pool of water; the white sheets in which the men had wrapped themselves and the yellow fox skins on the standards were reflected in the pool. I shall never forget the beauty of the sight. At night there was a lunar rainbow.*

*The men swept the water with brooms and dug little channels to drain off the water and strewed sand, and in the morning decorated the booth again.*

Indians, Mexicans in wagons, and Navajos on horseback in gay blankets began to assemble. I remember particularly an old Navajo chief on a white pony with his three wives trailing behind him. The drums began. The two parties of racers grouped themselves. Very queer Desiderio looked wearing only gold rimmed spectacles and a red spotted breechcloth. (He was the baker at Santa Fe Indian School home on holiday, and they caught him and obliged him to race.) They raced from opposite ends. By and by the Navajo went from house to house, filling their blankets with gifts and bread.

But I have forgotten to write the real subject of my letter. About 10 o'clock the Belgian priest from Santa Cruz arrived and your parents were married. Priests were usually from Spain at that time because the Spanish, coming north from Mexico, were the first European settlers in the region. With this influx, most pueblo people understood and spoke Spanish.

*Ruin of the Old Mission at Santa Clara, ca. 1910* as it looked when Freire-Marreco stayed at that Pueblo. Later rebuilt, it is still in use. Copy of Diapositive, Fred Harvey Collection, Courtesy of the Smithsonian Institution, National Museum of the American Indian, Neg. No. N31752.

*The night before, your mother had borrowed my white silk shirt waist. The nuptial mass was said in the cottonwood booth.* Probably because the church was in ruins at that time. *There was another couple whose names I have forgotten, possibly a daughter of J.D. Gutierrez, for I saw the wedding trunks in his house. When Santiago, the sacristan, went along asking each one, "Has desayundo?"* (Have you had breakfast?) *Your father, Sekang* (Little Leaf), *had to answer, "He bebido café"* (I drank coffee); *so only your mother could take the Sacrament.*

*I can't remember any more of the day, but at night Santiago escorted me back to my canvas house. We passed a group of Apaches sleeping on the ground wrapped in their blankets and a little drunken Apache, seeing a woman, came after us calling. Don Santiago laughed and translated: "He say, 'Do not leave me, I have plenty of watermelons.' Arrived at my tent, he said, "Maybe you scared, I sleep under your table." But I could not let him lie on the wet floor. The water was leaking through the roof; the blankets were all wet; I put up my umbrella and slept under it.*

*Next morning we stood waiting to wave to the train.* Waving was standard procedure to stop the "Chile Line" train at Santa Clara Pueblo, not a scheduled stop, in order to board.

*I began to shiver, and by the time we reached Buckman, where for some reason we had left the horses, I was in a fever. We had a hard time riding to the Rito de los Frijoles; at one place the trail had partly washed out and the ponies refused to cross it, Santiago had to gather rocks and build it up again. The last part of our journey he dismounted and ran through the trees in the misty moonlight, the ponies following him: As he said afterwards, "By gosh, I run all same as coyote!" Lastly there was the long steep descent to the camp. I dismounted with difficulty and cried on Miss Abbot's neck. Dr. Hewett excused me saying, "These folks have had a hard trip."*

*Your parents had a nice neat house not very far from the Squash Kiva, furnished with table, chairs and bedstead. They wore citizen dress except for dances. They went to mass at Santa Cruz.*

*Santa Fe People Leaving Train. Pueblo Santa Clara, New Mexico.* The Denver and Rio Grande Railroad spur, familiarly called the "Chile Line," no longer exists. There was neither a station nor an attendant there. 1903 photograph by George H. Pepper. Courtesy of the Smithsonian Institution, National Museum of the American Indian, Neg. No. N32500.

She mentioned another encounter with Pablita's parents, this time when a loud disturbance coincided with the marriage of a local couple, a schoolteacher and a widower. *We had a rather disagreeable schoolmistress who lived in Juan Naranjo's house. She married an American carpenter from Espanola. At night a party of Americans came out to give them a cencerrada* (noise-making to disturb newlyweds) *because he was a widower. I was alarmed by the loud shouts and went stumbling over the furrows of a maize field in the dark and took refuge in your parent's house. Your father explained the noise and lighted me back to my tent.*

*The last time I saw them was when I called to say goodbye about nine o'clock one night in 1911. I heard afterwards that your father said, "Saiya came to our house in the middle of the night!"*

*It is that long ago! I have had so much pleasure in recalling those happy days, which seem as clear as if it were yesterday. Is your father alive and well? I wonder if you would send this letter to* **El Palacio** *when you and your family are through with it?*

*I enclose the negative of your parents in case you wish to have more copies made: please return it to me; and a few prints taken that day for you to keep, except two that are marked.*

*Please do not call me madam. Umbi awinge—iwe sayagi any dintung* (your village called me grandmother in their language). *Sengidiho I kwomi* (Farewell, stay in good health).

As a Postscript: *I have just found 32 prints taken in 1938 I think, by Miss Blackwood, Demonstrator in Ethnology at Oxford. You will find your father among them. I am sending them on loan, but keep your father's.* (Courtesy of Pablita Velarde)

Beatrice Mary Blackwood, 1889-1926, was a British anthropologist, ethnologist and linguist who spent parts of 1924, 1925, and 1926 in the U.S. so the photographs may have been taken earlier than Freire-Marreco's date. Retracing Freire-Marreco's trips, Blackwood then helped catalogue Freire-Marrece's collection for the Pitt Rivers Museum.

❦ ❦ ❦

After living at Santa Clara for only a short time, Freire-Marreco reassured her sponsors that she was perfectly safe, an issue that seemed to be of great importance to her family and benefactors. However, she was discouraged and somewhat critical, probably because she had been ill. Perhaps, too, she had found living conditions at the Pueblo strenuous. Even though she had obviously become fond of the Native people, she reported some disappointment in their secrecy toward whites and expressed also a lack of progress on her fieldwork to Somerville College through Helen Darbishire. She stated that things were going badly, but then pushed herself forward. Thanking Darbishire for her letter of July 22 that had been received at Santa Clara Pueblo, Freire-Marreco wrote her reply a month later.

My work so far has been among Indians with whom it was perfectly safe to stay alone, and there were white people within easy reach. I don't think it at all likely that I shall make any expedition into the real wilds, it is so difficult and expensive to find nomadic groups at all; my wildest field will probably be Santo Domingo, where I hope to go sometime in September. There they are a little more like savages, but I think I shall stay with the trader's wife at Thornton, two miles off, and ride in and out to the pueblo. Another thing is the slowness of methods here is necessarily so great, that it would be almost useless to bring out another worker for a short definite time. The people here are extremely proud and secretive, and very much on an equality with white people, in their estimation at least. There is a fixed determination to frustrate the inquisition of white people, veiled under the forms of politeness in the Rio Grande pueblos, expressed in open hostility among the Keres.

The only possible attitude in the first case is that of a discreet and well behaved visitor; what attitude is possible in the second case I don't yet know. It seems that this is one of the most difficult fields in the world, and if I had known anything of it beforehand I would never have come; and I must say I wish Miss Fletcher, with all her kindness, had been more explicit about it. The fact was, I believe, that she thought of me chiefly as a pupil for Dr. Hewett's School here; and he is a splendid teacher and well worth coming to learn from; but that's not what you sent me over to do!

You must not think that Dr. Hewett does not do everything possible to forward and facilitate my work. He is splendid about it, spares no pains to get me opportunities, and without his very wide local knowledge and influence I should have no chance at all. Everywhere in the Rio Grande area his name is a password with Americans, Mexicans and Indians. He has given me the services, and sometimes the whole time, of one of the best informed and best disposed Indians in the territory, Santiago Naranjo, from whom I have learnt all the little that I have learnt so far. Besides this, the School has treated me most generously in the way of expense, lending me tent and bedding, providing me with transport, and in every way helping out my resources. I am most grateful to Dr. Hewett and to the School: what discourages me is what they acknowledge, the difficulty of the field. Mr. Harrington, the ethnologist on the staff, has just come *in to camp: he declares that the only way to get real information is to pay a man in each place to come to you privately. Well, that's all against my training, and against the concrete method which requires you to observe events in their natural setting; it seems most unsatisfactory in the way of information, because only a treacherous and mercenary person would come to you so; and candidly, I have'nt the courage for intrigue In short, I don't mean to.* Later in her stay, there is a change in attitude by Freire-Marreco toward this approach to information gathering.

*Well, now that I'm here and have spent so much of your money already I think I'd better stick to it, and I may get some observations of everyday native customs worth having, but certainly I'm not going to set the Thames on fire with any great discoveries. If any friends in Oxford enquire, you may as well begin in good time to say that things are going badly.*

*Perhaps I take a particularly gloomy view because my horse has a sore back and I've just had an attack of malaria; and I haven't told you any of the pleasant side, the fascination of the Indian character and the Indian home-life. I love the Santa Clara people and could live there for the rest of my life with pleasure, and there are two families there that love me a little, too.*

*Best love to all the Senior Common Room when they meet again. Best love to College, in fact, which daily has my very grateful remembrance, and I only wish I were likely to do their generosity more credit.*

*We start at five tomorrow, so no more tonight.*

As a Postscript: *If Miss Fletcher is still in England when term begins, I do wish you would try to get her to see you in College: she is absolutely fascinating and enchanting, quite a wonderful type, and I believe she would enjoy Somerville: do try. Mr. Myres will have her address.* (Somerville, Darbishire, 19 Aug. 1910) Due to Freire-Marreco's suggestion, an invitation was extended to Fletcher to read a paper at a meeting at the Royal Anthropological Society meeting. Fletcher consented.

Once her health and spirits had improved, Freire-Marreco, clearly felt guilty about her previous complaints, so wrote apologetically to Darbishire. Also, she now had hopes of getting further removed from what she called "civilization" and of accomplishing some of the goals of study she had planned. The letter to Darbishire was quite self-effacing.

*I am a good deal ashamed of the letter I wrote you last month; it was much too doleful about opportunities of work, and I fear it was expressed in terms most ungrateful to Miss Fletcher, to whose introduction and advice I owe so much. It is no excuse to say that I wrote it with a temperature, because people have no business to write letters then!*

*At the end of last month I had several consultations with Dr. Hewett and Mr. Hodge, the head of the Bureau of American Ethnology, who was in camp with us. An expedition of four members of the School of American Archaeology will be going to the Lower Colorado country early in December, to complete a study of the Mojave tribe which Mr. Harrington has begun. It is proposed that I shall go at the same time, or possibly a month earlier, to study the neighboring Yavapai or Chimaweve. Both of these tribes would be particularly interesting from the point of view of contact with the Mohave. They are quite simple primitive people, and have not the reserve which makes the Pueblos so hard to do rapid and systematic work with. It is supposed that in the course of November and December I might do them pretty thoroughly. The cost of this expedition would probably be more than I could meet, but the Bureau of Ethnology is willing to pay for a piece of the work of that sort, out of next year's appropriation. Their plan is to pay for a piece of work ready for publication, and the amount would probably be $300. Would the Somerville Committee be willing to let me go on these terms and to have the results published in the Bureau of Ethnology Reports and Bulletins? I imagine that it would be no disadvantage to secure publication in that way, and the Bureau Reports are so widely circulated that they are as accessible as any English publication. I should be able to quote freely from the sociological material in any special work on Authority.*

*Until November, I propose to stay in the Rio Grande valley, fishing very gently for information in Santa Clara and San Juan. At the end of this month I am going to Taos for a day or two. I think I am making progress in friendships here, but whether they will tell anything of importance remains to be seen. I came here again on September 4th, and am quite settled down to a comfortable though solitary housekeeping, in two little wood and canvas houses with a porch of branches between. I do all my own housework, such as it is, and cooking, only*

I have a girl to fetch water twice a day. I entertain a good deal, mostly old ladies who are willing to teach me Indian medicine; and really you never know what the pleasures of hospitality are until you do your own cooking! What a useful member of a reading party I shall be ever after this! I think I shall hire myself out in College to conduct camping parties and wash, bake and cook for them. I never was half so well in my life. The climate suits me admirably, and so does living out of doors. I simply cannot realize how far I am from England and all of you, with a fresh set of scenes and people almost as familiar as Oxford, in fact more familiar than College will be with all the freshers when I come into residence.

The house Freire-Marreco occupied at Santa Clara Pueblo: Her drawing of her living arrangement she sent to Helen Darbishire dated 16 Sept. 1909. Courtesy of the University of Oxford, Somerville College.

1991 photograph by L. Blair is the dwelling, by then in ruins, of her 1913 house.

This is a pleasant busy well-fed time of year in the pueblo; women are cleaning wheat by hand—a slow and soothing process, and men are up the canyon at their fruit gardens drying peaches and melons for the winter. Sometimes the whole family moves out to a little hut near the garden, so as to watch the fruit at night and enjoy a casual camp life. Until six o'clock in the evening the village is quite deserted: it is also unusually clean, because women are not throwing their kitchen refuse into the plaza as usual.

*Girl with Water Jar, Pueblo Santa Clara, New Mexico.* The water source, Santa Clara Creek, was shared by all the people of the Pueblo and transported in this manner to their homes in jars of this shape that helped conserve moisture and eased pouring. Courtesy of Smithsonian Institution, National Museum of the American Indian, 1904 Churchill Collection No. 27029.

*Platform for drying fruit and meat,* located in a canyon not far from Santa Clara Pueblo. This way to preserve food assured a winter's supply or survival after a failed crop. Courtesy of University of New Mexico, Maxwell Museum of Anthropology, W.W. Hill Collection No. 84.55.477.

  *P.S. My Indian name is Ta-yo-povi, (flower of the sedge). I have another, but I fear it's not quite kind, for none of my friends will disclose it.* (ibid. 16 September 1910) There were two almost identical versions of her other Tewa name. Tewa nicknames are not only descriptive, but can be cruel. Older residents of Santa Clara remembered her as "Aunt Whiskers," while at Hano on the Hopi Reservation, some 200 miles distant as the crow flies, she was referred to simply as "Whiskers." Many years later her English housekeeper and companion confirmed this personal attribute of facial hair; it had been the housekeeper's task to tweeze the surplus hair.

🦋 🦋 🦋

On September 4, 1910 Freire-Marreco had taken up residence at Santa Clara Pueblo and lived there until late November. From there she made side trips to Santo Domingo and San Juan Pueblos. On October 4th she was in Nambe, followed by Tesuque on the 7th or 8th, and Taos Pueblo on the 25th. Though the narrow gauge "Chile Line" Railroad ran through Santa Clara Pueblo, her travel between pueblos was usually on horseback, sometimes bareback.

*View of Pueblo, Santa Clara, New Mexico.* The two story-building on the right, mentioned in a Freire-Marreco letter, no longer exists and not until recent years was another second story home erected at the Pueblo. Courtesy of Smithsonian Institution, National Museum of the American Indian, 1904 Churchill Collection, Neg. No. N27041.

In a short note to Hewett, Freire-Marreco was learning not to accept so-called facts just on the word of others. *I am almost certain that I was wrong about the customs of marriage of Santa Clara, of which I spoke to you. I think I was too hasty in accepting a white person's generalizations.* (Museum of New Mexico, Hewett, dated only Wednesday)

Showing great concern for the welfare of the Santa Clara people, she appealed to Hewett for help. Santiago had asked her to explain the new *police arrangements*, which were causing *a little trouble* at Santa Clara. It concerned Clara True, the Bureau of Indian Affairs school teacher in the Espanola area, who had lived in the Rio Grande region with her housekeeper-mother for a number of years. She had a good reputation among the Santa Clara people for helping settle their affairs, such as land disputes with the U.S. government. A strong-willed and determined person, she aggravated those who held opposing views and was criticized as one who interfered and assumed authority she did not have. She was even labeled "She Devil of the Rio Grande" by some government officials.

*The Indian account of it is this: Miss True has got seven Indian policemen and one white man to keep the Indians from drinking. Donociano "had a bottle" last Monday week, and these new policemen took it away from him; he asked the white man what their authority was, but he would not explain beyond saying that "it was Government." The white man offered Donaciano a job, but D. wants to know, "Who is the boss?" Some Tesuque men, who had a bottle in Espanola on August 12, were detected by these new policemen and taken into court, and no-one would tell them what sort of new police they were. It has nothing to do with Mr. Crandall and his police, and no notice has been given to the governor of the pueblo (which seems to be the main grievance). Altogether, the people are a little troubled, and Santiago wants to have something authentic to tell them.* As Superintendent of the Espanola, NM, Schools, Crandall also had some authority from the U.S. government to intervene in pueblo affairs in order to help the Native people.

This 1904 photograph was taken in the Espanola, New Mexico school district. From left to right: Superintendent of Schools Crandall, Mrs. Crandall, Mrs. True (Clara True's mother), Clara True (a teacher in the local schools) and Col. Frank Churchill (United States Indian School Inspector.) Freire-Marreco undoubtedly knew these people during her stay at Santa Clara Pueblo. Courtesy of Smithsonian Institution, National Museum of the American Indian, Churchill Collection, Neg. No. N27031.

Freire-Marreco said she was passing on the *rambling account* just as she had received it the day before. She had told *Santiago that Miss True was probably authorized by some other department of the U.S. government other than that by which Mr. Crandall was employed, and that she would try to find out more precisely.* Miss True being away at present in the Jicarilla Apache country, the anthropologist asked Hewett who best to approach for more information. She expressed a fear of *giving offense by asking questions of the wrong people,* and acknowledged that the local officials were *at the very least a little sensitive.* (ibid. 13 Sept. 1910)

Two months later in another letter to Hewett Freire-Marreco praised Clara True's accomplishments, but also expressed a small doubt.

Her own analysis of the situation was strengthened by her studies of governmental interactions with pueblo leaders.

*An official like Miss True—thoroughly capable, energetic, and conscientious—is predisposed by her very successful experience of reservation administration to wish to play the part of providence to the Indian community. She can do, and is doing, so much more for the people than their own officials can do. She is naturally impatient of the timidity and occasional stupidity; naturally and unconsciously, she encourages the people as a whole, and individuals too, to look to her direct as the agent of the Central Government, without the intermediation of the native organization. Equally naturally, she finds it easier to work with individual Indians and groups who will look to her and to the Central Government, and who are somewhat estranged from the native political organization. I speak (as do the Indians themselves) with the most sincere admiration for Miss True's work on behalf of the Tewa Indians; I can well believe that centralization of this sort may be in accord with the intentions of the U.S. Government. I am only concerned to point out that the difficulties of the Native officials are increased and that this has something to do with the present anxiety for recognition and definition of their authority. (ibid. 24 Nov. 1910)*

As far as the U.S. government was concerned, Freire-Marreco had been right to question True's actions. J.D. DeHuff, Superintendent U.S. Indian School, Santa Fe told Clara True in no uncertain terms that she had behaved badly. *I have been thinking considerably over the proposition of what happened last Saturday evening and I feel that in order that there may be a proper understanding on the part of all concerned, I believe I ought to make this statement to you in writing.*

*It would seem that you arranged with Juan Pajarito to take a number of boy pupils from this school and stage a dance or Indian ceremonial at La Fonda (Hotel in Santa Fe) for the benefit of a special affair given for visiting women last Saturday night. I knew nothing of this until you called me up on the phone about 6 o'clock in the evening. Juan had asked me about two o'clock in the afternoon if he could have the boys to stage a dance in the city that night. I told him that if he had the permission of the Governor of the Santo Domingo Pueblo I thought it would be all right.*

Now as a matter of fact I have been requested more than once by the Governor and the Santo Domingo Council not to let the Santo Domingo boys stage any ceremonials in the city without their consent. Furthermore the Indian Office has stated to me that objection has been raised with the Office to my allowing the pupils of this school to stage an Indian ceremonial under any circumstances and the Commissioner has very plainly stated to me his desire that I desist from anything of the kind.

I must therefore in justice and protection to myself and out of deference to the properly constituted Pueblo authorities in Santo Domingo make it an absolute requirement that anybody who wishes the services of my pupils for any purpose whatsoever must consult with me before coming to any agreement with any one representing those pupils. This is a rather delicate matter and I hope it may be taken in the spirit in which I am presenting it. I personally have no objections to those Indian ceremonials but there are people who would object to them and if it should happen that in spite of the restrictions that have been placed upon me I still go ahead allowing my pupils to stage these ceremonials, you can readily see how I am going to find myself involved in serious difficulties. (Smithsonian Institution, National Archives, Bureau of Indian Affairs file, 25 May 1925)

There is no evidence that Freire-Marreco was ever involved with the officious Clara True. The English anthropologist's life was not so worrisome as she carefully made sure not to interfere in or try to change the lives of her Santa Clara hosts.

🦅 🦅 🦅

To Myres she painted an interesting word picture of her personal relationship with some of the Santa Clara people and their practices at the Pueblo's harvest time. It seems she no longer feared being away from "white people." *The copy of your lecture on the Value of Ancient History—thank you very much for sending it—arrived yesterday, and I am reading it at a little Indian ranch, six or seven miles up the Canyon from the Rio Grande valley; within the limits of semi-mountain flora, scrub-cedar, willows, oceans of golden-flowering sage and rabbit-brush, and a mountain stream rushing over the stones.*

*A Shrine on the Loma above Santa Clara 1911.* **Not identified further, the shrine appears to be on a mesa and probably no longer exists. Courtesy of University of New Mexico, Maxwell Museum of Anthropology, School of American Research B. Freire-Marreco Collection No. 84.55.480.**

My friend, Mountain-hoarfrost, shares with two brothers a little ranch here, inherited from his father, orchards, cornfields, hay and pasture; there is a one-roomed adobe cottage, within sight of the caves where he and his wife lived when they were young and poor before any children came.

Here we came yesterday afternoon from his town house in Santa Clara Pueblo to pick the last of the apples—himself, his wife, his son Snowbird, myself, and a modest selection from his children and dogs. We all slept (or not) in rows on the floor, ten mortal hours from dark to sunrise, relieved only by a shot at a coyote about 2 a.m., and breakfasted on fried liver and yesterday's tortillas. Unfortunately, the house is not his home, and so I did not see Mountain-hoarfrost sprinkle the *cornmeal this morning, though there is a typical apparatus for it remaining from his father's time.* She probably was referring to a hand-crafted ceramic container for sacred cornmeal usually mounted on the wall of a Pueblo home.

A boy sitting in a cave at Puye Ruins, New Mexico, the ancestral home of the Santa Clara Pueblo people. Beatrice Blackwood of the Pitt Rivers Museum, School of Anthropology and Museum Ethnography, University of Oxford took this photograph in 1927 when she retraced Freire-Marreco's trips in the southwest United States. Courtesy of University of Oxford, Pitt Rivers Museum of Anthropology and Museum Ethnography Ref. No. BB B5 126N.

She liked spending time with Mountain-hoarfrost and was delighted to see that his family studied her as much as she studied them. *I love the family too well to do any anthropologizing on them; but it is great fun to see them doing it on me! At breakfast this morning I was telling them about fox-hunting and the breaking-up of the fox. They exclaimed in horror, "when they* might have kept the skin whole to dance with!" I hastily added that at least the tail was preserved with care to hang in the house; and I fancy they got about as correct a picture of English habits as I get from anything they tell me!

Telling is simply no good to me: I get endless false impressions unless I see things done and do them too. Mr. Squeers did not carry his admirable method far enough: You must go and clean it before you spell w i n d e r, not after. Consequently, my hands are sore with husking corn, drying melons, and splitting peaches for the winter.

She then led into her next thought—housekeeping. I am getting an insight into pueblo housekeeping—in some respects, a horrid insight, but thank goodness my appetite survives it. Even so; I fear they are "modified" by my company; Mountain-hoarfrost and Snowbird made a very unusual toilet this morning, and as for Foot-race, I washed him myself. But I wish you had seen us last night, sitting on blankets round the fire, gloating over a parcel of parrot feathers just received from the London Zoo—the firelight dancing on the plastered wall and on the Indians' warm human-colored faces. I can never think white the normal color after this. Parrots' feathers are ritually essential here, and very scarce: one village, fifty miles off, owns a live bird, and sells his moltings at fabulous prices.

She then delighted herself with thoughts of how Indians would perceive the information Myres sent her in a letter she had just received from him. In this company please imagine me reading your lecture, and laughing at page twenty two, and having to stop and explain to the Indians what sort of man you are—hombre qui mucho save las cosas de quanto hay (man that knows much about many things), a phrase that covers potsherds and other works of genius. I am so glad to get it here; I have read nothing for weeks except **Mine and Ranch Cookery**, and translations from post-Hellenic Greek and you do revive my belief in the whole business and primarily in the job that I am now making a failure of. I have been feeling merely an unsuccessful detective, and it is good to be reassured that Sociology is really a science and an art.

Departing briefly with an almost rhetorical question on the meaning of history and the importance of Indian events as compared to other groups: Can what happens on the Mississippi never be history as well as what happened on the Nile? And are you sure that what happened here has not escaped our notice being history?

At any rate, for what happens in this country is splendid. And if ever there was a people to whom Society and State were all in all, it is these Pueblo Indians. Sometimes they speak of it themselves "because that the way the Indian going to live." The day before yesterday I rode with Mountain-hoarfrost to the dance at Nambe, a small and decayed town, but in some respects more conservative than ours: he asked the news of a man there, and reported to me, "This people here going to take their corn tomorrow; the governor he speak to the people a week ago to be ready for tomorrow, and they all wait; no one he touch corn. Isn't that pretty nice?" he said with enthusiasm.

The present trouble comes with the attempt to merge these tiny sovereign states in the United States—authority is impaired. "These times the Uni'stai law pretty high"—and Uni'stai Government means a distant self-satisfied Bureau, and local officials openly corrupt. New-Mexican control, now to be substituted to some extent, will probably be worse. And added to all this, the attentions of ethnologists—the last straw! "All this long time no one asking the Indian questions, and now everyone asking him everything all the time!"

And there is in the history of Santa Clara, a real problem. There are two factions in this Pueblo, and just how and when they arose no one seems to know. I began by hoping it was intensification of the anti-solidarity sentiment between two phratries, the Winter and the Summer People, because it would fit in so nicely with Dr. Rivers and Anarchy Brown and the social-morphologists generally; but in this field you get a suspicion that things may also happen from particular causes, specific events, I mean.

Presumably this refered to A. Radcliffe Brown, an ethnologist then at the London School of Ecomonics.

W.W. Hill in **An Ethnography of Santa Clara Pueblo** (1982, 199-201) describes well the complicated reasons for the schisms between the Winter and Summer peoples as well as the splits between the progressive and conservative factions of each group that continued for years and still crops up in rumors. These rivalries often make it difficult for an investigator to obtain unbiased information.

*View of Santa Clara from La Loma, Summer People's Estufa 1911* as it was when Friere-Marreco was there. She was thought to favor the Summer People by the Winter People. Courtesy of University of New Mexico, Maxwell Museum of Anthropology, School of American Research B Freire-Marreco Collection No. 84.55.481.

Sir James Donaldson, 1831-1915, a British educator and classical scholar who helped establish compulsory primary education in Scotland was also one of the first to investigate relationships within the pueblos. He noted in 1890 the feud was then of several years standing, although previously all the people danced together.

*Now there are fifteen families who do not dance,* wrote Freire-Marreco, *and endless trouble arises from their periodical refusal to share in the four common works—to work on the ditch, to work on the wood-road, to sweep the plaza, and to work on the church. In this condition of pressure, it seems that the two things obviously not for mere life have gone to the wall—the church is in* ruins, and the plaza unswept. (But in every respect, compared to other pueblos, there is a decline in elegance of the Indians' sort—less dancing, less dressing, fewer home-made ornaments and conveniences; combined with comparative prosperity, getting and spending of coined money, decided rise in prosperity of some families who are able to secure elegances of the American sort, greater difference between rich and poor, and a beginning of hired labor between rich and poor Indians.) And even on the conservative-unionist side—the governor and cacique side—there are signs of another split, less than seven years old. "Seven years ago, when the Governor say something, all the people quiet, no one saying anything. This time, when the Governor say something, some people don't want. It is hinted that our present Governor is not the man to cope with these bad times—if the Governor a good man to speak, good with the head, then be all right. But Leandro be pretty old man, one hour say one thing, another hour say the other. What Governor shall we have next year? That rests with the cacique, and the cacique we may not criticize; he got a business to pick the best man." Like a shabby little old cardinal he looks; and it is an edifying sight to see him assisting at the ceremonies of the Other Church.

These personal relationships that led to pueblo conflict were of great interest and importance to Freire-Marreco. The matter of authority was exactly the subject that gained her the Fellowship and became the reason for her visit to the southwest United States. Her investigation into the structure of pueblo governments and outlining the various duties of pueblo officials led to her biggest contribution to the Rio Grande pueblos.

Returning to Freire-Marreco's letter to Myers describing her ranch visit during harvest time: *Before I finished writing this we had come home— wagon full of apples and family, myself escorting on horseback—and we fell in with a bunch of Mexican cows that had been poaching on our pastures, and we drove them three miles down the canyon—futile, but pleasant. Then we met a pinto pony mare with two Indian girls riding double, and a mule foal following, and to them we entrusted the further misguiding of the cows.*

*Also I had finished your lecture, very slowly and reluctantly reading the Blue Bird piece, because it was the last; and much wishing I had been there to hear it. Sorry though I shall be to part with it, I mean to present it to the School of Archaeology Library.*

*For weeks I have been trying to get Mr. Harrington to finish his phonetic scheme and let me post it; but he is just like the other **Notes and Queries** contributors! I suppose it is published by this time. I have only seen one report of this British Association's paper on mourning customs: it sounds as if it were on the same old lines, looking for ideas and object in view, instead of feelings.*

*I see that I have written enormously, you will never have the time to read it, but perhaps Mrs. Myres will be kind enough. You must not apply any Canons of relevance to a correspondent who has not a soul to talk to—to count it talking.*

*As a Postscript: Would it be too much to ask you to put this into an envelope for my mother instead of into the wastepaper-basket? It is so hard to keep the news up-to-date in writing home, and this would fill a gap.* (Bodleian, Myres, 6 Oct. 1910)

❦ ❦ ❦

Autumn was coming on when this letter was written. Freire-Marreco couldn't always find time to write all the news to all of her friends and colleagues back in England. Work came first and writing longhand was time-consuming. Evidence of this is contained in some October correspondence from her mother, Gertrude Freire-Marreco, to Mrs. John Myres. Although they had never met, Mrs. Freire-Marreco somewhat apologetically asked for information about Alice Fletcher who, on Barbara's recommendation, was coming to visit. She knew nothing more than that her daughter had great respect and affection for Fletcher and she was anxious to act in a manner pleasing to Barbara and acceptable by American standards.

The Myres were in the process of moving from Liverpool back to Oxford and a busy Mrs. Myres asked her husband to reply to this request. He complied with a long glowing report about Fletcher's many accomplishments and personal traits, reassuring the Freire-Marrecos they would enjoy her company. He added that he hoped there was good news from Barbara because he had not heard from her for some time, though probably because he had been so busy he had not kept in touch with friends. Shortly after he wrote that reply, John Myres received Barbara's letter of 6 October 1910 that she had asked to have passed on to him.

᯾ ᯾ ᯾

A colleague Freire-Marreco kept in touch with for years was John Harrington, the fellow anthropologist she had met as a fellow resident at Rito de los Friyoles. Although the professional relationship with Harrington lasted, it is difficult to organize their correspondence, because with very few exceptions his letters to her no longer exist. But it was evident that many items of mutual interest were discussed, no matter how far apart they were living and working, and the ones from her contain bits and pieces of information of interest to both of them. Her replies made it clear they had an ongoing dialogue concerning new information not previously published.

Here are a few examples:

*Thank you very much for your letter and the information about the K'osa (Pueblo clowns). It seems as if a study of the society would be exceedingly interesting from the point of view of psychology—the deliberate overexcitement expressed in such acts of perversity as you mention, and the forced gaiety kept up with some difficulty for many hours.*

*I will send you the color identifications as soon as I can get them, and two or three place-names. I asked Juan Guadalupe Naranjo what Kapo meant, and he answered without hesitation, "dew—what comes in the night and looks pretty in the morning."* A more modern interpretation of Kapo, Santa Clara's Tewa name, accepted by some, translates as "where roses grow near water."

*Cochiti: There is a space off the plaza adjoining the cacique's house, and anyone who walks over it may be seized by the kusole, taken into the house and initiated. This is the chief way of recruiting the society. Mothers don't like their children to go about alone for this reason. One man who is a kusole now was taken as a baby; his elder sister had him in a blanket on her back and walked over the space, and both were captured. Here in the Tewa pueblos it* is the same. When the k'osa make their "house" with ashes at a dance, any Indian who walks into it will be taken and initiated. Hence mothers hold their children fast.

She shared with Harrington much folklore and legend. *Quanto hay the coyotes were very bad. Once a coyote went to drink and saw the moon reflected in the water and thought it was a cheese. What a large cheese, he said—and really it was the moon in the sky. He went deeper and deeper after it, and was drowned.* (Gesture of a coyote's ineffective paddling with front paws.)

*When the old town of Santa Clara was further Northwest, near the bridge (i.e. where the line is carried on trestles quite near the pueblo),there lived a man and a woman, married, and the man had an eagle in a cage, young, and he took great care of it and gave it meat every day and it grew large. The woman was mad because the man took such care of the eagle—the eagle knew that the woman was not thinking right about him, and for two days he ate nothing. The man asked the eagle why he was like that, but the eagle said nothing. For two days more he would not eat, and the man asked him again and he told him that the woman was not thinking right about him. The eagle told the man to lie on his (the eagle's) back and shut his eyes and not open them till he bade him. The man did so and the eagle flew up, up, up. Then he landed somewhere and said, "Open your eyes." They were on a high mountain with a side steep like the wall of this room. The man would not climb down. The eagle said, "I am going away to look for some food for you, stay here till I come back." The man could not get down, the Eagle never came back and the man starved to death. Where was the mountain? Somewhere to the north.*

*Another time when this same man was already old (hombre grande), he was chopping with a stone hatchet at the top of a rock, to make a hollow to hold rainwater. And a piece of rock flew up and put out both his eyes; he was blind.* (Laugh here: it is a funny story.)

*Once a coyote and a wolf were running, the coyote fleeing and the wolf pursuing. They came to an ox. The coyote jumped down the ox's throat and into his stomach. He made a fire in the ox's stomach, and cooked the tripe and liver and all the things inside (indicating position) one after the other.*

*Quanto hay* people here were strong. Both men and women were swift. They used to run to the top of the *loma*; now they can't; if they run (gesture of clasping upper ribs with both hands.) (Smithsonian Instition, National Archeological Archives, Museum of Natural History, John P. Harrington papers 1907-1967, 9 Oct. 1910. Hereafter cited as National Archives, Harrington)

In another letter she patched together several examples of stories and legends. *The Santa Clara names for the quarters are:*

North *"towards the mountain"*

East *"towards the sun"*

South *"everything wash out that way"*—all the old towns have
      been moved towards the south

West *"everything go on that way, sun, moon, stars"*
But the only color identification I can get is red with North.

I asked about identification with the quarters, but I could not get it; my host said, *"asi namas dicimos,"* which might be a polite refusal to say more.

On the way from Santa Clara to Nambe you pass the following places. Taking the horse trail most to the Northeast—*"white dirt here."* A place where the whitening for women's shoes is procured. White leather moccasins are still desirable for special Pueblo events and occasions.

*"The lady mounts here"* is a large stone beside the trail. Formerly when Indians had few or no wagons, on the day of Nambe fiesta the women would set out early on foot from Santa Clara, the men would come later on horseback; here the men would overtake the women, and they would stand on this rock to mount behind the saddle.

Taking the horse trail more to the south, you pass *"hand mark put on here,"* a sandy stone beside the trail on which people used to put their hands as they passed. When Santiago was a boy it was about five feet high, now it is worn down to about three. How could even a soft stone deteriorate that fast?

*"Sand all colors,"* a region of colored sandy rocks between the Rio Grande and Pojuaque. Close to the Rio Grande you pass the old site of Pojuaque. The original name of the town, Posuwake, is said to be an Indian version of the name Pojuaque which dates to Mexican times.

*Flat stones for making tortillas are got from the Arroyo Seco, on the San Juan side of the river.*

*I am having a delightful visit here* (Taos Pueblo), *being treated, as far as I can see, just like an Indian visitor, except that I take the position of a man rather than of a woman.* (ibid. 20 Oct.1910) There are two photographs taken by Freire-Marreco at Taos Pueblo in her Album 34 for 1910 and 1911: PR No. BS1.10.14 and 15 at the Pitt River Museum, Oxford University.

Next when she wrote to Harrington, it was to thank him for his October 3rd letter. *Miss True promises to look up her notes and send you the color identifications for Santa Clara. She got them some time ago, I believe from Santiago! At any rate he told her the legend about the colors of corn: that once the Indian had only animal food, and once in a time of scarcity resulting from forest fires, they asked the cacique to find them a new food supply. All the people went up to Puye Ruins and danced for three weeks before the cacique could get any vision.*

*Then he learnt that he was to take six colored pebbles and put them in a hole with a large stone over them. The people danced for another long time, then they uncovered the hole and found six blades of corn growing up. These plants bore corn of the six colors.*

*I think you are quite right about Santiago's attitude to ethnology; he does not mean to tell anything that matters, and when he tells Dr. Hewett, even, that he will "tell anything he knows," I am sure it is with the reservation, "that is anything lawful." He told me so in plain language the other day; hay cosas que no so pueden decir* (things we don't talk about). *Though it is disappointing from the ethnological standpoint, I feel bound to respect his resolution; I am sure that no really religious Indian can tell; all the virtue of uncivilized rites lies in secrecy. But as you say, he is unnecessarily scrupulous about trifles—more so than he used to be; he says that the publication of books about the Zuni and Moki has made the Santa Clara people more cautious. He is adept at putting off the inquirer by appearing to be confidential and really telling nothing, and, if driven to it, he lies, "soberly, advisedly, discreetly and in the fear of God." I say this without any want of affection for him—as a friend he is admirable, as ethnological material he is baffling.*

*Puye Ruins, New Mexico ca. 1920* has changed very little. Evidence of occupation by Santa Clara forbears exists in the smoke-blackened ceilings of caves and holes in the rock face where viga roof supports once lodged.
Courtesy of the Palace of the Governors, MNM/DCA Neg. No. 42030.

*If you want to work Santa Clara, I believe the men to use are Pedro Baca and Pedro Cajete, and if possible Aniceto Sonasa, through Miss True. The first two know a great deal about both phratries, having changed sides. I can't get at them, because I'm supposed to be a hot partisan of the Summer side.*

*I am extremely sorry to be leaving, just as things are opening up a little and just as the winter functions begin, but I know I must go somewhere where publishable information can be got. I have had a very kind invitation from the governor and apparently from the council as well, to "come back and stay for a year and Leandro will teach me everything, religion and old histories and all,"*

*if I will be a sort of secretary to the governor. I wish I had a year to give! But I*
*doubt if they would consent to publication and of course, on those terms, I could*
*not publish without their consent. (This is confidential, please, except to Dr.*
*Hewett.)*

*Thank you for the charming translation which I have only just found,*
*the papers having stuck together. I wish I could appreciate your work as well as*
*a poet.*

*I wonder if you have seen anything in the papers about the Santa Clara*
*cattle-drive? We have only seven men in the town tonight, counting the cacique*
*and ojiki; all the rest are up the canyon guarding the cattle until the lawyer*
*comes; and although everything is most legal and orderly, they are all enjoying*
*the old fashioned flavor of the affair.* Presumably this refers to the abduction
of Native cattle by Mexican rustlers. (ibid. 4 November 1910)

🦋 🦋 🦋

It was November. By now Freire-Marreco's prime concern had
become the structure of government in all its aspects, particularly as it
related to the authority of the elected officials. Writing at great length
to Hewett, she evidenced a growing respect for the Pueblo people's
organization, particularly for having succeeded for such a long time; she
also criticized the United States government's lack of cooperation in
enforcing it. Headed: *Train west of Winslow. I should like to put in writing*
*a few points about the authority of the governor of Santa Clara. The three*
*arguments which Santiago (with the approval of Leandro) wished to present to*
*you are as follows:*

*1. The authority of the governor is essential to the existence of their*
*policy in its present form. If the Government of the U.S. recognizes no coercive*
*power in the governor's office, "under what authority are we to live? And if we*
*live under no authority, we shall be worse than the beasts."*

*2. The government is pledged to the support of the governors by President*
*Lincoln's gift of the second Staff, by which, as the Indians understood, the U.S.*
*Government ratified the action of the Mexican government in presenting the first*
*Staff.*

Commonly referred to as the "Governor's Canes," every Rio Grande Pueblo has two, one presented by the Spanish when they had authority over the pueblos and one by U.S. President Abraham Lincoln. They are in the Governor's possession during his term of office symbolizing his position and authority.

*3. The agents of the U.S. Government are very ready to use the power of the governor when it suits their purposes. It is only fair that they should lend a more consistent support to his authority.*

*As regards the first point, it seems to me that they are right in thinking that the existence of the pueblo, as an agricultural community, is bound up with the maintenance of the Native government. Cooperation is essential. And I do not think that the majority of the Indians are capable of any other kind of cooperation. Nor do I see that any hardship is inflicted on the few progressive individuals. Since the lands are not occupied in severalty and freely transferred by sale and bequest, the progressive individuals are perfectly well able to become richer and more prosperous than the non-progressives, and in fact they have become so. Pedro Baca owns four houses, Francis Naranjo two or three, Juanito Naranjo four old houses and a new one, but the acreage cultivated by them bears the same proportion to the general acreage.* Many pueblo people own more than one house today, usually at least one built by the U.S. government.

*The only limitation is that placed on the sale of land to non-Indians, in which the rule of the pueblo coincides with the intentions of the U.S. Government. If the Government needs to interfere at all in this respect, I submit that it might possibly see a danger in a practice which has been carried to great lengths in the Tewa pueblos east of the river, and has just begun to operate at Santa Clara: A Mexican woman marries an elderly Indian and, as his wife, acquires a house in the village and buys land. On her Indian husband's death, she marries a Mexican and this Mexican occupies, if he does not own, her holdings in the pueblo.* There is still some Santa Clara resentment concerning Mexican heritage of pueblo property, even though these disputes may date back generations.

*As regards the second point, I submit that the U.S. Government, having in view the very object of educating the Indians into conscious citizenship of the United States, should do nothing to weaken their sentiment of loyalty to the central government and the President. This sentiment has survived a series of disappointments which might well have alienated any people less reasonable and submissive. It is constantly said by the Indians in the midst of complaints of injustice or neglect: "but we believe that the Government of Washington loves us and desires to protect us; only they are far away and know nothing of what is done in New Mexico"—an excuse, however creditable to the Indians' sense of fairness, can hardly be gratifying to the responsible heads of the Indian Department.* Most Native people are good U. S. citizens as evidenced by their voluntary military service, especially in times of national war.

*In connection with this historical argument, I think there is very strong evidence that the office of governor existed prior to the Spanish conquest. I mean that there was a civil chief who presided over agriculture and public works, with certain religious functions still exercised by the governors. The Spaniards did not create this office, they only added the element of responsibility to external authority. But no doubt their recognition and the subsequent recognition by the United States Government, have done much to develop the office in its present form.*

*As regards the third point. The temporary opposition offered by the Indians to the work of the new "whiskey police"—a work which they confess to be necessary and beneficial—was largely due, I believe, to this—that the new arrangements were not communicated to the Indians through the recognized channels. It was said, "Why do they not tell the governors as usual? The new law is such and such; now keep all your people quiet." This slight to the governor's authority seems to have led to the unfortunate and futile conspiracy (in which the governor of Santa Clara did not join) to resist arrest for drunkenness. The governor of San Ildefonso encouraged his people to resist, and in consequence it was necessary to exact a public apology from him—regrettably weakening of his authority.* Alcohol has been a problem among Native people since Whites have provided it. Various other drugs more recently have infiltrated reservations creating even more problems.

*I venture to urge again, that the authority of the governors is worth preserving, weakened though it has been of late years, it is still a most valuable instrument of cooperation, perhaps the only instrument which the people are yet able to use, a serious check on wrongdoing, and an organ for the expression of a sound moral and educative sentiment*. Living in two culturally diverse worlds is always difficult.

*It would be very unbecoming in me—a newcomer, owing so much to Miss True's generous communication of her knowledge and experience—to criticize her methods behind her back to anyone but yourself. I desire nothing more than that the whole pueblo should cooperate with her heartily and unreservedly, as they have done in the last three weeks, without jealousy or suspicion. But if I did not mention this side of the situation to you, I should not be representing the views of those who charged me with their messages.*

*The whole question of the authority of the governors at Santa Clara is bound up with the recent political history of that pueblo. To view the facts very briefly, as far as they are known to me at present: During a period of uncertain length, but certainly covering more than thirty years, the two complimentary moieties, or phratries, of the tribe, the Summer and Winter People, have been assuming to a greater and greater extent the character of political parties or factions. Shortly before 1897 a movement of secession took place, by which the Winter People withdrew from participation in the government and ceremonies of the pueblo. The motives of this secession were far from simple: To some extent it was the outcome of mere party spirit, for fifteen years the appointment of the governors had been in the hands of the Winter People exclusively, and when (by the advice of the U.S. Indian agent) the staves passed to the Summer side, the Winter People simply declined to submit. Again, it was an individualistic revolt against communal control; it must be regarded as a Puritan movement, a protest against the enforcement of certain ceremonies which had become objectionable to the more progressive members of the pueblo. There were also other factors, personal and religious, into which I cannot enter here. It happened that in 1897 the governor Jose Jesus Naranjo, had a sum of $350 to distribute. Finally it was agreed by the Winter People that, in consideration of sharing in the distribution, they would obey the governor in the performance of the Four Public Works, namely work on the irrigation ditch, work on the public road, the repair of the church, and the periodical sweeping of the plaza; and the distribution of the money took place on those terms.*

*It seems that the Winter People have never carried out this agreement.*

The governor and council are afraid to take measures to enforce it by any legal process. At present, there is a movement toward reconciliation. *The governor and council are willing to meet the Winter People halfway by calling out only the heads of families or their substitutes, that is, one man from each household, to work on the ditch. The original custom was that every man should work on the ditch, which provides a living for all. Women are called out to help in repairing the church and in sweeping the plaza.*

Freire-Marreco offered a reasonable analysis of the situation. *The governor and council do not ask for a restoration of their ancient powers—they ask only for a definition of their powers, and to secure that, they are willing to accept a limitation of them. The four public works seem to them essential for the maintenance of the community life. Work on the church may seem unsuitable for public recognition; but it has been a most valuable bond of union and a meeting ground for members of the opposing factions.*

She continued to praise Pueblo people to Hewett and she actively desired to solve some of their problems. *You won't mind my writing to you, with all your long knowledge of the pueblo, as if I knew about it! I look on myself as your deputy and for the last three months, especially for the last ten days, I have been trying to soak myself in their point of view. Some things they hide from me as much as ever, but questions of government they speak of freely; and the more I see, the more I respect and admire them. What splendid opportunities of responsibility and self sacrifice we have lost in the process of centralization! I feel ashamed to think that a first-rate man like my own father takes no part in government beyond voting, while these poor farmers give up sleep and pleasure and money, and face all the calumny and ingratitude incidental to government, to serve their people. It is on small scale, but all the ancient republican virtues are exercised. And there is a serious joy in the sacrifice, too.*

*Of Santiago himself I think better than ever I did, and indeed closer knowledge of him brings me back to your own high estimate of his character. I learn from Sofia that he is still heart-broken for the loss of his father, and can't sleep at nights for grief, especially at this time of changing governors; that he has not been in good health and has had two alarming fainting-fits, when he supposed that his father called him away; they are badly off, and don't know how they will manage for two years without wages.* There was no remuneration for any pueblo official at this time and Santiago was the governor-elect.

*I never see anything but a decent manly cheerfulness. I must tell you one honorable circumstance, though I am not supposed to let you know it—the Mexican cattle having poached all the winter pasture, he had been intending to ask you to lend him $10 for hay for the two horses; but as soon as he knew that he might be made governor, he gave up the idea of borrowing, because he could not feel sure of repaying you without the usual summer work.*

*Also, his eyes are very troublesome—and after Juan Diego going blind after operation, he is afraid to go to the government physician. I remind him that you wanted him to see Dr. Massie, and if he can get leave of absence for a day or two, I think he will go into Santa Fe to consult him. All this sounds rather dismal, but I believe he rejoices in being governor all the same—the moral-advice-giving business is just in his line, isn't it?*

*I can never thank you too much for arranging my work here—this is studying Authority in Primitive Society at close quarters. I want to write also about my work, but I will finish this letter here for the post, in case I am invited to a council to take over the archives. I wish to goodness I could stay here as secretary as they want me to—but it's absolutely impossible. However, they've done without me very comfortably for several hundred years, so I needn't flatter myself that I am necessary.* (Smithsonian Institution, National Anthropological Archives, Hewett file, 24 Nov. 1910. Hereafter cited as National Archives, Hewett).

Perhaps a postscript and noted "Personal" on the reverse side of the last page of this letter Freire-Marreco tried to help a good man who she felt deserved a chance. *If Anastacio Naranjo is retired from the Forest Police on account of his eyesight, which may be at the end of this month, there is some hope of Albino's being taken on trial. If he can keep the job, he will have to keep a decent horse. Myself, I shouldn't think he is quite good enough, but he is very keen to try, and no doubt it will develop him. It seems he isn't such a fool as he looks to white people; the family say he is the best boy in the place, always at work, manages the farm well when his father is away, never stays down in Espanola, never drinks or smokes, sleeps at home every night like a child, and is learning to talk the language of the council.*

❧ ❧ ❧

With time running short, Freire-Marreco determined to make the most of it and carry her work beyond the Rio Grande Pueblos to pursue a course that would take her to a more remote region of the United States. A note to Edgar Hewett requested a meeting with him to plan a trip to Arizona. She also asked to meet with her colleague, John Harrington, about this journey. *I have not heard from Oxford yet: I expect they are waiting for a meeting early in October. But I hope there will be no difficulty.* Probably she referred to the gaining of permission for the proposed trip from the Somerville College Fellowship Committee who controlled her grant money.

The necessary travel arrangements were made for Freire-Marreco's departure for Arizona. Regretfully she missed seeing Harrington before she left Santa Fe, but in a letter left for him she expressed concern at not being able to attend important upcoming events at Santa Clara, as well as her usual financial need. *I do want to sit tight and see every item of the preparation for the elections on the 31ˢᵗ for five days. It will be none too much, if I am to work back into a confidential position after a month's absence.*

*And, if you'll excuse my asking—does the School pay your traveling expenses? If yours are paid, I should be very glad to escape spending $5 on railway and hotel; it is a very serious consideration to me just now.* (National Archives, Harrington, before 25 Nov. 1910)

# ❦ Yavapai Country, Arizona

Willing and able to travel farther afield, Barbara Freire-Marreco made a hoped-for trip to carry out her intention to study a different American Indian culture. Leaving the Rio Grande Valley, she had planned to undertake ethnological studies among the Mohaves on the Colorado River Reservation or at Fort Mohave Reservation both in Arizona.

On November 11, 1910 Frederick Hodge of the Bureau of American Ethnology wrote a glowing reference to Robert Valentine, Commissioner of Indian Affairs praising Freire-Marreco's qualifications, stating her plans and asking for letters of introduction to the Indian Affairs officials at these locations. On November 22nd Hodge was informed by the Office of Indian Affairs the letters had been sent. Hodge replied with a letter of thanks on November 28th. Interestingly, Freire-Marreco was already on a train west of Winslow, Arizona on November 24th when her destination had changed for some unexplained reason.

The best laid plans don't always work. A letter from Hodge to Valentine on December 14th revealed a last-minute change of field: *Circumstances were such that Miss Freire-Marreco found it impracticable to visit the Colorado River Reservations , and instead has gone to southern Arizona where she desires to make some studies of the Mohave-Apache at Camp McDowell and, I understand, at the Phoenix School. If you will be so good as to furnish Miss Freire-Marreco with letters of introduction to the superintendents of the Phoenix School and the Camp McDowell Reservation, I shall be greatly obliged, and I am sure her work there will be greatly facilitated.* (National Archives, Hodge, 14 Dec. 1910)

Now the subjects of her new study would be the Yavapai, a branch of the Athabascans, originally nomadic Natives who had wandered for centuries as hunters and gatherers, finally settling what is now central Arizona. They were markedly different from the Pueblo cultures of the Rio Grande who had traditionally lived in village groups and were descended from people forced to leave the Four Corners area about 1250 A.D., probably due to severe drought, to migrate in an easterly direction and eventually relocate in what is now New Mexico.

To help her make the necessary arrangements, again her fellow scientists and sponsors had provided letters of introduction. Communication was slow, but professional courtesy always prevailed. Valentine agreed to help in a letter and it paid off, for Freire-Marreco was soon ensconced at the Phoenix Indian School.

*United States Indian School, Phoenix* **as it looked to Freire-Marreco in the early 1900's. Native children of various tribes were forced to live and study in boarding schools such as this, as madated by the U.S. Government.** Courtesy of the Arizona Historical Foundation, Hayden Library, Arizona State University, Tempe.

This School had been established under the control of the Bureau of Indian Affairs when U. S. law required all Native children to be taken from their homes and sent to boarding schools, usually quite a distance, to be educated in white man's ways. This one housed different Southwest tribes until it closed in 1990 and all the records were all sent to the Bureau of Indian Affairs in Washington, D.C

Freire Marreco's time at the School was probably not very long as she soon reported to Hewett: *Mr. Goodman, the Superintendent here, is sending me out to Fort McDowell tomorrow. If you wish to communicate, the address will be c/o Supt. C. E. Coe, Camp McDowell, via Scottsdale. Mr. Coe sends to Scottsdale for mail twice a week.*

*Mr. Goodman tells me that a larger and less civilized group of the Mohave-Apache is settled near Camp Verde. If time allows me to visit them, I shall come back to Phoenix and go by rail to Prescott.* (Museum of New Mexico, Hewett, 25 Nov. 1910)

**Fort McDowell in Frontier Days, Arizona; Officers and Soldiers Barracks and Parade Ground with Verde River.** Travelers used this facility, there being no other accommodations in that area available. From an original photograph by G.H. Rothrock, Phoenix. Courtesy of the Arizona Historical Society, Tucson No. 20804.

Originally Camp McDowell, the Fort was established in 1865 as a military base to keep peace in the area. There had been continuing friction between neighboring tribes in the region, referred to as the Hualapai Wars that resulted in the imprisonment of the Yavapai on the San Carlos Apache Reservation. About 1900 the Yavapai began returning to their homeland and the Fort McDowell Reservation was formed in 1903. In 1906 the Bureau of Indian Affairs started negotiations to build a dam on reservation land in order to divert water to the fast-growing city of Phoenix. The resident Native people were given the option of remaining without irrigation water or moving to the neighboring Salt River Reservation and taking up residence with their traditional enemies. They chose to stay and fight the Central Arizona Project, eventually defeating the proposed Orme Dam.

Keeping in touch with Hodge from Fort McDowell, Freire-Marreco wrote to report her activities: *By this time you will have heard from Mr. Hewett that I have come to the Mohave-Apache Reservation. I am staying in the house of Mr. Coe, the McDowell Superintendent.*

*Do you wish me to collect any specimens of Mohave-Apache work? I daresay you are already well-provided with them. There are baskets of course; a respectable one would cost $5 and a fine one much more. Cradles, very like San Carlos Apache, neatly made of roots and twigs with buckskin covers would cost $3. or $3.50. The old men make buckskin caps, dyed with iqualla twigs and plumed with owl feathers. I gave $1 for one last week. The old men can make stone arrow heads, but only boys use bows and arrows. There is also a sort of kite, and the boys use bullroarers.*

*If I can get the medicine-man to come into town and make some Edison records, will the Bureau be willing to take the records at the price which they cost me? And shall I try to get some language records from other men? (One man here says that he is the only genuine Yavapai, and there are slight linguistic differences.) I am obliged to you beforehand, because I have not much money to risk.* Making Native speech recordings was an approach favored by those interested in linguistics, especially John Harrington. The scheme here never materialized.

She mentioned she would be in Arizona only until December 22nd or 23rd, then, she *must* be back at Santa Clara for the Christmas dances and the election. The word "must" emphasized her determination to witness the wheels of Santa Clara government turning. The postscript to this letter, written on the road, closed with a plea to keep expenses down: *Please don't cable me any authorization, because it would cost $20 to deliver here!* (National Archives, Hodge, 8 Dec. 1910)

❧ ❧ ❧

Little evidence of Freire-Marreco's hurried trip to Camp McDowell survives, but the short adventure was remarkable because she was able to collect some useful information in a short period of time. Detailed information and photographs of her visit with the Yavapai can be found in her Album 34 and Collection notes at the Pitt Rivers Museum, University of Oxford.

In a report a month after returning to Santa Clara, on January 28, 1911 she related some findings to Hewett. *In Arizona it was exceedingly interesting and promising, if only I were quicker and more competent. I spent many days trying various interpreters before I found the best one, and my genealogical informant went away before I had half finished, and I could get no one else to do the same work. Then I failed to get in touch with the most important group of all, two families called Dickens; it seems to me now that they would have known what the other families do not know, for instance about the very imposing pueblo ruin overlooking the river.*

It seems possible that Freire-Marreco was too hurried, though more likely these Native people had already started to lose their cultural inheritance, so much of which is now gone.

*The best work I did was with the medicine-men; three of them were quite confidential about their experiences, and I saw a cure performed.*

*I am sorry to say that I could not find the clans, though I tried many ways of getting at them. The obvious explanation is that I failed to get at the truth; it is also just possible that other forms of grouping have obscured or replaced the clans.*

Before General Cook's campaign, the Mohave-Apache lived in small local groups, two or three families at each spring in the hills; then came their thirty years of exile on the San Carlos Reservation, and now surviving groups of Mohave-Apache, Yavapai , and Yuma-Apache have all been localized afresh on the McDowell Reservation. The grouping of which people seem to be conscious depends on membership of these three tribes; there is a further vague classification into "Isapo" (people I know) and a vague local grouping of (people up above and people down below,) "mial and kowji." I think you might almost say that you see a tribe in the making; of course what they want to cement them is war, and that they can't have! From the sociological point of view it will be a pity if the Government allots the lands this year, because it will stop the process by which kindred elements are gravitating towards each other in a local grouping.

I found two young people, partly educated, who were anxious to write their own language, and taught them a little. I promised that, if I ever came back, we would write a grammar in partnership. I believed that the Bureau would publish it under our joint names. If Mr. Harrington goes to work there, of course that would be better still.

I got a much more favorable impression of the work of the Indian Service there, and I hope a more just one. There the superintendents are not ignorantly tampering with an existing civilization, but bringing decent living and order to people who need them badly. Mr. and Mrs. Coe at McDowell are very intelligent and sympathetic, and the people seem to trust them. (National Archives, Hewett, Jan. 1911)

# ❧ Return to the Rio Grande Valley

As she had planned, Freire-Marreco returned to the Rio Grande Valley in time for the Christmas dances on December 25th and 26th 1910. Because of her interest in the upcoming Santa Clara elections and the pueblo organizational structure, she wrote to Hewett expressing concern regarding the enforcement of inherited Native customs and the possible interference from the U.S. government's inconsistent and weak enforcement of regulations.

*Santiago Naranjo was yesterday made governor of the pueblo, Victoriano Sisneros—teniente, Candido Tafoya—alguazil (baliff and policeman), Florentino Sisneros—capitan, Marcellino Baca—fiscal (treasurer)—all fairly young and progressive as you see, and immediately after his election he dictated the enclosed letter to you. I have translated it literally, but I have to add some particulars which he mentioned in talking over the matter before hand, but omitted in the actual dictation.*

*On the night of January 1st he told me that, since the council had asked the cacique for a new governor this year, he had very grave fears that he should not escape the office, having been for so many years, teniente and alquazil alternately. As regards his private affairs, it means a serious loss—two years with no possibility of earning wages. He cannot leave the town at all this year, and next year he must be at every council as the governor's nearest adviser. And as regards public business, the present uncertainty as to the governor's authority makes the office extremely difficult to hold. He said that "if he came out governor" next day, his first business should be to write to you for help.*

*At present several men refuse to work on the ditch, and yet take the* water as if they had worked, "filling themselves with other men's bread," and do it with impunity. "Why do you not take the officials with you and break down their ditches?" I asked. "We dare not, until we know for certain the Government's attitude towards us; if we did it now, we believe that the men would take it into court, and we haven't the money to spend on lawsuits; besides, the Mexican law is entirely different from ours. Without the public works, especially the ditch, it is impossible for the pueblo to live." The system is, that all men should work on the ditch, the married men in consideration of the land they already occupy, the "boys" in consideration of the land they will have assigned to them on their marriage. But all that I have already reported to you verbally and by letter, and indeed you know it better than I do!

Secondly, I am to make it very clear that Santiago has not the faintest intention of using his power to enforce ceremonial observances of any kind— "only the public works by which the families of the pueblo must live;" as for customs, "how can anyone enforce them nowadays: they must be forgotten in time: let them be maintained by those of us who care for them, but we cannot enforce them." I quote the man's words, literally translated.

What is desired is an expression of the Government's wishes. "The Government does not know that everything is not well here." You know what complete faith they have in the good will of the Government at Washington.

Very soon the question of public works must come up: first the sweeping of the town on January 6th or 7th; then the repair of the church; then, in February, the main works begin—the ditch, and all the business of agriculture. Santiago has no desire to make a fool of himself and bring the authority of the governor into contempt by ordering what he cannot enforce; and for this reason he begs with the greatest seriousness and anxiety that the Government will give him some decided answer in the course of this month. If once the spring work on the ditch has been successfully enforced, the government of the pueblo will be possible, if not easy, for the rest of the year: if not, there will be a repetition of what Leandro has had to endure, and worse, because of continued impunity.

Some people say, as you know, "If the pueblo governors can't manage their own people, they aren't worth helping." But indeed any politician, any statesman, ought to sympathize with the difficult situation created by outside *interference, by the consciousness of another authority to which an appeal can be made. And don't let anyone say United States law ought to be good enough for them: First, it's Mexican law that they get in actual fact, in this territory; secondly, the Pueblos aren't ripe yet for the U.S. law, you must support their institutions and let them merge gradually into the legal institutions of the country.*

*I wish with all my heart that the highest authorities at Washington could be here and see for themselves the touching faith, the steady and much-tried loyalty towards "Washington" and "the President." I wish they could stand, as I stood yesterday, in the new governor's house, and feel the thrill of exaltation and awe that ran round the assembly as the Staves, President Lincoln's Staff in chief, were borne into the room; how all stood in reverent silence while the governor prayed aloud that he might be worthy to bear that great and heavy charge, the care of all the people, and to maintain those staves which are the very symbol and sacrament of authority. "God is in heaven, and these staves are on earth; and if a man will not obey the staves that are here before his eyes, how shall he obey God in heaven?"*

*Can you not make a personal appeal? If (I speak in entire ignorance of what is possible in America) you could bring it to the President himself, you would reinforce and establish for many years the traditional loyalty which now clings to the successors of President Lincoln. And if the authorities decide to help this governor, they will be helping a thoroughly conscientious, responsible, reasonable unprejudiced man, who is quite curiously free from mere antiquarian sentiment about customs and traditions, and only desires to keep the pueblo in working order as a machine for decent living. This pueblo is not going downhill like San Ildefonso; the population is well maintained; American ideas are being gradually absorbed; the people work for their living, they don't dance for it. But you can't afford, yet, to weaken the ancient bulwarks of law and order and morals; you must maintain them until the people have learnt to feel safe with United States law—and, I may add, there must be great changes in New Mexico before that can be!* (ibid., 3 Jan. 1911)

The enclosure mentioned in this letter, in Freire-Marreco's handwriting, bore Santiago's name. Santiago himself was appealing to Hewett for advice, asking him to act as an intermediary between his people and the U.S. government. The fact that Freire-Marreco actually wrote the letter showed Santiago's trust in her—an example of anthropology in action.

"*Senor Hewett, Amigo, I will say to you now in this letter that I have been made governor of this pueblo; and I am very sorry that (I fear) I shall not come to work again or leave the town to do any work of diligence for my family, because I cannot leave the town to do any work as I have done in other years. But, my friend, I am to serve you in everything that I can and help you in everything that I can.*

"*And also, I wish you to do me a favor if it is possible; to see what you may be able to do for me, I being governor of this pueblo of Santa Clara, and being your friend, Santiago Naranjo.*

"*If you determine to help me in this matter, I wish you to make known to the president, or to the government, to ask them how it will be best in this pueblo to enforce the public works, namely to sweep the town; to work on the church; the public road; and the ditch.*

"*This is what I desire, I desire you to do me the favor (to ask) how it will be best to carry out*—executor en estos trabajos (get the work done) *these works; and if you do me this favor, I desire that power may be given me, the right to discipline my pueblo* –corregir a me pueblo (correct or make right my town) *in these works.*

"*Friend, in those times, our rule was this, that in a public work every man should go to work, but now no; we are not obedient to the orders of the governor. And for that reason I ask your help and inform you how it was in those times. Now in these times, it is very different, for the reason that the sons of this pueblo are not obedient. And yet, without taking part in the work, I suppose that no single man has any right; and that is what I wish to know, friend.*

"*I suppose that a governor exists in order that his commands shall be obeyed*—creo que un gobernador esta para obedecer todos sus mandates, (I believe all the mandates of the governor should be obeyed.) *because the staff that President Lincoln gave, he gave in order that all the commands of the said governor should be obeyed; and therefore I desire that they shall obey me too if it is in any way possible, if the government will give me any power and right to enforce public works.*

"And also I will tell you another thing, that I am not enforcing leyes y costumbres (laws and customs), only and solely the common public works; in these alone I desire to be obeyed. And if you do me the favor to help me to enforce them, I desire that the president will give me a written order, and signed, to enforce these public works. I say this again, that he may believe that I am not enforcing costumbres.

"Therefore no more for the present, friend Hewett, and as soon as you get this letter, answer me the contents of it. I hope for this favor from you, and I shall be your friend in all that I can do."

Freire-Marreco added: This letter is intended to be shown to anyone whom you may think advisable.

Pressed for time and knowing she would be leaving the country soon, Freire-Marreco made another appeal to Hewett on the 5th of January. By a significant coincidence, the letter of which I send you a hasty translation arrived the day after I posted Santiago's letter to you. As you see, it is from the Down River pueblos to the Up River pueblos. The council here met to consider it last night, and I was also instructed to let you know what was going on. It was thought that you might be able to give information about the state of pueblo affairs in Washington which would make a great difference. I write this in haste for a man is going to the post. (Museum of New Mexico, Hewett, 5 Jan. 1911)

Even though Freire-Marreco was not allowed to witness the Santa Clara ceremonials, she gained information on the proceedings. She wrote what she had learned to Harrington. Alas, I didn't see the ceremony of making the governor: Leandro was kind enough to consult the principales about admitting me, and got a firm refusal; but luckily Juanito gave me a pretty full description the night before. I was at the council to "ask for a new governor," and got some idea of the traditional forms in which they speak, and today I hope to see the taking over of the archives. Pueblo archives were the personal responsibility of the presiding governor, so were passed from the outgoing to the newly elected governor. It is all most admirable and creditable to the people—what an astonishing means of education government is! I could never have believed that poor farmers would be as dignified and statesmanlike as these men are, or dictate *the admirable letters that have been given me to translate in the last few hours.*

*I hope Santiago forgives my getting information from other men! Really, if I stuck to him I should learn nothing. As he candidly remarks, it would be far safer if I asked no one but himself, "for if you ask another man, there is always a danger of your coming to something important." I am glad that we are on comfortably candid terms about it, anyway!*

She added a few more items of interest to both of them: *I have some cardinal trees now, they came without asking in a story, but they are modern imported trees, I fear. Will try again.*

*All animals were born from una pelotita de pinorcal,* (a little sap ball of pine); *it happened while the people were at Puye.*

*I find the Tewa more difficult than ever! That is, I can talk a bit to the children, but I can't write it with even a decent show of probability. You will have to correct all my stuff, if you will be so kind.* (National Archives, Harrington, ND)

Another undated letter to Harrington from Freire-Marreco must have been written about the same time. She listed all the newly elected officers at Santa Clara, probably all known to both of them.

Governor—Santiago Naranjo

Tiniente—Victoriano Sisneros

Alguazil—Candido Tafoya

Capitan—Florentino Sisneros

Fiscal—Marcellino Baca

She also requested a meeting with him to work for a few days before she left Santa Clara. A return trip to Arizona was not a reality because her time was nearly gone. However, because she now had the trust of the Santa Clara people, she had been given access to pueblo archives.

*I want to stay until Dia de los Reyes (Kings Day) January 6ᵗʰ at least, because I shall have a chance now to copy all the archives, and also Jose Manuel will tell stories almost every night now, if he doesn't go to sleep over them!* (ibid. ND ca. late December 1910 or early January 1911)

❧ ❧ ❧

Santa Clara was not the only pueblo having trouble enforcing its traditions and laws. Meetings between the Up River and Down River (Rio Grande) pueblo people led to a letter dictated to Freire-Marreco and addressed to all the New Mexico Pueblo governors. It was an invitation to discuss mutual problems and what actions could be taken. Originally written in Spanish at the Pueblo of San Felipe on December 19, 1910, it was an attempt to clarify the issues—and also a call to arms.

Translation: "We held a council in this pueblo of San Felipe, and at the said council were present the Governors of Isleta, of Laguna, of Sandia, and of San Felipe. But the rest of the pueblos did not appear at the said council, for the reason that they did not receive our letter in proper time. This council was called with the sole object and intention of consulting upon matters of importance and beneficial to our pueblos. We, the governors of the various pueblos of New Mexico, having the government of our pueblos in our hands, are practically without sufficient force of authority to govern our own people or to defend our rights or property, to exact obedience or to put our decisions into execution against anyone.

"All these rights are being taken from us, that is, by the white agent; and the same is true in regard to our land or to personal property. All this causes damage and ruin to ourselves and to our families; and if we go on in this same manner, we are ruined forever. Brothers, today in this council we all expressed the same opinion, that all this will cause damage and destruction to our pueblos: after discussion, we concluded that it is highly necessary that a delegation of the pueblos should go to Washington and place our complaints in the hands of the Commission of Indian Affairs; that we should make our petitions and present them ourselves and personally. We respectfully request your attention to this, Governors, officials, principales and sons of all the Pueblos of New Mexico, that you will come to transact, jointly with ourselves, matters which may be of benefit to our pueblos. We call this Council at the Pueblo of Santo Domingo, for the 20th day of January 1911. And desiring to receive your favorable answer in the manner most convenient to yourselves, and with salutations and good wishes for your prosperity, we remain your servants,

Bautista Zuni—Governor of Isleta

*Jose Felipe Jiron—Tiniente-gobernador*
*Francisco Chirina—Principale*
*Desiderio Jaramilla—Principale"*

(Museum of New Mexico, Hewett, 5 Jan. 1911)

The prospect of a meeting of all the Rio Grande Pueblos had an uplifting effect on Freire-Marreco. She informed Hewett. *We are just starting to a General Council at Santo Domingo: Leandro, Santiago, Victoriano, Francisco, Pedro Cjete and myself.* (ibid. 18 Jan. 1911)

Perhaps because of her persistence, she inspired others to take action to help the Pueblos solve their problems. Hewett, true to his good reputation with pueblo people, requested help on January 9th from Alice Fletcher, who had influence in high national governmental places.

*You will better than any one else appreciate the urgency of this case. I am placing all of the documents in your hands and I believe that your personal plea added to the excellent presentation of matter by Miss Freire-Marreco will have great weight at the Indian Office. I am deeply concerned about this case. Were it possible I would go straight back to Washington to take it up in person. Will you kindly explain to Mr. Valentine that I am unable to do so?* He was committed to an expedition to Guatamala.

*It seems to me that this is an opportunity to do a great and lasting good for the Pueblo Indians. I am certain that with their profound belief in and regard for the authority of the Government at Washington, a very brief and sympathetic admonition (not necessarily a mandate) from the President or Secretary of the Interior, to the effect that all should consider it their duty to bear their part in the public works of the community specifying particularly the work on the ditch but also touching upon the cleaning of the village and work on the public road, would have all the effect of a law with the simple and law-abiding people and could bring order and peace out of a condition that has been very unsettled and trying for years.*

*I know Santiago Naranjo as well as I do any living man. I know his fine character and high purpose and there can be no doubting his sincerity in this matter as he presents it. While it seems perhaps but a small matter, it is as worthy of our most earnest attention and the attention of the Government as it would be if it involved a province, for a great principle of justice is involved and an opportunity is here presented for us and for the Government to serve a most worthy group of simple, trusting and trustworthy citizens of the United States with whom a single word of admonition from the President would be more effective than would a law of Congress, with any other people whom I know.*

*Will you please take it up and do your very best with it and write Miss Freire-Marreco very soon as to what progress is being made? I am writing her about it today and am also sending a letter to the Governor.* (National Archives, Hewett , 9 Jan. 1911)

Fletcher responded to Hewett with two letters, unfortunately written after the General Council had convened and Freire-Marreco had left New Mexico. *I presented Santiago's matter to the Commissioner and I have had several interviews. There are difficulties in the way of an official letter. If I had more personal knowledge of matters I could have done more. I hoped to hear from Miss Freire-Marreco but I have no idea where she is and her parents do not seem to know her movements. They may know by this time.*

*I wrote to Santiago with the knowledge of the Office and while it may be a little friendly comfort, it may not be much. I told him that his efforts to keep the Pueblo clean and sanitary . . ... Those who used the ditch should help to repair and make it good for the people. I hoped the people would be law abiding. There has been some trouble among the Pueblos, just what I do not know, and a murder has been committed.*

*There are complications that I do not fully understand. I am very sorry Miss F-M has not written me. If she had, I might have been able to assess some of the questions which needed to be replied to in order to work intelligently.*

*I am sorry not to have better news for you concerning Santiago.* (Museum of New Mexico, Hewett, 18 Feb. 1911)

About a month later Fletcher expressed little hope. *Thanks for Miss F-M's letter. I will keep it for you. She has done well. I saw her here, and she and I had some valuable conversations with Mr. Valentine. The question touching the endorsement of Pueblo government on the old lines is one of much difficulty.*

*The commissioner desires to help, and is looking for a way to do so effectively. Santiago has received my letter sent after submitting it to the Authorities and I have a letter in reply written by someone for him, but not at his dictation which I regret. I doubt if I write again. It will hardly do any good.* (ibid. 4 Mar. 1911)

❦ ❦ ❦

Using her language and secretarial abilities at the General Council, Freire-Marreco had put the Pueblos' request for help in an easily understood form for the Bureau of Indian Affairs. Originally in Spanish—a language common to all the pueblos represented at the Council—she translated it into English, a copy of which is in the Smithsonian Institution's National Archives. It is not addressed, is undated, and unsigned. A Spanish copy with corrections and additions is in the Museum of New Mexico's Angelico Chavez History Library. The articulate and well-organized document led to a better understanding of the Rio Grande Pueblos' problems and improved relations considerably among the fighting factions within the Pueblos—a major accomplishment for Freire-Marreco.

*A General Council of the Pueblos of New Mew Mexico was called by the governor and principales of the pueblo of Isleta and held at the pueblo of Santo Domingo on the 20th of January 1911. Representatives of twelve pueblos attended, viz. Isleta, Sandia, Santa Ana, Zia, Jemez, San Felipe, Santo Domingo, Cochiti, Tesuque, Nambe, Santa Clara, and Taos.*

The letter of invitation stated the reason for calling the Council, a reason that was repeated by the representative of Isleta in the opening speech as a general proclamation: *that the governor and officials of all the pueblos find that they have not sufficient authority to keep order in their pueblos.*

The council discussed the subject of *Mexican and American encroachments on Indian lands, a topic* of much concern and debate.

*At the conclusion of the council, it was resolved:*

*(1) To send a written petition to Washington praying for the necessary support for their authority.*

(2) To ask the Government of the United States to send a commission to investigate the situation of the pueblos.

The delegates from the pueblo of Santa Clara were requested to draw up this petition, and the signatures of all the delegates present were given to them. The officials of Acoma afterward sent their signatures by post.

In order to carry out these instructions, the governor and principales of Santa Clara held several meetings on returning to their pueblo, viz. a meeting of their council to hear a report of the proceedings of the General Council; a meeting to inform Miss True of what had been done; three meetings of the heads of houses to adjust certain local difficulties; and lastly, a meeting of the five delegates to the General Council, at which notes for the wording of the petition were dictated to B. Freire-Marreco, an English visitor staying at the time in the pueblo.

They are agreed that the reason for this decay of authority is that it is doubtful whether the Government of the United States allows them to inflict any punishment for disobedience.

As a result of this Council meeting, Freire-Marreco then reviewed the situation in a communication to be sent to U. S. government authorities including the Commissioner for Indian Affairs in Washington. In 1909 the Pueblo Indians were informed, through their superintendents that in the future they would not be allowed to inflict punishment contrary to the laws of New Mexico. A General Council met at Santa Fe on June 19, 1909 and, with Mr. Crandall's assistance, drew up a petition, praying that their right to punish internal disorders, to settle internal disputes, and to enforce the necessary public works might be maintained. Mr. Crandall had already written a letter of enquiry to the Department on their behalf (office letter dated May 5, 1909), and he received an answer dated September 2, 1909, of which he sent copies to the governors of the pueblos in his district, stating that it was not the intention of the Government to prevent the governors of the pueblos from giving those orders which they had been accustomed to give. On the contrary, the government approves of the continued supervision of these matters by the governors and their subordinate officers, and it desires that the Indians give prompt and cheerful obedience to all just and proper commands of their officers in connection with such matters. Although

Freire-Marreco put the following in quotations, she probably edited some in translation.

"We agree," they said, "with all that was said by the writers of the petition of June 19, 1909, but we say, very respectfully, that the answer which they received has not the force which is needed. It is not enough for the Government to advise the people to obey the governors. In times past we have had letters of advice of this kind from our agents and superintendents, but still we are in uncertainty. What we all desire is that the President and Congress of the United States should tell us what powers they allow us to exercise, and by what punishment they allow us to enforce our orders. We shall be content to have our powers limited if only we may have them defined and certain. It is because we are uncertain that our affairs go wrong.

"We submit most respectfully whatever the President and Congress may think best, but here we will write what seems to us most necessary:

1. We all request that the President and Congress will maintain our authority to enforce the public works which are most necessary in the pueblos, because without them we cannot maintain our families and live in cleanliness and decency. These are: to work on the common ditch; to repair the church and cemetery; to work on the public roads; and in some pueblos, to herd the horses. In each pueblo the people can decide how they wish to work on the ditch, whether universally, or by acreage, or by head of families as we have amicably agreed in this pueblo of Santa Clara. But we cannot enforce these necessary public works unless we are able to inflict punishment on the disobedient.

2. We all desire that the President and Congress will authorize us to hold courts as before to settle disputes which arise between members of the same pueblo, as, for example, about boundaries, water, timber, and quarrels between married couples. In our courts the governor, principales and officials settle these cases without any costs, and both parties are generally satisfied. But we cannot judge these cases unless we can punish those who do not obey the orders of the court.

3. We all desire that the President and Congress will authorize us to punish disorders and drunkenness in our pueblos. We all agree that drunkenness is the cause of almost all disorder and disobedience, and we are all resolved to put

*it down, if the President will maintain our authority.*

*4. We have discussed what sort of punishment it would be right to ask the President and Congress to authorize. There were many kinds of punishment in old times, but one seems to us the best, namely, to impose a task of work for the benefit of the whole pueblo, for example, when a man has been drunk, the council orders him to cut so many posts to fence the common pasture, or, to bring wood and stones to mend the ditch. This is the punishment which we have imposed of late years, and this is the only punishment we wish to use in future.* Community Service!

*5. If the President and Congress will give us the authority for which we ask, we will not use it to enforce ceremonies or religious customs, but solely and only for the purposes which we have mentioned, namely, to enforce the public works, to repress disorders, and to settle disputes between members of the same pueblo.*

*"We beg the Honorable Commissioner for Indian Affairs, our friend and protector (Mr. Valentine) will commend our petition to the President and Congress. And we pray that almighty God, who has established the authority of the President and Congress of the United States for the good government and order of us all, may incline them to support us in these matters for the benefit of all our people.*

*"And further we beg the President and Congress, or the Honorable Commissioner, will send us three Commissioners to visit the pueblos, and to see how things are in New Mexico, and how we use our authority, and what the Indians suffer from the encroachments of Mexicans and Americans. And we beg that we may have good notice when the Commissioners are coming, in order that we may be ready to meet them, either in a General Council or in each pueblo separately, according as they think best."* (National Archives, Hewett ND)

❧ ❧ ❧

As was her practice, Freire-Marreco sent her personal observations of the proceedings at Santo Domingo to Hewett including thoughts not included in the official report. She also stated her regrets for leaving and, of course, thanked him. *Your kind and welcome letters to Santiago and myself were received a fortnight ago. Your letter, with the comfortable feeling that you are never appealed to in vain, was a great satisfaction to the new governor; and it has been carefully put away in the archives, which we are sorting according to dates so as to make future reference more easy. Incidentally I am learning something of the history of the last twenty years—one or two of the principales are always on duty to safeguard the archives, and their comments are sometimes interesting. But how exceedingly unreliable are their memories!*

*I want now to modify what I said in my last letter on two points. First, I think I was quite wrong in thinking that Miss True was hostile to the preservation of Native government. Really, I believe she is strongly in favor of it, though she sees the difficulties better than I do. And now she has the full confidence of both parties in Santa Clara, and all the best men are supporting her firm course of action about liquor.* However, the Bureau of Indian Affairs did not support Clara True's actions.

*Secondly, I find in the archives a succession of letters from agents and superintendents recommending obedience, and there is not force in them. And last year (June 1910) a committee appointed by a General Council of fourteen pueblos made an appeal through Mr. Crandall to the Department. I enclose copies of petition and answer; you will see that Mr. Crandall has put their case very well, and the Department's answer simply is this, "When we gave our ruling we did not consider what the logical result would be. Of course the answer does not give any authority at all, and the Indians say that advice is no use at all; they are quite competent to give any amount of advice; what they want is a definition of their powers. The fact is that the Department can do nothing—only Congress can give the necessary authority, and the better informed Indians are quite aware of this, and will not be put off with paternal admonitions". The Great White Father stage of intercourse is past!*

*The proceedings at Santo Domingo were, briefly these: Nine pueblos were represented: Laguna, Acoma, San Juan, San Ildefonso, Pojoaque and Picuris being absent. I was not allowed to sit. Taos, Santo Domingo and Sandia voting against my admission to the whole sitting, and Santa Clara men refusing to send for me on less than equal terms with the other delegates; but I sat on the* executive committee after the big meeting, and the business has been carefully explained to me.

Isleta opened the meeting, saying that they had called it to consider the unsatisfactory position of the governors, and proposing to send a delegation to Washington. Several Down-river pueblos spoke, showing a certain distrust of Isleta, and it looked as if nothing definite would be done. A written petition was proposed, but several pueblos were unwilling to give their signatures. Francisco Naranjo pulled the meeting out of the fire by what seems to have been a great speech: he explained that it was useless to send a delegation in the last year of this Congress, proposed that they should ask Congress to send a committee of investigation this year or else give free passes to Washington in 1912, and meanwhile that a written petition should be sent. He made a great impression, and the whole meeting decided to put the business in the hands of the pueblo Santa Clara, and gave them signatures beforehand for whatever petition the Santa Clara men should think best to write. Later on there is to be another Junta General at Santo Domingo to report progress.

We had one committee meeting that same evening, the Santa Clara delegates (Santiago, Leandro, Victoriano, Francisco N., Pedro Cajeti), myself, and Marcelino Aveita of Isleta, a very well-informed serious man; and another next day with that clever but dangerous person, Lorenzo Martinez of Taos. It was then that I saw copies of the correspondence of 1910, and understood that admonition would not serve.

On returning to Santa Clara, we had a council to meet Miss True; it was arranged that we should make out a written statement of what the Indians think the essential minimum of authority and that Miss True should show this to Mr. Johnson who will be here before long. Ceremonial and religious engagements have delayed this work, but I hope we shall have a full meeting of heads of houses on Sunday night. We ought to have had a preliminary council tonight, I think, but something unexplained stood in the way; and for a rarity I am sick in bed and have had no chance to urge it personally today. All this I will report to Miss Fletcher.

You will rejoice to hear of the splendid improvement in the relations of the two parties—successful joint action at the General Council, and simultaneously *a religious revival on the Winter side. I cannot tell which is cause and which is effect! Francisco has spoken about the governors' authority and about dancing for rain in a very surprising manner. His party came out yesterday with a very beautiful and important dance which has not been seen for about 26 years— everyone was happy and serious, and the hearty way in which our side swept for their dance ought to make it easier for them to sweep in the general cleaning next week. It is certain that they will join in putting forward this petition for defining the governor's powers; personally, I believe that they want a permanent reunion—that is, that Francisco is tired of being excluded from regular office, and means to be governor before very long. As you know, the old and correct rule is to have Winter and Summer governors in alternate years, and a Winter governor with a Summer capitan , and vice versa, the cacique and ojike concurring in the appointments. But from 1879 to 1894 the Winter side monopolized the appointments: in 1894 the agent thought to put things right by the very un-Indian expedient of giving the staves to the majority, and since then the Summer people have stayed in power, and Francisco's party have been in open revolt. (I omit endless complications caused by the secession of individuals and families from one side to the other.)*

*Now I am trying to suggest to the governor's side that reunion means:*

1. *Admitting the Winter people to power in alternate years.*
2. *Recognition of Jose Manuel as ojike, and that it is worth while to sacrifice the monopoly of power in order to return to the ways of the ancients.*

*What I don't say is that when Leandro dies all the brains will be on the Winter side and they are bound to get the upper hand somehow: the union will be made on far better terms now while Leandro lives. Neither Manuel Tafoya nor Santiago could hold their own against Francisco much less Eulogio! The one strong modern man on our side is Victoriano, and I suspect the choice lay between him and Santiago (perhaps you know that the cacique has a grudge against Victoriano): now the number of principales is made up, and Victoriano can't be appointed until someone dies. Victoriano was disappointed—he wanted to be governor—but he seems to be a man of principle and loyalty, and will be a splendid teniente. If, as I believe, Francisco's side are bound to come in to power before long, I want them to come in under safeguards of the old alternate regime: if not, we shall have just a swing of the pendulum, and another fifteen years of monopoly with a further decay of organization.*

*You will guess how very sad I am to be leaving the pueblo at this deeply interesting and critical time. However, they did without me for very many hundreds of years! If it might please God to give us a reunion on constitutional terms this year, and five wet years to cement it—already we have had two unusual winter rains, such as have not come since about 1905, and that has strengthened people's good resolutions. I have learnt here to feel with all my heart that nothing goes to the root of things but prayer.*

*There are great difficulties in the way of reunion, two being obvious even to me:*

*1. There would be six principales, or even eight.*

*2. The ceremonies would have to be safeguarded against the innovations of the Winter party. If their consciences won't allow them to conform, a complete reunion is impossible, and there must be many things which they have outgrown in these years of separation.*

*It is all as delicate as a butterfly's wing—one rash work might ruin all. Only Grace can bring them safely through. I hope much from their growing feeling that it is predestined—the cycle of years, the coincidence of events in the last few months—New Mexican Constitution, your map, the cow-business, this General Council, the winter rains. Their system of religious cooperation with natural processes ought to make them even more willing than the European politician to follow the trend of the times: and that is the way the prophecy fulfills itself!*

*I almost forgot to mention work. The opportunities, though still slow and scattered, are very good, now that both sides are equally kind to me. I have given up asking questions, and people begin to tell a little about religion of the middle layer —I mean, there are three strata:*

*Top layer—Catholic, to be talked of freely*

*Second layer—Montezuma, the Mother, the Sun and Moon*

*Bottom layer—Costumbres, not to be spoken of*

*My six months in America have been most valuable and most instructive* to me, and whatever disappointments there have been have come from my own want of competence and energy. I cannot thank you enough for all the splendid opportunities you have provided, and for all the many kindnesses, and most especially, for the chance of knowing and loving the Santa Clara people.

I wish nothing more than to come back, and I am grateful for your plans which make it possible for me to come—if only my family will let me. As far as I know, I must stay in England until June 1912; but if, by that time, your plans for the School's work were still the same, I should be very happy to come over in the fall, lecture at Santa Fe or wherever you wished, and make another visit to the Mohave-Apache in the Christmas vacation. I should like to live at Santa Clara, and undoubtedly I should get, in time, a great deal of information which ought to be preserved for the future, even if it is not permissible to publish it now. And now I have guest-friends at Santo Domingo, with whom I could stay from time to time, and perhaps get to know a little of that pueblo. Their hospitality was charming—they even gave me a small speaking part in the drama with which they entertained the visitors!

I suppose that I must leave Santa Clara in ten days' time and, after a few days in Santa Fe with Mr. Harrington, go on to Washington and thence to New York. I will get the Santa Clara medicine paper done before I leave, and I think I shall submit it to the principales, so as to be open and above-board with them, and show them that I have not written anything about the Medical Society. Goodbye and thank you very much. (National Archives, Hewett, 28 Jan. 1911)

❧ ❧ ❧

As Freire-Marreco left the Southwest from Lamy, New Mexico, on the outbound train, her most glowing thank-you was to Somerville College. The date was February 17, 1911. *Today I have actually started for home, and the first letter written on the journey ought to be to you, to begin a long series of thank-yous that I shall be saying to you for so many years.*

*You have given me the time of my life! Wherever it has been a failure, it has been from my own want of energy and perseverance. I have left undone*

VERY much—I have not given a fair trial to the methods about which I learnt at home—I have been too timid, and above all, too sleepy! But oh, what a time I have had, especially since Christmas! What scope to live and be a real person! And what endless kindness: today when I look back on the whole outing, it seems a long string of kindnesses. The lady on the boat asking me home to stay with her; the Church of St. John at Boston; Miss Fletcher at Washington calling me "my dear girl" the first day; Dr. Hewett's constant "We can arrange all that for you;" the schoolmistress at Santa Clara (whom I did not like) always kind and hospitable; the agent's wife at McDowell taking me into her house for a month, and the agent lending me horses; the old magician talking and talking all the afternoon, and his grandson and grandson's wife heroically coming out in the dusk to see me home. And oh, my dear Santa Clara people, always making allowances and sparing me expenses "because you come from so far away;" and I can't begin to talk of the endless goodness of Santiago and Filomena and Sofia, who have been father and mother and sister to me. And people at Santa Fe, hospitable and friendly; and Harrington (whom I used not to like either) pouring instruction into me at every minute of the day, and packing my things, and writing me a flaming testimonial at the last moment—which I enclose a copy of it—it is not all true, but that's no great fault in a testimonial. And behind all these happy experiences lies your immense kindness which has made them all possible.

I am going to Washington for a few days, partly to report to Mr. Hodge and Miss Fletcher, but chiefly on business of the council at Santa Clara.

I hope to catch the Laurentic, February 25th from New York. Train coming- goodbye. (Somerville, Darbishire, 17 Feb. 1911)

# AN ENGLISH INTERVAL

As a second generation anthropologist, Barbara Freire-Marreco considered herself fortunate to live at a time when mutual respect was growing between scientists on both sides of the Atlantic. Even during the one-year hiatus between her two field trips to the States, her trans-Atlantic communications continued, and she contributed to the spirit of cooperation developing among her American and European colleagues.

Upon returning to England, she reported to the scholarship sponsors who had funded her sojourn in the United States. Two copies of this report, almost identical, still exist—one at the Museum of New Mexico's Angelico Chavez History Library, the other at Somerville College Library, Oxford University. Both are dated April 27, 1911 and addressed to Helen Darbishire. With gratitude she thanked Somerville College, also crediting her American benefactors.

This report included a summary of her 1909-1910 American expenditures, including what she considered her "extravagant expences." The costs would have been significantly greater except for the liberal hospitality of the School of American Archaeology. Her tally:

*Outfit about  30*
*Sea passages  32*
*Railway fares  28*
*Expense between Atlantic & Santa Fe, to and fro  34*

Expenses in camp   13
Visit to Arizona   35
Specimens & carriage about   8
Living expenses, wages, presents, cables, postage   98
Total pounds, about   278

Of this, 130 pounds has been paid from the Fellowship allowance, 40 pounds from my own funds, and at present I am indebted to my father for a loan of 108 pounds. The expenses of the Arizona visit will be covered by payment from the Bureau of Ethnology if my report is accepted.

Her reckoning of 135 pounds for expenses up to August 1912:

Summer term   15.00
Vacation work   20.00
Three terms in Oxford   60.00
D.S.C. fees & other exp.   40.00
Total   135.00

I hope to pay off another 45 pounds, leaving a deficit of 28 pounds.

Dr. Hewett has suggested that I should return to Santa Fe, perhaps in the winter of 1912, to lecture on Social Anthropology for the School. The salary would cover the traveling and living expenses, and I could go on with the Pueblo work at the same time, and undertake another piece of investigation for the Bureau of Ethnology.

A postscript marked omit, was added to the Museum of New Mexico Library's copy. I brought home a small collection from New Mexico and Arizona, perhaps eighty specimens in all. Many of them illustrate the native uses of plants in medicine; others are specimens of pottery, dancing-ornaments, amulets, and household utensils. Considering that there will be a deficit on the expenses of the expedition, it seems more appropriate to spend the Fellowship Allowance on actual work and traveling, and to assign the 40 pounds of my own which I have spent to outfit and on specimens. I propose, therefore, to present the specimens to the Pitt Rivers Collection as from myself. Although no longer complete, this is one of her collections now housed at the Pitt Rivers Museum in Oxford.

❧ ❧ ❧

After settling back in England and reflecting on the past year's fieldwork, Freire-Marreco felt her time in the United States had been worthwhile and fulfilling, especially when she lived and worked in the Rio Grande Pueblos. She had learned respect for Native people, developed affection for many of them. Now it did not seem impossible to make a return trip, and her focus was directed toward that end.

Meanwhile, she took up the British academic life again. Although officially living at the parental home in 1911 and 1912, she spent time also in London and Oxford, at the London School of Economics and various Oxford colleges. She again wrote book reports and edited *Notes and Queries* for the Royal Anthropological Institute. Mentioned in correspondence, she read at least one paper at an Oxford Anthropological Society meeting during this period.

𒀖 𒀖 𒀖

Freire-Marreco and John Myres probably met many times in 1911 because of her frequent visits to Oxford, where she continued to consult him and to place great value on his opinion. There is almost no correspondence between them at this time undoubtedly because of the face-to-face encounters. What notes that have surfaced are concerned mostly about meeting publication deadlines for *Notes and Queries*.

Myres shared many interests with his protégée. Her details of New Mexican Pueblo life fascinated him. On August 27th she wrote: *Blanket weaving is almost gone from the Rio Grande: they buy Hopi dresses, Navajo and Mexican blankets. Pottery has gone from Taos; they get it from the Tewa Pueblos. Baskets are almost gone, upriver from Santo Domingo; they buy from Apaches and the Hopi. Even in the little Tewa group of six villages, belt making is almost limited to the Pueblo of Tesuque.* She would have been delighted to know that many of these crafts are now thriving arts.

The rest of this letter is included because it seems curious: If Freire-Marreco had had a more modern understanding of healthy diets she would not have requested the following information, but would have realized the foods introduced by whites to the Pueblos and reservations were replacing a more nutritious diet that had worked for centuries in the Southwest. *I wish you were out there for a bit to understand them! Sir, what do you make of a civilization without oil or butter, without sugar or honey, without wine or beer? Maize, lean meat, beans, pumpkins—that was the pre-Spanish diet. Since the Spanish came, apples, peaches, apricots, melons added: When they are dried for winter, they give a fair proportion of sugar to bulk, but in summer, I know to my shame, one overeats oneself on them trying to satisfy the longing for sugar. I suppose buffalo gave some fat, but they hunted it for a short time in the year; the other meat was venison, rabbit, birds of sorts. Spaniards brought cows, but you can't wean calves artificially in such a poor country, and there is no milk to drink south of Picuris or Taos, and no butter anywhere. They salt the milk. Why?*

*I want to know: Were the pre-Spanish actually ill off? Did they lack something necessary to comfort in lacking sweets and fat? One thing looks like it: As soon as American trade reaches a Pueblo tribe, they become great customers for sugar and lard—<u>carloads of lard</u> —and coffee three times a day—it's not for nothing that the Santa Fe Railroad starts from Chicago! Coffee and sugar are luxuries, lard is a necessity.*

*Another thing I should like you to see is the little donkey caravan competing with the railway from Espanola to Fernandez de Taos, carrying paraffin. Also the queer parasitical white traders and hawkers in Indian towns, bartering luxuries for necessaries. The Indians swap their good corn for sugar, coffee, even apples—in January a basket of apples is bartered for a basket of corn! Muy Tantos los Indiaos (very foolish the Indians). Why, I met an American and a Mexican in partnership with a cinematographer and they rake in corn and chickens at the doors. And also, Pueblo Indians used to trade in such bulky perishables. How could it pay? No shell currency there—they took bread and meal into the Comanche country to buy buffalo hides; and took their lives in their hands too. And more lately, it was thought worthwhile to peddle two donkey-loads of apples right up to the Jicarilla Apache.* (Bodleian, Myres, 27 Aug. 1911)

Professor Myers had better and more current knowledge of nutrition. His answer: *I am just off to Portsmouth for the British Association Meeting, but I should like to answer your questions shortly before I go.*

Meat, though lean, would I suppose give enough fat to support human life, and I believe there is a small quantity of oil in beans, but clearly, from what you say about the lard trade, they were very short of fat of any kind. The same about sugar: probably maize contains a little and sugar is not essential, so I understand, as long as you have starch or other carboniferous matter such as is supplied by most kinds of vegetable tissue. The great value of sugar is that being soluble and combustible, it goes straight to the spot, repairing damage and restoring energy far more quickly than anything else. Is is for this reason that it is so valuable for children, and also let me add for fractious drivers and tent-pitchers after a long day's march. I always carry lump sugar in my pocket to play catch with as soon as we have unpacked the loads for the night. At the same time, life without sugar or fat can hardly be cheerful, and probably not permanently wholesome.

The use of coffee which you emphasize points somewhat in the same direction, because one of the physiological effects of coffee is to produce a nervous stimulation which simulates warmth such as would be produced in reality by a dose of sugar. It is for this reason that coffee is so much used by drivers and other people who live exposed lives.

I should like to see the donkey caravans competing with the railway. It would remind me of the competition of bullock traffic with the railway in Cyprus. There, in fact, they postponed the construction of the railway for many years, lowering their freight tariff for a while whenever the railway project was mooted.

I should like to talk over these and similar matters with you more at length—perhaps next term. Meanwhile, we shall pass through London, and in that case we should be delighted, if it should be possible, to arrange to come down and spend a night with your people. Will you please thank them very kindly for this pleasant thought of theirs? Probably the more convenient time would be as we return in October. (ibid., 30 Aug. 1911)

With the realization that one could get along without a lot of sugar and fat, Freire-Marreco returned to other interesting facts she had learned at various Pueblos. *Thank you very much for the full answers about food and trade. About starch compensating for sugar: after a while as your taste gets purged of butter and sugar, you come to detect a sweetness in dry bread, especially wheat bread, and a richness in maize bread: but tortillas made of store flour are dross to my mind! Thanks for the hint about sugar when you camp—but Indians are hardly ever fractious till they get colds on the chest, and then they are as bad as children.*

*An example of trade of surplus for luxuries? Necessaries? I forgot—the Indians at Santa Clara have ceased to grow their ceremonial tobacco: the Spaniards just across the river grow it, and the Indians buy it with pottery. Pottery is made by women and costs nothing but time. When Santa Clara people take pottery to Taos, it is not barter, but a gift, for which a return is expected sooner or later. The Sia (Zia) Indians, who have a poor water supply, make a large regular supply of pottery and barter it for corn (1) with a white trader, (2) with the Indians of Santa Ana and Jemez.* (ibid., 31 Aug. 1911)

҂ ҂ ҂

Because Freire-Marreco was in England at this time and had personal contact with her British professional associates, her important exchanged correspondence was with American colleagues and U. S. government officials. Her concern with the seemingly unsolvable conflict between long-standing tribal problems and U. S. government organization is shown in a long plea and explanation to the Commissioner of the Bureau of Indian Affairs in Washington, Robert Valentine, a man she had met through Alice Fletcher. The following dramatic and impassioned letter reveals a broad-sweeping comprehension of the Pueblo situation and her insightful analysis as to the solution. *When you were so good as to listen to me at the end of February, I don't think that I put my point to you at all clearly. To tell the truth, I had allowed myself to be taken by surprise, having persuaded myself that the measure of support for our authority which the Indian Governors had desired was, if not easy to give, at least obviously desirable. Your explanation made me see the difficulties in the way of granting this support, and especially, that it would conflict with the policy of individualization and centralization on which the Government has been working for many years.*

*I think the point I ought to have submitted to you is this: Can you not make these communities into communities of civilized men? And would not that be a better piece of work, sociologically speaking, than to break up in the hope of getting some few civilized individuals? Progressive communities of civilized men; with land owned in severalty by all means (though the climate will probably continue to impose joint irrigation and common pasturage): but this is not inconsistent with the sociable village life which makes these Indians cheerful, dignified, humane. In fact, it is the condition which the modern experiments aim at creating.*

*If you pursue a policy of disruption—or rather, if you allow disruptive tendencies to have their way here, you will not be building something among irrevocable ruins (which has been your work among some other Indian tribes), but deliberately breaking down a living healthy organization. The very difficulties or readjustment of which the Indians are conscious prove that it is alive and healthy—only a few dying inbred communities like San Ildefonso find nothing to complain of. The progressive Pueblos complain of very healthy growing-pains!*

*Miss Fletcher said to me that she has had to weep over Indians for many years—to be content to save thirty percent of the individuals of broken tribes, but here there need be little to weep over. I believe that the bad years of timidity, resentment and brooding formalism are over and gone. You have the people alive, reasonably prosperous (at least self supporting), improving, suggestible, civilizable. A few of the smallest villages will die out, it seems, but they are exceptions. It is difficult and complicated, but surely it is as healthy and hopeful a problem as ever came before an administrator.*

*The whole tendency of the day is towards centralization and individualization. We are becoming a conglomeration of individuals, held together by no bond more immediate than the State. Mr. Commissioner—if you will allow me to speak freely—I believe that you are a practical sociologist: I cannot believe that you will be content to sit by and see tendencies take their course, even if they are tendencies towards a convenient uniformity. I can guess that Congress and your public (like ours in England) expect you to do so. To acquiesce in the tendencies which they discovered was the way of the doctrinaire sociologist of the day before yesterday, and consequently it went the way of the half-educated public of today. But in plain truth, what is the good of having men trained to discover these currents unless it is that they may be energetically effective to control them, and turn them into more hopeful channels. And to do that, the sociologist must not be ashamed of a little empiricism.*

*It is as a means toward the Community that I ask you to support the Native organization of the Pueblo Indians. I don't ask you to save their art or their religion—I know it can't be done. I don't want you to keep the Pueblos in a glass case for anthropologists to look at. I don't want to be antiquarian, and so won't even ask what the better educated public of (say) 1950 will say if it realized that the immense confederation of the United States could not find room for almost the last republics of an ancient pattern left in the world.*

Although some fighting still exists today in and between the Rio Grande Pueblos, several organizations now promote cooperation and coexistence among the Pueblo peoples. As a small point in the larger battle she was waging, Freire-Marreco had dismissed efforts as futile to save their art and religion. She would be surprised and pleased to learn that these fundamentals have not only survived, but thrive in many areas and on many levels in the twenty-first century.

A heartfelt plea from her delineated exactly the dilemma of the Pueblo Indians. Continuing, she summarized all she hoped for their future. *The Pueblo Indians, under mask of reserve and suspicion, are so extraordinarily suggestible! If you will recognize their magistrates you can make them your instruments for education—for Americanization in a good sense—and carry out all the changes you think necessary without a struggle and without a shock. Just as, on a small scale, you see a tactful schoolmistress enlist the authority of the governors on the side of education, while a half-educated person alienates them by discourtesy or neglect.*

*In a few years' time, you could make them believe that all the Government's instruction were the logical fulfillment of their ancient laws! I am contradicting some of the antiquarians here, but yet I don't think I am talking nonsense. Within the apparent rigidity of conservative form, the spirit of Pueblo tradition is exceedingly fluid; you can put new wine into those old bottles— already it has happened many a time. I speak from the evidence of many of their* institutions. For instance, the possession and demise of land in severalty is no doubt an innovation upon an older tenure, but now the Tewa Indians, at least, take it to be a part of their ancient customs. Only make the Native machinery your instrument, and you can do all you think needful and have the people thank you for it.

When the Bureau of Indian Affairs has acquired the right to control and protect the Pueblos (and I hope with all my heart you may acquire it), what other machinery of control can you find more suitable than this which already exists? Why, among the reservation Indians, the Bureau has set up a machinery of chiefs and Indian judges which is just a pale ghost of the living system of the Pueblos!

I fear that I write too hotly; and worse still, that I write as if I were addressing the general reader rather than an expert authority. You will pardon it, I hope, and believe that only your own kindness and patience encourages me to offer you an opinion.

This reminds me: You said something about the public indifference to Indian problems. Would it be useful or a hindrance if I were to send something on this subject to a popular magazine? Something in the way of criticism from a foreigner's point of view. Naturally, I would not send it without your sanction. (National Archives, Bureau of Indian Affairs, Valentine file, 29 Apr. 1911)

In his response sent to her, Valentine condoned Freire-Marreco's attitude and stated his course of action, enlisting the help of the Commissioner of Indian Schools under his jurisdiction. *I am very grateful to you for your letter of April 29th, and shall reply to it more fully later. I have sent a copy to Mr. Shelby H. Singleton, who is making a careful preliminary study for me of conditions among the Pueblos, pending my own trip to that part of the country, which I still mean to take, but which has been postponed owing to the necessity of my being in Washington during the extra session of Congress.*

*Mr. Singleton has for seven years been council and secretary of the Citizens' Association of Chicago, and consequently has had great experience, both in investigating work and in studying first hand, of sociological conditions. I am sure that he will have the courage, as I hope I shall, to adopt a particular method in any particular case, even if it seems to be out of line with our general policy. You did not put the case at all too strongly.*

*It strikes me as a very fine idea that you should write a popular magazine article, expressing your views. I feel we cannot have too much discussion of this subject from all points of view. I shall take pleasure in writing you further, when I have given the subject some mature consideration.* (ibid. 6 May 1911)

Singleton, the Supervisor of Indian Schools under the authority of the Bureau of Indian Affairs, Department of the Interior, had agreed with Freire-Marreco, but with modifications. He wrote her on July 25th from Chicago of their mutual views. *At the request of the Commissioner of Indian Affairs I recently spent a month in New Mexico investigating matters relating to the Pueblo Indians. In that connection Commissioner Valentine handed me a letter which he had received from you under date of April 29th. I was greatly interested in the views expressed in your letter and after a month's contact with these people in a number of their villages, I found myself strongly in sympathy with your suggestion that the Native governmental machinery of the Pueblos be utilized as an instrument for their civilization. In the course of a somewhat lengthy report to the Indian Office upon my investigation, in discussing the request made by a General Council of the Pueblos held at Santa Clara on May 18th, 1911 that the local authorities in each Pueblo be given power to enforce regulations for the performance of necessary public work and for the preservation of order in the villages. I said:*

*"Great stress is laid by all the Pueblos upon this request. They declare that not only the prosperity, but the very existence of these communal villages depends upon the granting of such powers. Their reasons for making this request are set forth fully in the statements formulated by the two General Councils and I am satisfied that some means must be devised in the near future for strengthening the hands of the local Pueblo authorities so that they may be able to enforce the public works necessary to the well-being of the villages and to punish those who commit minor offences.*

*"I am satisfied that if the Pueblo Indians are to survive in any desirable way, the Indian Office must utilize what is best in their old form of government. Recognition of the Pueblo government in the manner here open to us will result in the destruction of the old formalism. We can make the government already existing in each village by granting certain powers of self-government. This can*

be accomplished by incorporating the village under our laws.

"This is desirable . . . in time to change a so-called pagan community into a civilized one. The change will be so gradual that the Indians will not know when it came. The Governor will become the Mayor; the Captain of War, the village policeman; and the Junta will become the town meeting. Community work will represent our tax system.

"Many years ago the Pueblos voted and acted as jurymen. An Indian agent, who probably had some ulterior motive, arranged with the Indians that he would issue a certain amount of blankets and other goods to them and have them exempted from taxation if they would agree to stop voting. As a result of this informal bargain, the Indians in the Pueblos have not voted during recent years.

"There is reason to believe, however, that they are citizens of the United States and as such are entitled to the ballot. I would recommend that the necessary steps be taken as soon as possible to determine in the courts the status of these Indians as to citizenship, in order that the Government may adopt a permanent policy in dealing with them.

"If these Indians are allowed to vote it is feasible for them to elect one of their numbers in each Pueblo as Justice of the Peace. This would give them the power to punish minor offences. While many of the Indians are ignorant, it is the opinion of those who know them best that they are well qualified to exercise the right of franchise as most of the Mexican voters. If they asserted themselves by voting they would undoubtedly be less harassed by Mexican trespassers, since they would occupy a stronger position politically.

"In trying out any plan along this line, I believe that it would be feasible, with the aid of Miss True to induce the Santa Clara Indians to take the lead in testing the proposed innovations. If these worked well in Santa Clara Pueblo, it is probable that there would be little difficulty in inducing other Pueblos to follow the example of Santa Clara.

"I am convinced that these Indians, who have for three hundred years retained, almost unchanged, their ancient form of government and customs, are coming to the point where they will be willing, if properly handled, to take decided steps in the direction of civilization. For some years many of the men of these villages have been spending six months of the year working for American farmers *and lumbermen in the more Americanized parts of New Mexico and in Colorado and Utah. These bring home American ideas of government. This, aided by the educational work among the children, is leavening the whole lump of Pueblo village life and is preparing the way for better conditions."*

I believe with you that these Pueblo communities can be made into "communities of civilized men" and that this would be a far better piece of work, sociologically, than to break up the communities. I understand from Commissioner Valentine . . . taken in the immediate future to have the question of Pueblo citizenship finally determined. If it is finally decided that they are not citizens, the Indian Office will be in a position to deal with them with a freer hand. In any event it should be the aim of the government, for the present at least, to preserve these unique communities.

If you have written the proposed magazine article, which you mentioned in your letter to Mr. Valentine, I will be glad to know what periodical it will appear in as I would like very much to see it. (ibid. 25 July 1911)

Despite Singleton's support for many of her thoughts, Freire-Marreco was not ready to agree with his proposals. He seemed not able to fully accept the capability of Native people to govern themselves. Indeed, it is hard to accept his patronizing attitude. She responded: *Two serious objections might be made to these suggestions: first, that such a recognition of Indian authority as is here proposed would be undemocratic in principle; secondly, that it might defeat the very object which it is intended to serve.* (ibid. Nov. 1911)

She again emphasized the need to preserve the governor's authority and prestige, as well as independent elections. Defending the pueblo peoples' intelligence, she urged only support, not change, from the U.S. government, insisting that their present laws were quite adequate and only needed enforcing.

᪾ ᪾ ᪾

Politics and government weren't her only concern. Anthropology flourished in her heart and mind, and she was ever preoccupied with her fieldwork, past and future. While in England, Freire-Marreco kept in touch with Edgar Hewett in a professional and friendly way. She considered him her American mentor, and he seems to have accepted that role. She wrote to him, summarizing her last weeks in the States and informing him of what she had observed concerning the internal politics at Santa Clara Pueblo.

*I hope that you have had a very successful season, and that all the members of the expedition* (the aforementioned Quirigla) *have come back safe and well. I heard through Mr. J. L. Myres that you had been laying out an archaeological park with a fringe of fruit garden, among other things!*

*I want to report to you about the governor's business at Santa Clara.* Those in attendance at the meeting were named and that they had announced they had produced a petition to present to the U.S. Bureau of Indian Affairs in Washington.

*They were unanimous in wishing to entrust the presentation of the petition to Miss True. Accordingly I wrote out full notes of the points agreed on by the General Council, and these were handed over to Miss True with the signatures of all the delegates, on or about the 7th of February.*

*When I was in Washington (Feb. 19-25) I spoke to Miss Fletcher and Mr. Valentine about this petition. Mr. Valentine naturally answered that he could say nothing until he had received the petition itself. I have heard nothing of it yet, and it looks as if Miss True had not sent it in. It is rather important that it should be sent in without more delay, if only for the credit of Santa Clara with the other Pueblos. When you are in Santa Fe, would it be possible for you to see Miss True and talk about it? I fear that she has had a good many troubles lately, and perhaps it has been impossible for her to see about it. And if you have time to meet the governor and principales of Santa Clara, would you urge them that they are bound to see the petition through, by their promise to the other delegates? If Miss True has not time to do it for them, they ought to ask someone else to write it, or write it themselves.*

*I learnt some things in Washington which I could not write to the Santa Clara people, but which you ought to know, if by chance you do not know them already.*

*(1) Miss True does not possess the confidence of Mr. Valentine or of the*

*Assistant Commissioner in the very least, although they acknowledge the value of her temperance work.*

*(2) Mr. Valentine seems prepared to support Mr. Crandall as his subordinate and to accept the responsibility of his actions—which, of course, is very proper.*

*(3) The legal opinion is that the shoestring grant in Santa Clara Canyon is not merged in the reservation created by the Executive Order of 1906, and therefore, Miss True was mistaken in advising the Indians to take up and hold cattle trespassing on the shoestring grant which remains the private property of the Pueblo and as such subject to the trespass laws of the Territory, and not to the regulations which apply to reservations. That is, the Santa Clara Indians have put themselves in a bad position by the action which they took, and they may get into trouble.* The Shoestring Grant was a long narrow strip of land along Santa Clara Creek in dispute between the Pueblo and the Spanish population.

*(4) I understood the Commissioner to say that Miss True left the Indian Service on Dec. 31, 1910. None of the Indians knew this in February certainly, and they were only too anxious, SN (Santiago Naranjo) especially, to put as much responsibility on her as possible. They were asking her to support everything they did. Of course Miss True would not wish to deceive them. I believe she thought that I knew she had retired—but it does not seem a very safe situation.*

*Mr. Valentine seems to have got the impression that the Santa Clara people are rather a turbulent set. I hope Miss Fletcher may be able to persuade Mr. Valentine to visit New Mexico in the summer, and if he sees the Santa Clara people, he will almost certainly change his mind. Only the quiet safe people like Leandro, Santiago and Francisco must do some of the talking, and not leave it all to Victoriano Sisneros and Pedro Baca. V.S. and P.B. are splendid people in their way, but they speak English and think it manly and American to be rather disrespectful to officials!*

*As for the internal affairs of the Pueblo of Santa Clara, they were very hopeful when I left in February. The reconciliation between the two parties, which seemed to start from the cattle business on November 4th and was so much stimulated by the arrival of your map at the end of the month, took a fresh impetus from the General Council and the necessary cooperation of the leading men in that business. The dance of the Winter People of Jan. 27th had a great effect; and a new though informal agreement about the public works was made at the end of January with every sign of good feeling and good intentions on both sides. Leandro and Santiago on the one side and Francisco on the other all showed to great advantage and I think that Santiago did particularly well in taking a more frankly conciliatory line than Leandro himself would have been inclined to. I had a very sensible letter from him the other day, saying that the common work on the ditch had been done without trouble, and that he intended to make some small improvements in the irrigation this year.*

*As for your very kind and very much appreciated offer of lecture-work in Santa Fe later on, my family are not at all inclined to give me a definite answer about it yet. I can only ask you to keep the offer open if you can and will. My own wish would be to come over for the winter of 1912-13, but I cannot count on being able to do it.* (Museum of New Mexico, Hewett, 2 May 1911)

She enclosed a copy of her report to the Fellowship Committee, including the accounting for her stay in New Mexico, along with some articles she thought would be of interest to him.

Another letter from Freire-Marreco in May sent to Hewett reiterates that the report resulting from the Santo Domingo Council meeting had been turned over to Clara True; her own personal feeling was that if True did not take action, the Santa Clara people should. *I had a letter yesterday from Francisco Naranjo, saying that they are having trouble about the cattle of the Mexicans. I wonder if you know what it is? I fear it means that they are in trouble about impounding the cattle last November. If the Pueblo has to take up a collection for any legal expenses, if they let me know I will pay my share as a householder, which I was in November.*

*I expect you are tremendously busy, but if you can find time to send me any news of what is happening I shall be more than grateful. I wish with all my heart that I had given stronger advice about prudence and discretion—I was too ready to flatter them and Miss True, which was no true friendship. But indeed they both seemed to know their own business much better than I did.* (ibid. 9 May 1911)

Freire-Marreco's trust in Clara True's abilities—or intentions—was faltering. Apparently True herself became uncertain about her effectiveness because she later appealed directly to Hewett, asking him to intervene in the affairs between the Bureau of Indian Affairs and Santa Clara Pueblo.

*This note in haste to say that Mr. Singleton, the man who broke up the Chicago race tracks and police pools, is here quietly investigating Indian Affairs. I have asked Mr. Singleton to see you for various reasons, among them the chief to substantiate Santiago's statements concerning the availability of water in many of our canyons, Ojo de Agua, Chupadero, etc. The cattle men are falsely representing that there is no water anywhere outside Santa Clara Canyon. This should not have any weight but it has a little, which I deem it best to refute. I had Santiago with me when I showed Mr. Singleton personally several springs and told him of others. I suggested using you as a final authority on the topography of the country. It is entirely feasible for the Forest Service to open up other sources such as are made elsewhere. This new line of argument we are making destroys the last pretension of Jim Lease and the cattle gang. So far we have made good, I think. We took Mr. Singleton to the end of Santa Clara Canyon and showed him a good many things he could not otherwise learn. Thanking you for the favor we are asking and also for the map which has been and is being of so much service.* (ibid. 13 May 1912)

Clara True reported the news of Shelby Singleton's visit at Santa Clara Pueblo to England. On receiving her letter and another from the Santa Claran, Victoriano Sisneros, Freire Marreco wrote her thoughts on the matter, presumably to Hewett.

Although the letter is unsigned and nowhere to be found, a postscript summarized the outcome of Singleton's inspection. *Postscript: Since I wrote this letter, I have had letters from Miss True and Victoriano Sisneros with very hopeful accounts of Mr. Shelby Singleton's inspection. It seems that Mr. Singleton is inclined to recommend that the governor and council should be recognized as a mayor and corporation. Mr. Singleton went up the Santa Clara Canyon with Miss True, Santiago, and Pedro Baca to see the boundaries.*

*But no doubt this is very old news indeed to you on the spot. My excuse for writing is only the very anxious interest that I feel in the whole business.* (ibid. 13 June 1912)

During this interlude in England, Freire-Marreco had other things on her mind besides Clara True and Indian-U.S. politics. Ever mindful of her social relations she sent a note, along with some books, to Hewett that again showed her efforts not to offend Pueblo friends. This would no longer be offensive. *I enclose a little paper on Indian dances in relation to Indian social organization: It is very slight, but I hope it may interest you. I know you will be so kind as to keep it out of the School library (where Indians might see it) and out of the local papers; I would not have it mentioned to them for anything! There is nothing secret in it, of course, but the mere occurrence of such names as Tano in print would annoy the Indian.* (ibid. 5 Nov. 1911)

Hewett replied: *Many thanks for the books which you have been kind enough to send us. They will form a valued addition to our library. Your paper on the Indian dances will, as requested, be kept for private use.*

*I am intending to give myself the pleasure of a visit to England next spring. Mr. Marett has been kind enough to ask me to speak before the Oxford Anthropological Society and I shall take pleasure in complying with his request. We are all glad to know that you are to come back to us next fall. Could you arrange to be here by August first so as to take part in the Summer School?*

*You have spoken of wanting to do some work in our local archives. You will be pleased to learn that we are finding a good deal of interest in them. Mr. Tipton, probably our best authority in old Spanish, is going through the documents in the Federal building for the purpose of noting everything relating to land titles. In connection with his regular work he has very kindly undertaken to make note of all the documents that come under his notice which would be interesting to us. These memoranda I shall be glad to place at your disposal when you want them.*

*Is it your purpose to prepare the Bulletin on the Yavapai before next June or will you wait until you return to America? Kindly advise Mr. Hodge as soon as convenient when you expect to have the manuscript ready.* (ibid. 21 Dec. 1911)

Freire-Marreco had in fact, been keeping in touch with Frederick Hodge, the man who headed the Bureau of Ethnology and who she had met in Washington and then again at Hewett's summer school. In fact, there is more correspondence with Hodge than with any other American colleague during this time in England. Sometimes their letters crossed in the mail, making the dates referred to difficult to follow. *I am thanking you and the Bureau daily, when I look at your splendid present of publications. They will be a comfort to me for the rest of my life. I hardly like to mention it, for it seems ungrateful—but the set does not include either volume of your **Handbook of American Indians**. It would be a very valued possession if I could have it, but of course I know it must be in great demand everywhere.*

She went on to mention her work in progress concerning the newly recognized science of ethnobotany that had been initiated by John Wesley Powell. Powell, 1834-1902. Probably best known for his exploration and survey of the Colorado River, Powell contributed much to the knowledge of the natural history, geology and ethnology of that area.

The ethnobotany publication, to which she referred, did not appear until 1916 in a Smithsonian Report. She wrote: *I have nearly finished the longest chapter of my report of the McDowell Reservation, namely, that which deals with the doctors. I can't complete it until I get my plant specimens back from the University of Colorado. The chapter runs to about 30,000 words at present; a little more must be allowed for the plants; and all the rest of the report will probably be another 30,000 to 40,000.*

She added that she also wanted to get the criticisms of Dr. C.G. Seligmann, an experimental psychologist as well as an anthropologist. Charles Gabriel Seligmann, 1873-1940, was a Professor of Ethnology at the University of London who did most of his field work in the South Pacific Islands and Africa. *Would the Bureau allow me to publish any of the material in a different form in England: For instance, could the **Folklore Society's Journal** print any of it? Or could I write a semi-popular article for the **Nineteenth***

**Century** *or the* **Contemporary Review**? *It would be an advantage to me here if I could do it, but of course I am quite prepared to hear that I can't!* (National Archives, Hodge, 7 May 1911)

Hodge answered: *I am very glad to learn from your letter of May 27th that the Bureau publications, now safely in your hands, are proving such a comfort which will be increased, I hope, when our present grist comes out of the mill.*

*Pending any definite arrangement that we may make later, there is no reason why you should not publish the semi-popular articles in one of the English magazines, but I do not think it would be desirable to give the Folklore Society more than a foretaste of the folklore side of your proposed paper, if by doing other wise it would give the final product the appearance of being secondhand.* (ibid. 9 June 1911)

Freire-Marreco to Hodge: *I have been writing a short paper on a sociological question (the relation of the individual to society in uncivilized life) in which I have used some facts about the Mohave-Apache and their dances by way of contrast with the Pueblo institutions. I read the paper at Oxford the other day, and now the Somerville Fellowship committee wants me to print it without delay because it will encourage the subscribers to the Fellowship fund. So I think of sending it to one of the reviews.*

*But have you any objection to my using the Mohave-Apache material? I have treated it so summarily that I do not think it can come into comparison at all with the future* **Bureau of American Ethnology Report**. (ibid. June 26, 1911)

On the same day Hodge had written to Freire-Marreco. *Your letter of June 16th has just reached me. I see no objection whatsoever to the publication of the paper proposed, nor to the draft on your Yavapai material necessary to its preparation. Should similar questions arise I would suggest that you use your own judgment, in order to save time.* (ibid. 26 June 1911)

Freire-Marreco thanked him *for your letter of June 9th. I am very much obliged to you for leave to publish the semi-popular articles. If I communicate anything to the Folklore Society, I will not give them the paper to print, but refer them to the forthcoming* **Report**.

*The most important part will be the section on the Dreamers—medicine men—Dr. Seligmann tells me that most of the material in this section is quite new in kind. The rest is incomplete in many respects, and certainly needs another month to complete it!*

*Did I tell you in my last letter that I have great hopes of coming out again in October 1912? I have some plans for an enquiry into all the Pueblo Governments, but they would require the help of the Bureau of Indian Affairs; and anyhow it is too soon to think of them yet.*

*P.S. Have you any notes in the Bureau, not included in the published Reports, which would bear on the question of the caciques' office and authority in New Mexico or Arizona? If you could give me a chance to see any notes of the sort, I should be more than grateful.* (ibid. 18 June 1911)

Hodge replied to Freire-Marreco referencing a recent letter from Dr. Hewett respecting the plans for continuing the joint work of the School of American Archaeology during the forthcoming fiscal year that would commence July 1st. Hodge recapitulated. *Hewett writes as follows: "In my plans with Miss Freire-Marreco with reference to her Yavapai work no one was obligated to anything, but I expressed the hope that she might prepare something acceptable to the Bureau and that enough might be paid for it to cover the expense of her expedition. The sum of $200 would be entirely acceptable to her and I should be very glad to have that amount set aside in the distribution of this year's allotment for joint work."* (ibid. June 26, 1911)

Hodge appreciated the political and social contributions Freire-Marreco was making on behalf of the Pueblo Indian governments. He wrote to her two weeks after receiving her letter. *Your letter of June 18th has reached me, and I am gratified to learn that you have such bright hopes of coming to our Southwest again next year.*

*After all the work that has been done among the Pueblos, there are few results so far as the social and governmental organization of these Indians are concerned. The Bureau has no unpublished manuscript material on the subject, although Mrs. Stevenson probably has recorded a good deal of data relating to the Taos (Tigua) and the Tewa. She has resumed her work at Santa Clara and will devote particular attention this season to the material culture of the Tewa.*

Matilda Coxe Stevenson, (Mrs. James), 1849-1915, was tutored in ethnology by her educated husband. She was associated with the Bureau of American Ethnology and explored in the Rocky Mountains, but her research focused mainly on the New Mexican Pueblos, especially Zuni and Taos.

Hodge continued: *Have you read Bandelier's **The Delight Makers?** It is based on Pueblo life, especially of the Tewa and Queres (Keres) in prehistoric times.* (ibid. 30 June 1911) The book Hodge spoke of is now considered a classic novel of the region. It was written by Adolph F. Bandelier, 1840-1914, a Swiss-American archaeologist who worked in Central America, Mexico, Arizona, and New Mexico, and was a Director of the New York Museum of Natural History. Because of his profession, the book presents accurate historical fictionalized data concerning early life in the Rio Grande Pueblos.

In late August Freire-Marreco wrote Hodge of the difficulty of getting American books in England: *You were so very kind as to say that the Bureau might be able to lend me some books which I could not get, transmitting them through your agents in London. I find it very difficult to get Mr. Bandelier's works, and I should be exceedingly grateful if you could lend me copies of his papers dealing with the history of the Pueblos, the Spanish occupation, and so forth. I am working on the question of the Native government of the Pueblos of New Mexico as influenced by Spanish and American administration, for some lectures which I have to deliver in Oxford this autumn.*

Always seeking to broaden her professional knowledge and contacts, she asked about the works of Frank Hamilton Cushing, who had recently published a paper on the Zuni that she found interesting. Cushing, 1857-1900, was an American ethnologist who led expeditions in Florida and excavated in Arizona. Associated with the U. S. Bureau of Ethnology, he authored several works, mainly on Zuni Pueblo. *A second favor which I make bold to ask, though I have less hope of your being able to grant is this: In the **Third Annual Report**, p.xxix, I see it stated that Mr. Cushing began a paper on the "Sociologic and Governmental Institution of the Zuni." Is his Ms. in the possession of the Bureau, or any rough notes intended for it: I should think it a* *great privilege if I were allowed to read it.* (ibid. 30 Aug. 1911)

Six weeks later Hodge's letter told Freire-Marreco that most of the Bureau's copies of Bandelier's writings were out at present, but he was willing to send his own copies of his **Final Report and Contributions,** as well as the library copy of **The Delight Makers.** *When you have finished with them they may be returned through Wm. Wesley and Son, 28 Essex Street, Strand,* the London agents for the Smithsonian Institution.

*Cushing's paper, to which you refer, evidently consisted of rough notes, which were absorbed, in all probability, by the paper which I am sending. The reference to the Zuni pilgrimage to the Atlantic is probably Cushing's articles in the* **Century Magazine** *for December 1812 and February 1883, bearing the title "My Adventures in Zuni," and Sylvester Baxter's papers, which I am including with the books mentioned above. Kindly keep the latter under your eye, as I do not think they can well be duplicated.* (ibid. 1 Oct. 1911)

Freire-Marreco then wrote a thank-you letter to Hodge. *It is most kind of you to lend me your own copies of Bandelier's* **Final Report and Contributions,** *as well as the library books and papers. I will take great care of all, and return through Wesley.* (ibid. 1 Nov. 1911)

His reply showed he'd been promoting his associate's writings. *Mrs. Matilda Coxe Stevenson, whose present address is Espanola, New Mexico, wrote me that she has just had a peep at your paper on "Two American Indian Dances," (1911,* **Sociological Review***) and asks if it will be possible for her to procure a copy. I shall be very glad if you can find it practicable to meet Mrs. Stevenson's wishes. I am sure the paper will fall into appreciative hands.* (ibid. 7 Dec. 1911)

❦ ❦ ❦

Because of their close association while Freire-Marreco was in the Rio Grande area, it is strange that only one letter to her colleague John Harrington during this interim in England was found. *I have just been reading your "Brief Description of the Tewa Language" in the* **American Anthropologist,** *and am extraordinarily interested by the paternoster at the end.*

*If we meet next year, you must tell me how you got it out and whether Ignacio volunteered "ugly magic" and "that horned dead man" or not.*

*Will you just put in this envelope, if you have time, the name of the linguistic group to which Mohave belongs?*

*Are you finding "dreamers" among your present subjects? Are the people in general given to hysteria or auto-hypnotic seizures, or do they show any other signs of nervous instability? Do the "dreamers" show any such signs? What is their general health? Do they begin to "dream" as children? Any developments at 12 or 14? Any women "dreamers?" Do they see lights go up in the sky, hear voices, feel themselves cut open?*

*I have a nice feather for Diegito, and will send it to find you in Santa Fe in August.* (National Archives, Harrington, 19 June 1911)

Planning to be in residence at London and Oxford until the following June, reading and writing up her notes and giving some lectures, she ended somewhat wistfully, or perhaps with determination, *I hope to come out next September.* (ibid. 1 Nov. 1911)

🪰 🪰 🪰

An appendectomy on December 11th put a temporary halt to Freire-Marreco's letter-writing for the rest of the winter of 1911-1912. Early in the 20th century, an appendectomy could well be a life-threatening event, and her doctor required her to be bed-ridden for an extended period of time, only gradually returning to normal activity. She dutifully had her associates notified, including Hewett and Hodge. By spring 1912 it was evident that she had recovered and was back at work. Hodge continued where he had left off in December, writing her on April 20th in response to a note from her. *Your letter of April 12th has just come, and as you say nothing about your health, I hope it may be taken for granted that you have fully recovered from you recent illness.*

*Respecting your Yavapai paper, I have made such arrangements as will enable you to submit the manuscript at any time, even after July 1st. You will find enclosed a formal order, which our Treasury Department regards in the light* of a contract, so that the two hundred dollars ($200) allotted for the payment will be available from our current appropriation whether or not the manuscript is received during the present fiscal year, which closes June 30th. By this plan you will not be obliged to feel that there is desperate haste in finishing the paper, although, naturally I should like to have it as soon as you can see your way clear to send it. (National Archives, Hodge, 20 Apr. 1912)

Freire-Marreco responded in late June, not responding to the Yavapai paper, but with very specific requests for another ongoing project. *The editor of the new edition of the British Association's handbook for travelers,* **Notes and Queries on Anthropology,** *desires me to ask your leave to quote the classification of "Basketry" from Bulletin 30: that is the right-hand column of page 133, and first twenty lines of 134.* **Notes and Queries** *is intended to help amateurs and beginners to make useful collections and observations, and certainly nothing could be more helpful to them than those very clear and comprehensible figures.*

*If you consent to this, would it be possible for you to add to your kindness by lending the blocks? If not, we could have the pages of Bulletin 30 photographed and make our own blocks, but it would certainly be less satisfactory.*

*The text of the book went to the printers today, the editor Professor J.L. Myers has gone abroad, and I am left in charge for the present. I have warned the printer to keep space for the plates until I hear from you and if you decide to lend the blocks and will post them as soon as you conveniently can, I can get them in without delaying the book.*

*We should be very glad of permission to include a diagram to show how gestures may be recorded. After so many years, I fear that you are not likely to have the blocks; or else I should venture to ask you to lend that block as well.*

*I hope I have made this request in proper form! I never had to borrow plates before, and I am so much afraid that I haven't asked politely enough! Please put it down to me and not to the absent editor.* (ibid. 28 June 1912)

Hodge gave permission and urged Freire-Marreco to make full use of the material she requested as well as any other Bureau of Ethnology publications. He also assured her that the blocks for the basketry illustration were being sent.

Freire-Marreco's return to the United States was planned to be in 1912. When she actually left England in the autumn of that year, no formal itinerary in print had been set for the continuation of her research, which was still under the auspices of the Somerville College Fellowship. She did know the previous year, however, that the scholarship funds were still available when she mentioned her destination of the proposed trip in a letter to Hodge. His response revealed the future tableau of her trip.

*It is good to hear of the prospect of your visiting Hano in the winter of 1912. You will find the Tewas there are more susceptible to the wiles of the ethnologist than their Rio Grande kindred!* (ibid. 11 Oct. 1911)

# ❧ ANOTHER AMERICAN ADVENTURE ❧

## ❧ The Hopi Reservation, Arizona

Her health intact, financing available and parental approval granted, Barbara Freire-Marreco sailed again to the United States toward the end of 1912. Her U. S. colleagues, aware of her intended visit to Southwest Indian country, once again helped pave her way. She hoped to go to the Hopi Reservation in Arizona by way of Santa Fe and Espanola, New Mexico. This would not be an easy trip, for in late 1912 the journey would take her on steam trains and wagons or on horseback. Letters of introduction were again flying through the mails on her behalf.

Edgar Hewett, now a most devoted supporter of Freire-Marreco, wrote to Lorenzo Hubbell on November 15th to enlist her safe passage. Lorenzo Hubbell, 1853-1930, a very well known American throughout the Southwest, had established trading posts on the Navajo Reservation and also hosted travelers in his remote corner of the United States, at a time when very few accommodations were available. His main trading post at Ganado, Arizona, where Freire-Marreco probably stayed, is now a United States National Monument. Hewett's letter to Hubbell said: *This will introduce to you my good friend, Miss Freire-Marreco. She is on her way to Hano, and I know that you can be of greater assistance than any one else in seeing that she is conveyed across. I assure that she will greatly appreciate your kindness, and I need not tell you that I will also.* (Museum of New Mexico, Hewett, 15 Nov. 1912)

Whether Hubbell assisted or not, by early 1913 Freire-Marreco had arrived in Arizona. She had traveled by train from the East Coast and eventually the last leg by more primitive conveyances to Hopi country. Established on the Reservation in January, Freire-Marreco wrote to her ethnologist colleague John Harrington. Though her letters are headed Polacca, Arizona—the location of the nearest Post Office—she was actually living atop First Mesa in old Tewa Village, sometimes called Hano.

Watercolor painting of Tewa Village in 1905 by H.B. Judy, an artist and photographer, who accompanied Stewart Culin on an expedition to Hopi country sponsored by the Brooklyn Museum of Art. Painted only seven years before Freire-Marreco's visit, a Corn Clan house on the left is thought to be the one in which she stayed. Note the stone shrine. Courtesy of the Brooklyln Museum of Art Archives, Culin Archival Collection, Collection Expeditions: Tscshudy paintins [2.4.037].

The world of instant communication did not exist in 1913. Telephoning was considered an extravagant expense, and of course email was yet to come. In reviewing the exchange of correspondence, it now seems remarkable that the U. S. postal service operated so efficiently in spite of slow modes of transportation, especially in remote areas.

Correspondence with Harrington increased during this time, particularly with discussions about the Tewa language. The many pages of Tewa phonetics Freire-Marreco sent to Harrington are now in the Smithsonian's National Archives. They also exchanged information concerning the Hopi/Tewa culture, everyday life and crafts. A note to him, whom she had seen in Santa Fe, on her way through read: *Thank you very much indeed for the films and paper so promptly sent. I enclose cheque with many thanks. I am truly sorry to see that I left owing you $1.50 for Maria—I went around with it in my hand looking for you on the day that I left, but I suppose I forgot it at the last.*

Probably this reference was to Maria Martinez of San Ildefonso Pueblo. Maria and her husband Julian worked as custodians at the School of American Archaeology in Santa Fe at that time, where Edgar Hewett encouraged them to produce innovative black pottery that was polished to a gun metal finish on which a black matte design was painted, gaining them fame and influencing much of the pottery produced in the Rio Grande pueblos to this day.

A paragraph followed discussing various Hopi/Tewa language sounds with some comparison to that spoken in the New Mexican pueblos and then told of her problems of acceptance by the Native people in her new location. *Usual difficulties arising after the first three weeks—other families jealous of my hosts and saying things. Whereas in Santa Clara it would be said that they were telling me secrets, here it is said that I am a witch and that we talk bad things with the door locked. Of the accusations I prefer this one, because one really can deny it! There was an agitated meeting to cross-examine me two nights ago, and everything I had with me which they thought suspicious has been packed up and sent back to the railway, and I am told I may consider myself cleared, but really I hope no one will get smallpox just now, it would be awkward for me. My hosts are standing up for me nobly. It shows the importance of the genealogical method. I snubbed one man for his intolerable forwardness, and found too late that he is the p'o'ae turyjo's (a Hopi official) sister's son; and he has stirred up all this trouble.*

*The weaving here is absolutely delightful, and the needlework not bad, in spite of hideous yarn. I am learning a little of each. Fancy being invited to sit all day in a nice painted estufa! And no one cares.* (Not so at Santa Clara.) *The rubbish heaps are full of prayer-plumes—and the kitchen storerooms full of masks. I took food to a society and they returned me a prayer-plume. Indeed it was well not to bring Santiago!—it would have opened . . .* (National Archives, Harrington, 8 Jan. 1913) This had not been mentioned previously as a possibility in her correspondence. Her comment would have been interesting, but it is not legible.

Again Freire-Marreco wrote to Harrington sometime after January 8, 1913. *Things have quieted down a bit, after a shocking waste of time for me and much discomfort for everyone who was kind to me. They are repairing the kiva now in preparation for a long ceremony, and I hope it will occupy their minds for a bit! How incredibly nice but oh, how incredibly tiresome Indians can be!*

*You say the Hopi language is "a dear"—not half such a dear as this Arizona Tewa, which really has left all its faults behind in New Mexico.* (ibid. after Jan 18, 1913) Undoubtedly this was due to the Hopi Reservation's isolation, while the Rio Grande pueblos had been infected with the Spanish and English languages of a more populated location.

In her next letter, Freire-Marreco posed questions to Harrington: *Can you get me a Tewa word for "chastisement," castigo (punishment), applied to sickness, misfortune, etc. And is the same word used for punishment inflicted by officials; that is, cutting off water from fields, beating, putting in the stocks? Should be very grateful for early answer. Your long letter I will answer soon—at present rather harassed and not well. And how do you say "they give advice," referring to elders visiting a sick person?* (ibid. 28 Jan. 1913)

In a short note to Harrington on February 10th she promised to mail the Yavapai manuscript, which was material collected on her former trip.

She hoped to continue her field work with the Yavapai, but her plans were very uncertain. Again she told Harrington she feared *a fresh set of difficulties with the caciques.* Unintentionally, she may have been too close to sacred ceremonial material, uncomfortably so for the Hopi/Tewa caciques.

She also wrote to thank him for the answers to previously asked questions: *Thank you very much indeed for the translations that I asked for, and the ceremonial terms—very good of you to make time to send them. I have written to have the Yavapai manuscript sent to you at Santa Fe. I am very glad that you think of making two visits. I am quite uncertain when I shall go there. I want to stay here as long as I possibly can, the stuff is so good; but my position is precarious, one party being determined to get rid of me. After a fortnight's peace and quiet, they have just now got up a new fuss; but I hope to outlive it. If the worst comes to worst, I must take my interpreter away with me, but I haven't got enough on-the-spot observations yet to make that profitable. So you may see me any day, or not for a long time. I have sent my important notes to Keam's Canyon, in case of real trouble. . . .*

*The migration stories don't go beyond the last starting place. Just now I feel very doubtful about the value of these traditions, mere guesswork about ruins, so much is a reflection of present-day customs. Even where they can quote a dance to match the legend, it is quite possible that the legend is based on a misinterpretation of the ritual. Their archaeological naivete is astounding.*

*By the way, Santiago writes to ask, "Is it time that I had told you that he would answer questions?" I reply, that "you meant that you were asking the questions on my account to help me." But be kind of careful.*

*They have finished a splendid Scalp-dance, a regular cycle of Tewa songs, ten or twelve of them and one that I have heard already at Santa Clara.* (ibid. 10 Feb. 1913)

Freire-Marreco attended all the dances that were presented during her stay at Hopi. An unnamed dance not mentioned in the correspondence was held in Sitsumove village (her spelling) on January 25, 1913. Proof of her presence there are her photographs she loaned to Professor Ridgeway, now located in the Cambridge University Library Archives.

*Ohoiki'l dance, Hano.* January 25, 1913. One of five photographs Freire-Marreco took on the Hopi Reservation that she gave to William Ridgeway , accounting for their present location. No number. Courtesy of Cambridge University Museum of Archaeology and Anthropology, Ridgeway Papers. The others not shown are:

*a. Sitsumove. Branch planted at the Kaje t'ee.*

*b. Bluefaced katcinas at Sitsumove 1913.*

*c. Old man sprinkling cornmeal on the bluefaced katcinas as they pass the Sitsumove Kaje t'ee near which a tree has been planted for the dance.*

*d.* The one illustrated here.

*e. Ohoiki'l, the plaza shrine of Hano, called Khaye t'ege, fetish house.*

Labelled simply *Pueblo Indian,* this photograph was taken by Freire-Marreco while watching a dance presumably at Hano, First Mesa on the Hopi Reservaion, February 1913. Courtesy of the University of Oxford, Pitt River School of Anthropology and Museum Ethnography, Neg. No. BS1.SA.22A.

🦋 🦋 🦋

About the same time, an interesting transition had begun. There is a gradual change in the Freire-Marreco/Harrington professional relationship, showing them on a more equal footing. Expressing respect for her success in gaining information from Pueblo people, perhaps due to her experience living with them, Harrington now asked her advice on how to obtain ethnological data without offending. Her response: *The only plan I can imagine for getting at the Galisteo lady is to arrange with her through John Dixon to come to the Santa Fe School to see her children, if she has any there,* or to make some other plausible errand to Santa Fe. I don't see how any other way would be safe, and even then you would have to take care that the Santo Domingo children did not see you with her! I don't believe that letters to the governor would do the faintest good.

You ought to be here, too! But that is true of every place where an Indian lives. I can't say I find it easy yet, but compared to New Mexico, the Tewa is straightforward and audible; I feel I only need time to get a vocabulary. It is emphatic, accented, one word distinct from the next. You would get it in no time.

So much is happening every day that one person can't cover it all. Just now I sit indoors all day with an interpreter, and only join the family circle at meals and after supper; and I can't help missing a score of interesting things.

I could have spent all my time here well, and yet it is the little that I learnt at Santa Clara that makes it easier to learn here. As to plans, I need another three weeks here; and I think it very important to be back at Santa Clara with all the stuff and test it on them, and claim certain favors that they promised me. I don't really know whether to make a very short visit to the Yavapai, for genealogies mainly, on the way; or to come right back to Santa Clara before the planting begins, and go to Yavapai afterwards. It means an extra train fare. Anyhow I fear my trip to Grand Canyon and the Pacific must stand over, to save time and money. She never made that trip.

The Moqui sounds puzzle me very much, and I can't write them a bit.

Hawk and eagle feathers here are <u>very</u> dear. The men say, and perhaps truly, that they pay each other $2 for a good one! They wish I would buy some for them at the San Ildefonso price, they say.

About Philip Dasheno—he writes to me that he has "forgotten his own language and learnt to talk Santa Clara," but whether that is to be taken literally I don't know. He writes that he is going to marry a Santa Clara girl very shortly and bring her home, probably as soon as Lent is over. Dasheno was a Hopi who moved to Santa Clara whose descendants have remained there.

I sent you a few slips, to glance over and keep until I come, unless you are kind enough to correct the most obvious mistakes and let me see them before I leave. In working with Philip, it might be as well not to show him the

179

*actual slips as coming from me in case he has caught some of the New Mexican suspiciousness, but to use them along with your other Tewa material to question him on.*

*Tomorrow I hope to get to the past wanderings of the Tewa, and will send you all I get about them. But I won't keep this open for it, because the man has begun in the underworld, and perhaps we shan't arrive in New Mexico before tomorrow night. Isn't it quaint, that they always produce, as entirely new and exclusive information, the old stuff that one has seen in print for years? And I believe they are speaking the truth—one clan doesn't tell the stories to another, and an Indian has fewer chances of comparing stories than a white visitor has. Of course it also means, "Can't I have 50 a day more than the other men?"*

*By the way, the frankness of the Hopi-Tewa won't last long, I think. I bet you anything two or three Santa Clara men come here next year when they see how easy it is; and a Laguna man who was here for a month has been telling the people that they tell too much to white people.* (ibid. 4 Feb. 1913)

Many of the notes Freire-Marreco sent to Harrington contain only fragmentary but nonetheless interesting information, for example: *the Hopi call us Hanu—also supposed to be a Hopi nickname for the Tewa (but the Tewa use it freely).*

*Two informants said: "The Hopi call us Hanu. Some place, our home, far away east, is T'anu; maybe Hano is their mistake for it. Its right name is Tewa'oywi. The people talk about Tanu, but don't know where it is. When we first came here the Hopi were not kind to us, and maybe they call us Tanu just anyway."* (ibid. 5 Feb. 1912)

Freire-Marreco's information about how Tewas came to live with the Hopis was original at that time. Her informant thought the only justification for it was that some clans, all late arrivals here, came by way of Zuni; whereas the Corn clan came by way of Keam's Canyon. *"The Hopi are always calling us Hanu but we are Tewa. All the clans started together from Tsaewagi."*

Tsaewagi, a former home site in the Santa Cruz Valley near Espanola, New Mexico. Established after the Pueblo Revolt, it was inhabited by Tewas from nearby pueblos, while others in fear of retribution by the Spanish after they had killed two Roman Catholic priests, started a migration that led them to the First Mesa on the Hopi Reservation. 1986 Photograph by L. Blair.

Translated as Wide White Gap, Tsaewagi was inhabited by some of the Tewas after the Pueblo Revolt of 1680, in an attempt to escape the wrath of the Spanish after a particularly bloody skirmish, following at a later date by a circuitous route. *They halted at the ruin where one halts at midday on the mesa trail from Santa Clara to Cochiti. Some stayed behind here and came afterward by the Zuni road.* (ibid., 8 Feb. 1912)

This is the generally accepted version, with some variations of how some Tewas settled on First Mesa. Today the Corn clan claims to have been the leader of the Rio Grande Tewas to the Hopi Reservation during a several year wandering migration from Tsaewagi. Further, the Corn clan claims it was their Corn Mother that led the Tewas from the Zuni group north to their present home to join other Tewas on First Mesa. These are said to have been some of the last to arrive and are referred to as those "who came from the bottom."

Ten years later, Freire-Marreco was still putting together information about the Tewa migration. *About Ts'ae wa pi'i: The form I got at Hano was Ts'ae wa di and occasionally Ts'ae wa gi, and the explanation volunteered was "maybe there is a hill with a white horizontal strip. Everyone agreed that Tsaewadi is our home; we all came from the same place, Tsaewadi," but I think their knowledge of it was very slight. My best informant said: "It was from Tsaewadi that they came. The Mexicans live there now. When we got tired from hunger (about 1850) some of us went over, and the Tewa told us we ought to sell the land and get money for it. But none of us have been able to go over and do it."*

*Another time this Corn clan man said that "when the people left Tsaewadi they went to Ts'ele kju. They stopped there, and some ladies had babies and were left behind there; the others started without them. So when those came on afterward, they came by way of the Zuni road; but the first lot came by the straight road; stopping, living awhile, cooking provisions and starting again. They came to Tse putsu (in Navajo language) near Gallup; you see it near the road. Next they came to Ganado, P'o'iwe, and here they stayed a long while. One of the a-b-a-j-u they were carrying escaped there, so there is lots of water there. That's why we call it our water there, Tewa bi p'o. They stayed a long time at P o le'I, Keam's Canyon. On the south side, up at the old school plant south of the superintendent's office, there is water yet. Another of our a-b-a-j-u came out there. The water jumps there, like boiling. At the solstice, the Tewa go there to get little stones and dirt to put inside a certain rattle." That's all I wanted to say about place names.* (ibid. 16 Jan. 1924)

❧ ❧ ❧

During her stay with the Hopi-Tewas, Freire-Marreco kept in touch with Frederick Hodge. In an undated note, she informed him also about her standing with the Native people that might affect her immediate plans. *I am very uncertain of my own dates. Things here very pleasant and interesting, but precarious.*

She consulted Hodge on a variety of subjects: *Would you be so very kind as to identify this metal for me, or have it identified? Probably the locality from which it was obtained could be determined to some extent by a person acquainted with Southwestern minerals. Would you send me word about it, and post the specimen and identification to Henry Balfour Esq. M.A. University Museum, Oxford, England?*

*Were you able to get my Canadian herbs determined? And could you post them, too, to Mr. Balfour?*

In the photograph on page 40, Henry Balfour, 1861-1939, was one of the first anthropology diploma recipients with Barbara in 1908. He had a great interest in the natural sciences and is credited for classifying collections while serving as curator of Oxford University's Pitt River Museum from 1891 to 1939.

Reporting some findings, she continued: *A Tewa man here has just found out that he can imitate the vegetable-dyed wool, pale green, by boiling the store yarn with baked sheep dung and fresh sheep's dun, mixed. Of course it wouldn't deceive an expert, but it would perhaps deceive an amateur.*

*If anyone else thinks of coming here, please warn them not to bring sea-water. I got into trouble with mine—very improper to carry it without proper credentials—and I had to send it away to Santa Fe, along with some Indian corn and tobacco that I had with me.* (National Archives, Hodge, 29 Jan. 1913)

In answer to her question regarding a metal bracelet Hodge replied: *The National Museum reports as follows on the bracelet which you sent, and which I am today forwarding to Mr. Balfour. The metal of the bracelet is brass containing free copper. According to Dr. Hough the bracelet is not in the least unusual and the source of the metal has always been traceable to civilization.* (ibid. 24 Jan. 1913)

The man referred to, Walter Hough, 1859-1935, was an American ethnologist who did field work in Arizona and New Mexico. Hough also worked at the National Museum and served as president of the American Anthropology Association. Little brass jewelry is produced now, though novice metal smiths sometimes start working with brass, a less expensive material, to gain experience and only when feeling competent, will attempt working silver and perhaps even later, gold.

❧ ❧ ❧

Some of the most interesting Freire-Marreco correspondence from the Hopi Reservation was to John Myres. After she had settled and grown more comfortable in her situation, she sent word back to England. *I write to you, to wish a happy and hopeful year to Mrs. Myres and yourself, in the family circle of the Corn clan at Hano. All frowsting indoors, all busy: one son threading shell beads, another boring turquoises with a drill, another embroidering a wedding dress, one daughter drying newly ground cornmeal (and attending to her nephew's hair meanwhile), another making suds of yucca root to wash the men's heads. The mother is out at a relation's house, making blue wafers.* This is traditional Hopi piki made from a very thin batter of blue cornmeal and water, spread quickly by hand on a very hot flat stone, peeled off almost immediately and rolled into a thin tube.

*As for the stepfather, who is an elderly shepherd from Oraibi, he is weaving woolen leggings of old fashion, with undyed black and white wool—and what do you think he is producing? Purely and solely <u>shepherd's plaid trews</u>* (traditional close-fitting plaid trousers sometimes worn by Scotsmen) *in a beautiful herringbone—and I am taking notes of him with the aid of the new edition of* **Notes and Queries**: *we ought to have given more terms—eg. selvage; and the sort of heading by which the warp threads are fastened in pairs before the warp is transferred to the loom; and shade-sticks; and no doubt heaps of others. When I come home, I look forward to seeing* **N. & Q.** *in its complete form: meanwhile the proof I have with me is very useful. There are various blameless works done here: woolen weaving in twills, with and without color effects—the chef d'oeve being cloth in dark blue, cotton weaving, plain checker; cotton warp with woolen weft, colored wool design introduced with a needle and battened down; colored wool* embroidery on white cotton cloth, stitches parallel with the warp threads, odious commercial yarns introduced in the embroidery and color-design weaving and a tendency to modify designs, e.g. proper design for a wedding dress is butterfly and squash-blossom, but one weaver-and-embroiderer is introducing a zigzag which really belongs to the color-inserted weaving, not to embroidery at all.

Contained in her letter to John Myres, Freire-Marreco's drawing of a twill design to illustrate some weaving as done by the Native people on First Mesa, Arizona. Courtesy of University of Oxford, Bodleian Library, Room 132 Duke Humphreys Library, Myres file, 10 Jan. 1913.

I saw two things lately which I wished you there to see—one, near Espanola, a little caravan of loaded burros trotting along the railway line, the Mexican trader running after them with his gun on his back. The other, at the pueblo of Santo Domingo—the goats coming home at night, and the goatherd with his drill under his arm. He had been making shell beads as he watched the goats, and with strings of these beads he would presently go to the Navajo country and *buy more goats. But a horrid shock is in store for the Santo Domingo people. The Hopi, their chief customers, have this year learnt to make beads themselves! One Hopi boy went to Santo Domingo and bought 25 pounds of shells from the trader. You should have heard how those Santo Domingo people scolded me! They said, "You have no right to take out those shells. If your people make beads, how are we to get our woolen dresses?" Last year three shell necklaces with moderate turquoises and bits of pink shell, if carried to the Hopi, would bring a black dress worth $10 in money; at the beginning of December 1912 six would do it; now, January 1913, you can hardly get a pair of knitted socks for each string of beads. The only possible revenge seems to be for the New Mexican Indians to start weaving, but the Hopi feel secure that no one can ever learn the pattern.*

*These people are kind of unsophisticated compared to the New Mexicans. They don't make a fuss about your asking for information; they are more apt to accuse you of witchcraft or intentions that way. I have had to send back to the railway some Indian corn and tobacco which I thought would be acceptable here. I had no business to carry it without proper credentials, so a board of inquisitors decided. They seemed really scared, but the person at the bottom of it all was a man whom I had snubbed—he really needed it, but he is the chief's sister's son— wish I had stuck to the Genealogical Method.* This incident had made quite an impression on Freire-Marreco as she had repeated it to other associates.

*Language here is very jolly—they say "L," which their relations in New Mexico can't say, though they can sing it. Lots of words are longer here. Manners on the contrary are much shorter; and if you want to appreciate the Spaniards, come here where they didn't stay long enough to have an effect. Very few Spanish words in this language; only horse, sheep, leather, cow, bull. Some of these Tewa say "sh" for "s" approximating to the Hopi sounds; and "ky" for "sh", likewise Hopi.* (Bodleian, Myres 10 Jan. 1913)

On Easter Eve, Freire-Marreco again wrote to Myres. Although somewhat disjointed, this letter contains some of her miscellaneous thoughts and experiences. She was learning much in a short period of time. *I was delighted to get your letter from the "Baltic" and suddenly I remembered that there was a real world where Troy and things like that lived—I had quite forgotten it among the lively shadows.*

*Greek politics and order in nature—you ask me if there is any nomenclature of the sort here. I haven't made it out here, so far. The things in nature that matter are sky phenomena and wild animals, I think; the New Mexican Tewa, with their strong officialism, naturally say that each sort of animal has its "governor." There are no buffaloes now because "their governor has taken them away." At least, I suppose they mean the modern, official kind of "tuzjon,", but "tuzjon" also means the old-fashioned religious migration—leader of the stories.*

*Cushing has a very engaging paper in which he says that the Zuni say that clouds, water and so on are controlled by various sets of six invisible persons, a counterpart of the sixfold organization of religious societies in Zuni itself. I haven't the reference here. It was read before the Washington Anthropological Society, I think.*

Frank Hamilton Cushing, 1857-1900, the American ethnologist excavated mainly in Arizona, served with the U. S. Bureau of Ethnology and authored several books, most on Zuni, a Pueblo on which he was considered an expert, although ridiculed by the Zuni people.

***Notes and Queries*** *is most useful to me—its chief fault is, that Mr. Owens who is collecting at Second Mesa, likes it so much that he borrows it all the time. He says, he is checking over his notes by the technological section.* John G. Owens, an ethnologist from the Field Museum in Chicago at that time, published extensively in the ***Journal for American Ethnology***. In all probability Freire-Marreco had met him previously on her way through Chicago.

*My section on Authority is a horrid reproach to me here. I have made all the mistakes that I warned the reader against, treating prestige chiefs as if they were officials, and making them strain their authority without giving them support. They're only just getting over it, poor dears.*

*Just now we have an epidemic of influenza. I've got one patient here in bed, doing quite nicely, but if <u>all</u> the Corn clan get it they'll just have to lie on the floor as usual, and they all seem rather peevish this evening; it looks threatening.* No medical help was available in this remote location at that time and many Native people died during influenza epidemics.

She pondered what it meant to be remote as opposed to being "in the world." Her reference to "my people" may have been to distinguish the Tewa Corn clan people, with whom she lived, from Hopi clans on nearby Mesas. Or, "my people" might have implied that she felt more accepted as an extended part of the Corn clan family.

*I am not sure that my people are very much "aloof from the great world," perhaps I have given you a wrong impression. Here, to be sure, they are 100 miles from the railway, but they buy flour and sewing machines and all that sort of thing, and would like to see more of the world if they could. In New Mexico "the world" is quite close to them, but they keep it aloof by a deliberate effort. But what is "the world" of the New Mexican or Arizona white man, after all? Not very wide or very civilized; really the great world—law, religion, monarchy—was under Spain, in the first half of the XVIII century, not chiefly railway, flour, sewing machines, automobiles and land-grabbing and inferior newspapers. There was a drunken Navajo at Jemez Feast this November who said to the policeman, "You daren't take my bottle away: I'm a Democrat now!" and I think that is their nearest approach to American political life.*

*The patient's father and mother have come and insist on spending the night here, so no more; only warm thanks to you for writing.*

Probably written later: *P. S. The jolliest word here is "pin az." "Az"—to think, just ordinary thinking, conjecturing, guessing. "Pin" is your diaphragm, the place where you have indigestion. So "pin az" is to think effectively, eg. to think rain—there used to be a special house for doing it. A successful dance, is "pin az'i." A strange bird "has much pin az," so have prayer-feathers, and katsinas and doctors and heads of societies. By the "pin az'i" song of the Blue Corn Girls as they grind, clouds arise. It implies effort—"they try their best."*

*If you know a man who, as you believe, "pin az" is strong, you can adopt him as your father in order to recover from illness. One of your clan uncles is that kind of man: it does not prevent his being dreadfully downtrodden in his wife's house. "Women do not think," so our clan uncle tells me and quotes a song:—"my wife, poor thoughtless thing."*

*Then how is it that the last chief of Moenkopi was a woman—presumably she thought? Well, presumably she did, she used to smoke like anything. His niece,* out of his hearing, said of <u>course</u> women do think. Her own husband's mother was a chief, and he is only chief because he has no sisters.

She goes on to write some bits of information regarding Native trade that she thought would be of interest to him:

*Trade 30 years ago used to be like this:*

*Havasupai, buckskins, red paint, and baskets <—> Moqui, woolen goods. Moqui, woolen and cotton goods and the surplus of the buckskins <—>New Mexico pueblos, shell beads, turquoises, asses, Spanish goods.*

*There were two intermediary towns, Zuni and Laguna. A Moqui man might trade with New Mexico in several ways:*

*1) Wait for the Zuni and Laguna traders to come with beads and blue dye and fetch woolen dresses. Zuni makes its own beads, Laguna gets them from Santo Domingo. Sometimes Santo Domingo men come through to Moqui with beads, and take away woolen dresses and coats.*

*1 donkey = 1 woolen dress*

*1 pint blue copperas as dye = 1 woolen dress*

*3 strings shell beads = 1 woolen dress*

*2 turquoise earrings (strings of beads) = 10 woolen dresses*

*2) Go to the November dances at Zuni and take woolen dresses and cotton dresses and Havasupai red paint, and buy beads and parrot and macaw feathers. I don't know the old rate of exchange there, except that two knife blades full of Havasupai paint = 1 bunch of short parrot feathers.* Havasupai paint is colored earth used to smear on bodies before dances. In dry form it was measured by dipping a knife blade into the dirt.

*3) Go through Santo Domingo (but they aren't very safe people) and take dresses for beads.*

*4) This is the dashing thing to do: go right up to the Tewa towns on the Upper Rio Grande and get buffalo skins. The Comanche used to come to Santa Clara with buffalo skins on purpose to meet the Moquis. Also the Santa Clara people went to the Comanche country with bread and meal and bought buffalo skins ready for the Moquis.*

*1 woolen dress = 1 buffalo hide.*

It wasn't worthwhile apparently for the Moqui trader to go up north to Taos: the Taos people had only buckskins, red paint, and Apache baskets to offer, just what the Havasupai had quite near home. When I say Moqui (now commonly referred to as Hopi) I include the Tewa village on First Mesa.

That, roughly was the west to east line. But at Zuni starts a tremendously important southward line to Sonora and Mexico and possibly to Jalisco judging by the feathered basket with Seler figures in the **Bureau of American Ethnology Bulletin 38**: (he thinks it is a collar!). By this line the turquoises went down and the macaw and parrot feathers came up. And which way went the art of inlaying turquoise, malachite and jet in pitch, up or down? Zuni would be the place to study trade! There seems no doubt that Zuni was "Cibola"—the one fact about the northern world to the XVI century Mexican Indian—"as large as Mexico City"—the doorways crusted with turquoises. It still had great prestige—1600 inhabitants. Think of Cushing and Mrs. Stevenson both spending years there and never telling us a word about trade!—driveling about "theurgists" and "priests" at the time. Not one useful word written since the XVI century. But a nice American girl has just gone there to work up the language, and I hope will get something solid.

Present-day modifications—blue copperas utterly gone out, white traders bring indigo. Buffalo gone, hence Moqui no longer come up to Santa Clara. White traders begin to supply turquoises and beads, six or seven years only. But the one woolen dress = three strings of beads held perfectly firm until this last year.

The money prices are interesting too. Right on the spot where it is made the Moqui woolen dress fetches $10—$15, between Indians. At Santo Domingo beads are $1.50 a string. Woolen dresses only fetch $10—$12 all over New Mexico, but the Moqui trader can afford to sell them so, making his profit by bringing beads and turquoises to sell on his return. Buckskins are worth $20

If a Moqui man embroiders a cotton dress and takes it to Zuni and can find a man with $50, the man will give him the $50, but if he takes it up to Santa Clara, he will only get $23—$30. Because they haven't got the $50, any of them, up there.

One more thing I must add: In New Mexico and Arizona, pottery doesn't travel far <u>unless there is a famine</u>. It is too heavy and troublesome for even traders. But in the old famine times when women got desperate to save their children's lives, they would make pottery and travel in search of a market, or send their young boys. So Santo Domingo pottery went to Taos and every spring, Sia pots went to Jemez, Sia being chronically poor.

I see the Santo Domingo split-leaf-in-a-panel on some pots here, but it may be an independent invention.

Freire-Marreco's drawing of the Santo Domingo leaf design as used on pottery, when she was staying on the Hopi Reservation, in a letter to John Myres dated March 22, 1913. Courtesy of University of Oxford, Bodleian Library, Room 132 Duke Humphreys Library, Myres file. *The Pottery of Santo Domingo Pueblo* by Kenneth Chapaman, 1938, page 134 described it well: *Nearly all have a bilateral symmetrical arrangement of two wide stripes at each side, which may be modified forms of leaves.*

In the big famine here 60 years ago, I can't find that they exported pots. Too much starving country to cross before you could reach a market with heavy pots. Instead the women tramped into New Mexico with their babies and sold them there to save their lives. How different from the floating pottery of the Mediterranean.

🦋 🦋 🦋

This is a Tewa song, they danced to it last month:

Strophe: "I am going eastward. So I say, my wife will make me waferbread, will make me parched sweet-corn meal, with that I will provision myself when I go eastward. At the Tewa town" (i.e. New Mexico Tewa) "when I arrive there my clansmen there and I will stir it into gruel, we both will drink it, we both will laugh . . ."

Here she inserts a little explanation: but all those verbs are subordinated grammatically, to the final "we will laugh," so in the antistrophe, all are subordinate to "she will throw." The song continues:

Antistrophe: "My wife mine, without thought, taking prayer meal with her going up on the roof top will throw meal eastward, buffalo he will find for me, expensive things he will find for me. So she will say, in all directions she will throw meal." (ibid., 22 Mar. 1913)

# ❧  A Quick Visit to the Yavapais

In the spring of 1913, Freire-Marreco left the Hopi Reservation and made her way south to what she referred to as the Yavapai or the Mohave-Apache Reservation, now known as Fort McDowell and the Salt River Pima-Maricopa Reservations, near Phoenix. The trip materialized thanks to the efforts of Frederick Hodge. His letters of introduction and commendation to both the Superintendent and Acting Commissioner of the Bureau of Indian Affairs preceded her. There is only one letter from her written at Camp McDowell, via Scottsdale, to confirm her stay of only two weeks with a very few photographs and some notes at the Pitt Rivers Museum, Oxford .

This time proved to be a frustrating experience for her in her quest for information, due to the preoccupation of the Yavapais with a court case regarding the previously discussed water rights. Her contribution was in the role of translator between the Native people and the U. S. Government court in Phoenix. Disappointing as far as her field work was concerned, she spent much of her time waiting to see the Yavapai who were preoccupied with legal matters. In spite of this she was somewhat gratified, as she reported to Hodge.

*I am getting some useful work here with the Yavapai and am thankful that I came. I got some false impressions last time about marriage customs in particular.*

*P. S. In a previous letter I asked if you could lend your Pueblo Indian Clans. I shall be truly grateful if I find it at Santa Fe on my return thither; I shall need it badly.* (National Archives, Hodge, 26 Apr. 1913)

Hodge complied as her reply, written after she returned to the Rio Grande area, testified. This trip to visit the Yavapai was financed by the Bureau of American Ethnology, and therefore she immediately reported her accomplishments and expense account to him. *Thank you very much for the copy of your Pueblo Indian Clans, and for your letter of May 5th.*

*I enclose an account of my expenses on my visit to the Yavapai. You will see by the annexed journal that living expenses were incurred on several days when no actual work was done; but this was unavoidable: there is always some delay in getting a conveyance to McDowell, and my work was interrupted, first by the visit of a mission party, then by the session of the Federal Court, for which every possible interpreter was subpoenaed. I was obliged to follow my people to Phoenix and snatch what time I could with them, whenever they were not in court.*

*The work done is a follows: 1910 vocabulary revised with a better interpreter, corrected and enlarged.*

*Kinship terms entirely reworked with an older informant.*

*Information obtained about social morphology, war, marriage, trade, chieftainship of Yuma-Apaches: These differ widely from Customs of Mohave-Apaches, and in consequence any general conclusions must be modified in many respects.*

*Pima kinship terms obtained, with illustrative genealogy.*

*Two short Tonto vocabularies, to determine that the people who call themselves Tonto do in fact speak an Athapascan language.*

*I am now working at my additions to the ethnobotany paper: as soon as possible after that, I will send you the Yavapai notes, not ready for publication but for incorporation with the notes which I left at Washington. I shall have to take the whole thing to England to combine it and put it into shape.*

*I am going out to Santa Clara on Monday, and I expect to be there for two weeks, possibly three. I hardly expect that you will be able to get my accounts passed in time to let me have the money at Santa Fe (though I should be glad of it for my return journey), and it cannot be mailed to reach me here by May 30th. Please hold it for me until I come east.*

*I fear that I give you much additional trouble by being so chronically under-financed—I am so sorry! But the Hopi trip was very expensive.* Her Yavapai itinerary:

> *April 17 Midnight, arrived Phoenix*
> *18  At Indian School, making arrangements*
> *19  By Pima team to Salt River*
> *20  Sunday*
> *21  By Pima team to McDowell; visited camps;*
> *engaged interpreter with Mrs. Shafer*
> *22  8 hours work, interpreter & informant*
> *23  half day work, interpreter & informant, interrupted by preaching*
> *24  visited camps*
> *25  8 hours work, informant*
> *26  half day work, informant, interpreter*
> *27  Sunday*
> *28  All English-speaking Indians went to Phoenix on subpoena to Federal Court*
> *To Salt River, half day with Pima informant & interpreter*
> *29  To Phoenix, 2 hours with informant at Court House*
> *30  All in court, no work possible*
> *May 1 Two Tonto Apache vocabularies obtained at Court House,*
> *4½ hours work*
> *3 & 4 Short times, informant*
> *4  Left Phoenix*

An itemized account illustrates a very different economy in 1913:

| | |
|---|---:|
| *Railway fare: Ash Fork to Phoenix* | 7.80 |
| *Phoenix to Santa Fe* | 26.50 |
| *Pullman* | 2.50 |
| *Charges on baggage, expressing manuscript* | 2.75 |
| *Hotel expenses, three days* | 3.20 |
| *One week's board and lodging, McDowell* | 5.00 |
| *Team Phoenix to Salt River* | 1.50 |
| *Team Salt river to McDowell* | 5.00 |
| *Hire of saddle* | .25 |

| | |
|---|---|
| Meals and provisions and washing | 8.30 |
| Carfares, postage | .95 |
| Stationery | 1.30 |
| Interpreters and informants: Yavapai: | |
| 8 hours | 1.50 |
| 8 hours | 1.50 |
| 3 hours | .60 |
| 3 hours | .60 |
| 8 hours | 1.50 |
| 8 hours | 1.50 |
| half day | 1.00 |
| 2 hours | .40 |
| 4 hours | .90 |
| 8 hours | 1.50 |
| Various short times @ 1.10 | 12.10 |
| Pima, 2 half days | 2.00 |
| Tonto Apache, short times | .90 |
| | $80.05 |

The expense account Freire-Marreco presented to the Smithsonian Institution:

| | |
|---|---|
| Railway & other transportation | $46.00 |
| Wages and stationery | 16.30 |
| Personal expenses for 16 days | 17.70 |
| | $80.00 |

The Smithsonian Institution to Barbara Freire-Marreco: $80.00 (ibid. May 1913)

# ✒ Goodbye to the Rio Grande Valley

Before returning to England, Freire-Marreco had a three-week visit with her friends at Santa Clara. Although she had been away in Arizona, her efforts to help these Pueblo people with their many problems—including land disputes—motivated Edgar Hewett to take action as he had promised, by trying to clarify the relationship between Santa Clara and the U. S. Government. He wrote to Santiago Naranjo, by then the Pueblo governor. *As I promised through Miss Freire-Marreco I went to Washington in December and met the officials of the Indian office, to see if I could help in any way with the question of the Indian lands. I was sorry that I could not get time to go to Santa Clara and meet the people of your Pueblo, and talk it all over before I went to Washington, but you know how very busy I am. Instead of stopping in New Mexico, I went straight from California to Washington and have just got back.*

*I do not know how much I was able to help. I found the officers there all anxious to carry out the plan that Mr. Wilson has been working on, and which I am glad to see is what you all want. I know that what you want most all, however, is that the decision of Judge Pope concerning the Pueblo Indians, shall be set aside. If that is done, it removes the principal danger that your people are in. As you know, that case was appealed to the Supreme Court of the United States, in the hope that it would be found wrong and set aside. Mr. Wilson has made a strong argument for the Pueblos in that case and you may be sure that he has represented your people well. I specially want to let you all know how hard he had worked upon this case for you, and how well he has handled it. He is very anxious to win it for you, and if any one can, he will do it.*

*I found that there was so much before the Supreme Court that the case had been laid over for some time, and what I did was to try to get it advanced so as to have it settled quickly. I now have a letter from the Indian office in Washington, saying, that the case would come up for trial on the 24*<sup>th</sup> *of February. So I think the principal good I was able to do was to help get the case brought up for trial soon.*

*Now we must all do everything possible to win this, and you can depend upon Mr. Wilson. As soon as this is decided we will know what to do next. Please assure your people that we are going to back them up, and if it is possible see that no wrong is done them.* (Museum of New Mexico, Hewett, 16 Jan. 1913)

〽 〽 〽

Before leaving the United States, Freire-Marreco attended to unfinished business. Mentioning one ongoing project, she wrote to Harrington from Santa Clara Pueblo. *The Tewa botany paper should have been with you before this. I was working on it three weeks ago, but then three very bad pneumonia cases, all in the family of a dear friend here, have taken up my whole time. But if the two surviving patients go on well, I hope to work this afternoon and tomorrow. I am adding a good deal, but maintaining the general arrangement.*

*Thank you very much indeed for the corrections of words in the songs. I am making the alterations except in the few cases where there is really a difference in the two dialects.*

*If it were not for the pneumonia, I would have had the time of my life here at Santa Clara these three weeks—you can imagine the luxury of being openly and publicly instructed with the sanction of the authorities. Of course the busy time of year is a hindrance, but the worst hindrance is that I come from nursing so dreadfully sleepy and stupid!*

*Dr. Hewett told me, informally, that he intended to offer me work. Believe me, I am truly gratified that he should—to have me working for the School, and not less gratified that you should recommend me for it. I am obliged to put it quite out of my mind for the present, because of engagements in England, business and domestic, which I cannot break. But the School is, I hope, a permanent institution, and I shall be very glad to feel that I might make an application later on with hopes of favorable consideration. Whenever, or if even, I am able to join the School, certainly my first business will be to learn phonetics, and I will try to make some progress in England meanwhile. Certainly my work is much damaged by the want of phonetic training. I will never go out again without a phonograph, either.*

*Shall you be in Santa Fe in August? If Dr. Hewett has one of the Hano men to demonstrate weaving, you might do some phonograph work on him.*

*I have got material for a little paper comparing the uses of kinship terms at Santa Clara and at Hano; I intend it as a friendly and respectful revenge on you.*

*No, I don't know anything about mesquite. If I did, I would certainly wait for you, and I regret that I haven't that chance of obliging you. I am sorry to hear what trouble you have had in California. I think, in our sort of work, we have quite enough personal difficulties with the Indians to wear us rather thin, and we certainly needn't add to them by being mean to each other! There are enough neglected tribes to give us all a chance, I should think.* (National Archives, Harrington, after 26 Feb 1913)

🦋 🦋 🦋

As her second American adventure was drawing to a close, Freire-Marreco's thoughts turned toward her home in England. Reluctantly she was leaving the United States because obligated, but also with the hope to return. En route there is evidence she made stops enroute in Chicago, Washington, D. C. and New York City.

Her always interesting letters to John Myres provide information regarding her travels as well as Native cultural tidbits and personal opinions regarding her American colleagues. From the Sisters of Charity, St. Vincent's Sanitarium in Santa Fe she wrote:

*Thank you so much for your letter written on shipboard, and getting your work to the printer—it must be a great satisfaction. I thank you for the chance of writing to Mr. Bandelier and going to see him in New York. I have wished to know him for a long time. It is too bad that he should think himself unappreciated, when really, he is like the bird in the Hopi legend who put down a little dry earth in the water of primeval mud and so allowed human beings to get a footing.*

*I wish I knew what Mr. Cornford said about the Moqui*—must ask you as soon as I get home. Francis MacDonald Cornford, 1874-1943, was a British philosopher from Cambridge University. A professor of Ancient Philosophy, he lectured mainly in the Classics.

*I have been wondering what, exactly, the "governor of the buffaloes" ought to mean. An alcalde? A hereditary chief who could give his people away "if they were no longer dear to him?" A migration leader who watches and smokes all night? The Pueblo Indians seem to have had all those political institutions in turn, and I suppose the ideal polity of the buffaloes varied in the same way.*

*I can't remember when I wrote to you, but I think it was before I saw the most interesting sight of all—the huge old pueblo of Oraibi breaking up, rows of houses standing empty, the roofs of the kivas falling in, just a few people strolling round the quiet sunny streets.* A good reference to the split between the old and progressive Hopi cultures can be found in Harry C. James' **Pages from Hopi History**, University of Arizona Press, 1974.

*A few miles off, two brisk new villages have swarmed from Oraibi, breaking new fields and building new houses and new kivas as hard as they can go. One, Pakabi* (now usually spelled Bacavi) *looks very raw and new, but it is all complete and in working order—men cleaning out the springs, girls in full dress dancing beside them, katsinas running around the houses: although the migration-chief, who led them to the new site and faced their "murmurings" through a frightful cold homeless winter, wears the uniform of the U. S. Indian Police!*

*The railway towns like Winslow would amuse you too—the new pueblos of the Americans. The Winslow directory says: "It has cement sidewalks, an ample water-supply, and an up-to-date Public School System, and the lodges are in a flourishing condition." There isn't a Christian church in the place, but the kivas are all right, you see.*

*I went down to McDowell to revise work there, but most of the time had to hang about the federal court at Phoenix, where all the Indians I wanted were giving evidence. They swore (oaths) according to their <u>old</u> local grouping before they came to the reservation, the Prescott-Jerome people one way and Four-Peaks people the other way—it was not uninteresting. Also it was fun to hear a barrister examining his witnesses through an interpreter. They said such evidently unexpected things that cross-examination was hardly necessary.*

*Tomorrow I go to Santa Clara, with a big new dancing-dress for my estufa. I hope they'll dance for me. And after three weeks I must start home. The School here offers a job at $1500, but I ought to be at home for some time now. Please give my love to Mrs. Myres and say I shall be seeing her before long, now.*

Labeled only Santa Clara Dance, June 1913. These two photographs may well be ones sent by Freire-Marreco to W.W. Hill in response to a request by him for information for his planned publication. Courtesy of University of New Mexico, Maxwell Museum of Archaeology, School of American Research B. Freire-Marreco Collection Nos. 84.55.464 and 84.55.462.

Postscript: *For Geography of Asia: One Drelon was a missionary to the Hurons until they were annihilated by smallpox and the Iroquois in 1649. Then he was sent to the China station. Some years after, in "Tartary" (where abouts?) he confessed a Huron Christian woman who had come there as a captive, passed on from tribe to tribe. The only two Huron speaking Christians in all Asia, and they met!* (Bodleian, Myres, Whit Sunday 1913)

She recounted more of her activities to Myres in a letter written on board the S S "Cedric," and evidently mailed when she reached England.

*I took advantage of your introduction and called on Mr. and Mrs. Bandelier as soon as I reached New York—they were everything that is kind; and they asked me to stay a night with them when I came back from Washington, and that time Mr. Bandelier talked till 1:30 in the morning! Thank you so much for arranging the visit—I think it a great privilege. It seems to me wonderful that a man should be planning and fretting for new work at seventy! It was splendid, too, to hear him quote to support an argument—his memory so good, and his vast information so readily accessible.*

*One thing that has always puzzled me, about Mr. Bandelier's point of view, was cleared up by talking to him: I always wondered how he managed to preserve a cold judicial air in writing of Indians, how he managed to disguise his partiality for them (for I took it for granted, that, like all other workers in the American field, he was partial). Well, the answer is simple—he has nothing to disguise—he does not like Indians at all! What strange equipment for living among Indians so much. And yet they seemed to have liked him, probably just for being an honorable man.*

*In Washington Dr. Fewkes was so kind as to give me two afternoons of talk—a noble person he seems, full of adventure and happiness without the least eccentricity. He seems like a man who should have governed a frontier province two hundred years ago.* Walter Jesse Fewkes, 1850-1930, an American physicist, zoologist, anthropologist had a particular interest in primitive religions. He excavated in Mesa Verde, Mexico, and South America, was Field Director of the Hemenway Expedition and chief ethnologist at the Bureau of American Ethnology.

She also mentioned seeing the anthropologist and ethnologist Frederick Starr, 1858-1933, who was known internationally for his published liberal ideas. Associated with the American Museum of Natural History, he taught at several U. S. universities including Chicago, where he organized the anthropology department. *In Chicago I saw Professor Starr and heard him give a very slack lecture, and enjoyed seeing Mr. Owens again at the Field Museum. How beautiful that building is—and how natural in its shabbiness, streaky white and gray among the green trees! It looks like a real temple gone a little out of fashion. But they are going to rebuild it in marble and cut off many of its charming forlorn angles. The southwestern collections are magnificent, and the Northwest Coast too, and the large spacious picture-groups much finer than those at New York and Washington. But Washington has prehistoric Southwestern pottery most admirably arranged and shown—geographical groups in big cases across the sides, separate sites and local specialties in little cases, and comparative type-series down the middle of the hall.*

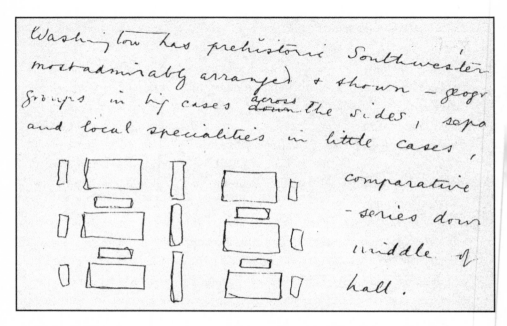

Washington has prehistoric Southwestern most admirably arranged & shown — geogr groups in big cases across ~~down~~ the sides, sepa and local specialities in little cases, comparative - series down middle of hall.

Freire-Marreco's drawing of the arrangement of display cases at the Smithsonian Institution in Washington that so impressed Freire-Marreco. Contained in a letter to John Myres dated July 5 1913. Courtesy of University of Oxford, Bodleian Library, Room 132 Duke Humphreys Library, Myres file.

*I hope you are all having a nice vacation, and possibly even a not-working one. I ought to work hard when I get home and brace up out of this bookless fogginess of mind.* (ibid. 5 July 1913)

Freire-Marreco left the United States for the second and last time. Although she hoped to return, she never again visited the people of Santa Clara Pueblo or the Tewa of First Mesa in Arizona. Except in memory and her writing, her American adventures were over.

# ❦ FROM A DISTANT POINT ❦

## ❦ American Connections

In 1913 Barbara Freire-Marreco was back in England to stay, and she took up residence once again with her parents at Potter's Croft in Woking, Surrey.

Correspondence became more infrequent between Freire-Marreco and her American associates. Although she was "across the pond," she never forget her Santa Clara Pueblo friends, and she soon started a practice she continued for many years, sending them presents. The Secretary of the School of American Archaeology received a boxful of gifts with this explanation: *I am sending you a parcel containing small presents for a few people at Santa Clara, hoping that you will be so kind as to forward them to Miss Richards, Santa Clara Pueblo, Espanola. They consist of parrot feathers, which cannot now be sent into the United States except as scientific specimens. As these are intended to cement scientific friendships at Santa Clara, I hope it is not improper to send them to the Museum as such! The larger parcel contains a pair of Hopi shoes.*

*If you have to pay any duty on any of these articles, or if the postage exceeds the value of the stamps which I enclose, please let me know and I will at once reimburse you. I hope that I am not giving you too much trouble.*

The Museum had sent to her their newly published magazine and she responded: *Many thanks for the copy of* **El Palacio**: *I hope that you will be able to publish it regularly as a delightful means of communication with absent friends of the School. I have read the first number with great interest.* This was the first issue of this publication from the Museum of New Mexico which continues to this day.

In the same letter she anticipated future issues: *I expect I shall receive a report of the Quarrai work next January, when I have paid my subscription.* (Museum of New Mexico, 8 Dec. 1913) Quarrai was the location where Hewett had been working, which explains her interest in this site. One of many ruins near the Rio Grande, it is located on the east side of the Manzono Mountains in central New Mexico, one of the Salinas group. It was abandoned, probably by Tiwa speaking people in late prehistoric times and then reoccupied in early historic times before it was again deserted.

Freire-Marreco, not only acknowledged receipt of the magazine, but reciprocated by donating books to the School of Anthropology and the Museum of New Mexico. One of her donations was especially noted, E. B. Tylor's **Anthropology**, *a book every student should read.* (**El Palacio Magazine**, Oct. 1914)

The January 1914 issue of **El Palacio Magazine** had previously reported the following story. *Miss Barbara Freire-Marreco, for several summers a student of the School of American Archaeology, is on the program at the annual meeting of the American Anthropological Association and American Folk Lore Society at the Museum of Natural History in New York City. Miss Marreco, who came to Santa Fe from Oxford, England, has chosen for her subject: "Tewa Kinship Terms from the Village of Hano, Arizona."*

No date was given for this scheduled presentation. At the time this was published Freire-Marreco was in England and no record of this lecture taking place has ever been found. It is likely that World War I disrupted any plans to appear in New York City.

Useful information she left behind in New Mexico was also recognized. The same issue also stated: *Historian B .M. Read exhibited a copy of a map of New Mexico originally made in 1779 by a civil engineer from Spain. It was made by Miss Barbara Freire-Marreco of the School of American Archaeology who had found the original in the British Museum at London.*

🕊 🕊 🕊

There were exchanges soon after her return to England between Freire-Marreco, Frederick Hodge and John Harrington concerning the publishing of the research she had collected while in New Mexico and Arizona, particularly concerning the ethnobotany of the Tewa Indians. Thirty of her letters on this subject, originally at the Bureau of American Ethnology, are now housed at the National Anthropological Archives: this correspondence also contains information about an exchange of books and bulletins with American colleagues.

Proofs crossed back and forth across the Atlantic with additions and corrections, making rather dull reading but explaining the delay in final publication. In its annual report dated 1914-1915 the Smithsonian explained that there would be a postponement in printing the work and announced it was awaiting extensive additional material from Miss Freire-Marreco. The delay was due perhaps to developing war conditions in Britain that affected communication.

🕊 🕊 🕊

In 1914 Freire-Marreco spent a month at Penelve in Leiston, a *quiet place in Suffolk.* (National Archives, Hodge 19 Feb. 1914) She was continuing to work on a promised Yavapai report as well as the ethnobotany material. Keeping in close touch with Frederick Hodge and ever curious relating to her work on botany relating to Native people, she sent a tobacco specimen to him for identification. As she requested, he submitted the specimen to the National Museum's Division of Botany, and a Mr. Standley verified her identification of it as N. attenuate.

A voracious reader, Barbara Frreire-Marreco relaxing at Penelve in Leiston, England, 1914. Taking a break from demanding academic and family obligations, she was working on manuscripts due the Smithsonian Institution.
Courtesy of Anthony Marreco.

Again from Suffolk, Freire-Marreco reported to Hodge and acknowledged that she had indeed been attending to work on the ethnobotany publication. *I will attend to the ethnobotany proofs as soon as I receive them. Will you please send two proofs, under separate covers, both addressed to me at Woking, one marked "to be forwarded," the other "not to be forwarded?" We expect to be in France a little before Easter.*

*I did not, when I wrote about the additional photographs, understand the practical difficulty of adding illustrations. I have written today for the photographs of the Oxford specimens and will send them for your decision; but I beg you will not let them be troublesome to you. If you decide to make a few additions, I suggest the views of the scenery and vegetation near the Tewa villages are more essential than photographs of a few museum specimens. We cannot show a complete series of Tewa artifacts in wood, gourd, etc., and the few photographs which I can supply are probably not very representative; whereas the views of the Rio Grande Valley, the Santa Clara Canyon and the flats near San Ildefonso are typical.*

*We have a very slow post here in Suffolk-your letter of the 19th only came today!* (ibid. 3 Mar. 1914)

Once back in Woking from Suffolk, Freire-Marreco thanked Hodge for sending the Yavapai manuscript and photographs. *No, indeed I did not wish to publish the Yavapai vocabulary and texts apart from the other material, but I hoped that they might be put in type, because they could be more easily criticized in that form. But if that would not be convenient, I should be very glad to have photostat copies, one for Mr. Harrington and one for myself. Am I right in thinking that a photostat copy is easily and cheaply multiplied? I am very ignorant of all these things, and can only hope that you will tell me if I ask for what is not practicable.* (ibid. 3 Apr. 1914)

Working on several projects at once, and in the same letter she mentioned her ongoing work on Pima kinship terms, which was information she had gathered in 1913 from the Yavapai in Arizona. Evidently still uncertain if she had all the necessary information, she asked for Hodge's help and also mentioned she planned to ask Dr. William Rivers of Cambridge to criticize her paper before she sent it to the Bureau of Ethnology.

Hodge replied: *Your Yavapai vocabulary, consisting of 754 entry cards preceded by the notes on General Characteristics, reached us safely through Wesley and the pages of "Sample Sentence Formation" were duly received with your note of March 10th.*

*I have already written to you with respect to the desirability of publishing the entire Yavapai material as a single memoir, and this plan you agree to in your letter of April 3d. With this project in view, it would not be possible for the Bureau to have the linguistic portion set up and printed in advance owing to legal difficulties in the way, the Public Printer not being authorized to accept merely a part of a publication—this for the purpose of avoiding the expense of putting matter in type and holding it indefinitely.*

*I shall endeavor to have the photostat copies of the vocabulary made as soon as possible.* (ibid. 15 Apr. 1914)

When Freire-Marreco next wrote to Hodge, it was to report progress. *I have a short article on "Pima Kinship Terms" with some miscellaneous information practically ready for the press. This information is the property of the Bureau, I think, since I charged for it last April on the basis of a day's expenses. Of course I don't know what you will think proper to do with it, but I wish you could put it in print somewhere, because it seems desirable that as many kinship systems as possible should be made accessible to anthropologists. There are about 3,200 words and a genealogical diagram.* (ibid. 13 June 1914) Hodge replied that he would do what he could to get it published, either by the Smithsonian Institution or in the **American Anthropologist**.

Freire-Marreco worked in spite of family difficulties, fulfilling her obligations to Hodge: *I send you herewith the revised manuscript of a short paper on the e diminutives in Tewa which I should like to offer for publication in the **American Anthropologist**. Possibly you may find room for it in the same number that my longer paper on "Kinship Terms" will appear. Mr. Harrington has seen the manuscript and agrees with the general idea.*

*I hope to mail Tewa Ethnobotany proofs from Tenerife, Canary Islands. My father's illness has made work very difficult this year, and now I am taking him away for a change of air. Please excuse a hasty note in the midst of packing.* (ibid. 9 July 1914) It was not clear what Walter Freire-Marreco's health problems were, but he was clearly not well at various times. As her upbringing demanded of a conscientious daughter, Freire-Marreco put family concerns first.

It was not until 1916 that the ethnobotany book was published. Titled **Ethnobotany of the Tewa Indians** by W.W. Robbins, John Harrington and Barbara Freire-Marreco, the piece was published as Bulletin 55 —a report complete in itself—by the Smithsonian Institution, Bureau of American Ethnology.

Wilfred William Robbins, 1884-1922, had attended the American

School of Archaeology's summer session when Freire-Marreco and Harrington were there. He was an American botanist, physiologist and pathologist. Associated with the University of Colorado as well as the University of California, Davis, apparently he didn't work with Freire-Marreco as closely as did Harrington, because no correspondence was found between Freire-Marreco and Robbins.

As a relatively new science, ethnobotany in the early 20th century intended to go beyond plant identification to include information about the people who inhabited the location of specific plants. In this case every aspect affecting the lives of the Tewa people was described, including the scientific identification of wild, cultivated and introduced vegetation. The information is specific, identifying each item and including its Tewa name. Covered not only was food, but also plants used in ceremonies, or as gifts, trade goods or medicine, emphasizing corn as used by Natives. Included were photographs and drawings. The data was new and the concept unique.

🦋 🦋 🦋

Hodge's reply to Freire-Marreco concerning the Tewa language: *Your manuscript on the e̱ diminutives in Tewa will be taken up for publication as soon as practicable. I fear it will not be possible to print it in a number of the* **American Anthropologist** *earlier than that for October-December, as the April-June issue is in press and the July-September number is to be devoted to special articles dedicated to the Congress of Americanists.*

*I greatly regret to hear of your father's illness, and trust the change of air and scene will prove to be beneficial in every way.* (ibid. 20 July 1914)

When Freire-Marreco returned from Las Palmas in the Canary Islands she found Hodge's letter waiting. *A most delightful number of the* **American Anthropologist** *has just arrived. But I am shocked to read of Mr. Bandelier's death.*

*My father is better for the change, thank you, but still far from strong.* In a postscript she expressed concern about a friend she was trying to contact, saying she feared *she may be in great difficulties on the Continent.* (ibid. 4 Aug. 1914) Trouble brewing in Europe with the onset of World War I had started to cause problems for European residents and visitors alike.

Hodge must have been relieved to send Freire-Marreco the following message: *After this long delay I am sending you, through Wesley, the two photostat copies of your Yavapai linguistic material; the third copy which you desired will be forwarded to Mr. Harrington who is convalescing from an attack of typhoid fever* (discussed later), *consequently I do not know when he may be in condition to take up the revision of the vocabulary. I am informing Mr. Harrington that the copy is sent to him at your insistence, and would suggest that you communicate with him in regard to your requirements as soon as you conveniently can.*

*I am glad to hear from your letter of August 4th that you returned to England before the commencement of the difficulties which I understand you are having in Europe, and also to know that your father's health is improved.*

*Postscript: I find that all shipments to European points are temporarily suspended. Will send by registered post.* (ibid. 19 Aug. 1914)

❦ ❦ ❦

Several inter-organizational memos and notes, once housed at the Smithsonian Institution, Bureau of American Ethnology, are now in the National Archives. Between a Mr. J.G. Gurley, a Mr. Gill, and a Miss Clark, all with the Bureau's Printing Office, they concern the difficulties of editing and publishing. To most they are of little interest.

While proof-reading some copy, Freire-Marreco felt compelled to write to Mr. Gurley to insure there would be no hurt to the Santa Clara people as well as to protect her personal reputation at the Pueblo: *The chief point is, that I object very strongly to having my name quoted in a book dealing largely with Tewa sacred places: It would be a great disadvantage to me later on at Santa Clara. I contributed the small paragraphs which Mr. Harrington quotes on the express condition that my name should not be printed, and I have repeated the stipulation more than once; so I feel justified in asking you to substitute "an investigator at Santa Clara" wherever my name appears. Very possibly Mr. Harrington has made this alteration in the page proof, but if he has overlooked it, I hope you will be so kind as to make quite sure that it is done.*

Always mindful not to offend Native Americans she added: *On similar grounds I protest against the appearance of Jim Naranjo's name on 40 RW. I know he would object strongly, and I think Mr. Harrington has left the name there by an oversight.* (National Archives, Harrington, 9 July 1914)

🕊 🕊 🕊

Correspondence between Freire-Marreco and John Harrington after her return to England in 1913 is scarce. However, her note to him in May 1914 displays not only a collegial exchange but the outright affection and concern she had developed for him.

*Your letter of May 11 came today; and first of all, I am sorry to hear of you suffering such excessive hardships, and I wish you would get yourself inoculated for typhoid—the French and American results of inoculation lately have been very good. American ethnology cannot afford to have you snuffed out just yet!*

*Secondly, I am truly obliged to you for finding time and energy to write to me under such circumstances. Your good advice shall be carefully applied. I hope to send you soon a short list of words illustrating a supposed interchange of j and s: meanwhile I will take care not to theorize about it in public. Theory is very dangerous, anyhow, for a person who knows as little about the Tewa language as I do.*

*What you say about the inconvenience of reciprocal terms actually identical is very forcible. I have some from the Pima which seem to be the very height of inconvenience and illogicalness, and yet, it seems they are used! A calls B my "grandson's mother," and B calls A the same! My informant admitted that it was not true in the second case but yet, she said, it was the regular thing. An equally illogical term is the Walpi one for grandmother's brother. As long as a boy is quite young, he and his maternal-grandmother's brother call each other "my little elder-brother!"*

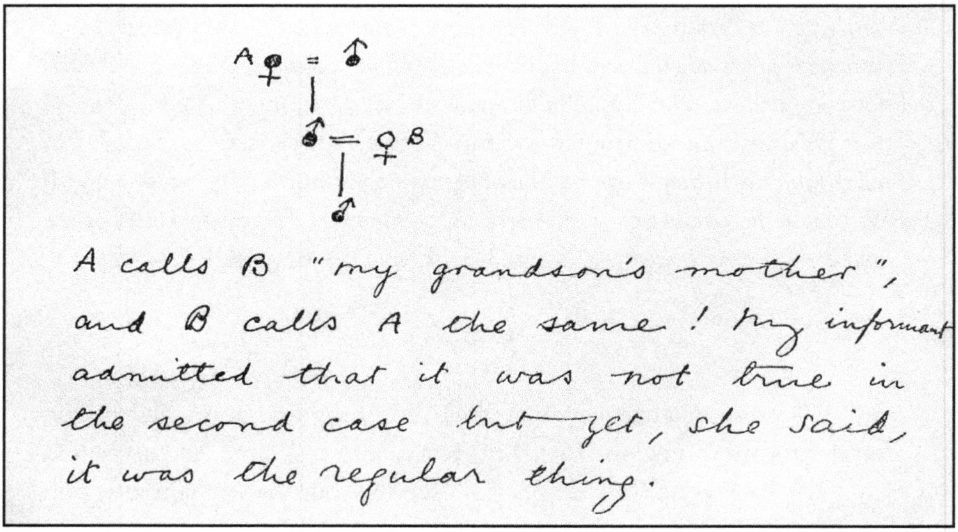

A diagram showing genealogical symbols, followed by handwritten text:

A calls B "my grandson's mother", and B calls A the same! My informant admitted that it was not true in the second case but yet, she said, it was the regular thing.

**A diagram of complicated Pima relationships Freire-Marreco drew in a letter to John Harrington on May 20 1914 in order to clarify her meaning.**
Courtesy of Smithsonian Institution, National Archives, Harrington papers.

I wish you wouldn't go on worrying yourself about that old relationship terms paper. It was quite obvious that it was a sort of accident, easily explained by the conditions under which you were working: and when your splendid block of Mohave work comes out, why, that trifle will be buried out of sight! I am _dreadfully_ sorry that you are having such a hard time and being obliged to spend your own money as well as your strength on the work. It is too bad, and I am most truly sorry, and admire the determination with which you carry on the work. I look forward to the publication of it to bring you the credit you deserve, in the States and in Europe. But, my "elder brother," I don't feel easy when I read —of your saying nasty words to yourself by way of consolation—it is so bad for the brain, and I should hate to see yours deteriorating in any way! Now you may allow yourself one large swear-word right here—qualifying the "impertinence of the woman" for preaching at you, for _swears_ are comparatively wholesome; but don't go muttering things to yourself anymore.

Thank you for verbal alterations to page two of the little paper, which I will make, and for the spelling corrections, and the suggestion about italics, and the indication of the glottal stops—all great improvements.

About the Hano d̲. Thank you so much for explaining it. I wanted to indicate the comparative heaviness and constancy of the Hano sound (which never varies to r̲ as in New Mexico Tewa) and which sounds to me very different from the New Mexico Tewa.

About a Tewa dictionary, of course I'm making a short Hano vocabulary, and keeping a sort of Tewa vocabulary in slips for my private use. But I know very little Tewa indeed—you don't realize how little. If ever you have time to make a Tewa dictionary, I should be glad to put my small amount of New Mexico Tewa material with yours.

You say that you got a Hano vocabulary at Santo Domingo. This is the first I have heard of it, and I am very much excited. Can't you print it soon, please, so that I can check my stuff on it? And do you believe it to be a kind of Tewa, or Tano? I shall be simply distracted until I read it in print.

Sorry the Tewa place-names came too late, but quite understand. I warmly appreciate your kind promise of letting me see the page-proof, and will suggest no additions. My chief object will be to have removed "Miss B. F-M says".....!

Would you object to telling me whether you are being paid for the T. E.Botany, and if so how? I don't know whether I am to be paid or not. I imagine not, for I simly volunteered to collaborate with you and Mr. Robbins, and had no commission at all from the Bureau to do the work. I was paid $40, however, for some work I did on it last summer in Washington—on the basis of so many galley proofs revised.

Thank you so much for thinking about the Yavapai vocabulary at the Bancroft Library. I'll take your advice and won't weep over it.

How I wish I were coming to San Diego, if only to see your collections! I don't think I have much chance. My father is very ill, and it is very unlikely that I shall be able to leave home next year with safety. Maybe my fieldwork chances are over for good—I wish I had made better use of them.

Prof. J. L. Myres of Oxford was in California this spring, but I suppose *you did not meet him. I think Dr. Marret is going out to Santa Fe in summer: please be nice to him if he comes your way.*

*Goodbye-good luck and good health. And get inoculated, please.* (ibid. 20 May 1914) It is ironic that she advised him to be vaccinated against typhoid fever and the next month he was stricken. It had been too late for an inoculation to benefit Harrington, but in Freire-Marreco's next letter there is no rebuff, only sympathy and thankfulness with just a little advice. *I am so truly sorry about your typhoid fever attack. I am not much surprised, though, considering what you have had to put up with. It is very kind of you to let me know, and I am thankful to hear that the most dangerous part of the illness is over. But you will have to make a patient and cautious convalescence. Don't think of writing to me until you are quite well and at leisure: there was nothing of any urgency in my letter; but some day I should like to hear how you managed to get to the railroad, and how your Mohaves treated you when you first got sick.*

*I remember well how kind you were when I was sick in Santa Fe— posting my letters, and giving me Tewa lessons and all. I am so sorry I can't return the kindness now!*

*By the same post I got a letter from Mr. Chapman to tell me of your illness and as a postscript he added a reassuring account of your progress just received from Dr. Hewett.* Kenneth M. Chapman, 1875-1968, was on the staff of Hewett's summer camp when Freire-Marreco attended, served as executive secretary of the School of American Archaeology as well as the Museum of New Mexico, was a research associate at the Laboratory of Anthropology, and a professor of Indian art at the University of New Mexico. As an artist, he illustrated his publications.

To continue Freire-Marreco's letter to Harrington: *Very little news here that would interest you. The English anthropologists who are going to the British Association meeting in Australia have to start next Friday, and I think some of them are coming home via San Francisco and will look in at the pueblos. I hope you'll be strong enough by that time to give them a few hints, and especially that you'll meet my dear friends and teachers J. L. Myres and R. R. Marret.*

*Very much sympathy and the warmest wishes for your good and quick recovery.*

Postscript: *What a good thing that you had already done such masses of work—it would have been worse at the beginning, wouldn't it? Sezwagi!—as they say to sick people at Santa Clara.*

*Please thank your nurse for writing the note to me, and ask her to use this envelope to let me know of your progress.* (ibid. 26 June 1914)

There was no more correspondence between them until February 1920, and then Freire-Marreco wrote from a new address: Pathway House, Mount Hermon Road, Woking. In characteristic fashion, she first discussed issues of interest to the receiver, saving her own important personal news for the end. *Your typewriter is just as it came to me, in its packing case, and it has been kept in the driest part of our house. Last summer I thought you would like to have it overhauled by the makers before it was shipped to you, but the firm has moved away and I cannot trace them. I was not ungrateful of your kind offer of the use the machine, but your letter of October 1914 speaks of a possible change of type, and so I never began to use the typewriter for fear it should afterward be necessary to return it to the makers.*

*Shall I have it shipped to you now, and by what agency?*

*Your kind letter of last summer suggesting the possibility of work under the Bureau of American Ethnology was warmly appreciated, though it would not have been easy for me to leave England. But I cannot allow you to say that the Bureau feels indebted to me: on the contrary, it is I who owe a great deal to the Bureau and have been too slow in repaying it.*

*Since Christmas I am engaged to be married, in April, to a friend whom I have known for some time, Mr. Robert Aitken.* (ibid. 2 Sept. 1920)

*With kind regards to Mrs. Harrington and yourself.*

After marriage she wrote from 11 Belsize Square, London: *Thank you very much for your kind letter of advice about publication, which I shall certainly have in mind. Before I publish any Tewa material, I ought really to finish up the Yavapai work for the Bureau of Ethnology. They paid me nearly $100 for expenses for it.*

This letter again addressed the matter of what was to be done with Harrington's typewriter, part of an ongoing saga that took several years to settle. *You don't say anything about your typewriter: what am I to do about it? As I wrote to you in the autumn, it has never been unpacked or used, and it may need to be put in order. The firm from whom you bought it seems to have gone out of business. Would you like me to send it to you, or to try and sell it in England for you?* (ibid. 16 Mar. 1921)

He did not respond to her requests that had begun in 1920 on how to dispose of the machine and over time she became quite exasperated. In June of 1924 she again offered to sell it for him because *it must be growing stiff in its case.* Then in October of that year she wrote more firmly, *do you ever remember your typewriter in my custody? My brother is selling the house in Woking, and cannot house it in his new small house, so you really must give me instructions, or I shall have to sell it to the best of my judgment and send you the proceeds. Now do write the answer while you think of it! Here is an envelope ready addressed.* (ibid. 23 Oct. 1924)

Finally in December, 1924: *I am very glad you have decided to have the typewriter sent to you, in spite of the heavy transportation charges, I believe you would have lost by selling it here. I was offered only six pounds for it!* (ibid. 8 Dec. 1924)

One wonders what the transportation cost must have been.

To return to Aitken's 1920 letter with other thoughts: *I am an admirer of Mrs. Parson's work. It seems to me very truthful and careful, and mostly free from cant of any kind.* Elsie Clews Parsons, 1874 -1941, known mainly as an American sociologist specializing in southwest Pueblo Indian religion, is still considered an expert in that study. Known as a modernist, she was respected as an ethnologist and served as a president of the American Ethnology Association as well as president of the American Folklore Society.

Also mentioned are two other American anthropologists, both at the University of California, Berkeley at that time. Robert Harry Lowie, 1859-1928, published extensively on Native cultures and was especially interested in their politics. He was Curator at the National Museum of Natural History, before going to Berkeley. Alfred Lewis Kroeber, 1876-1960, led several anthropological expeditions and published about North American, Mexican and Peruvian Indian sites. A proponent of the Boazian school of American anthropology, he furthered the linguistic classification of Native people.

*She* (Parsons), *Dr. Lowie and Dr. Kroeber have been very friendly, and have written more than once to offer facilities for the publication of my material; but undoubtedly I would rather have it published by the Bureau if they would not edit me too severely! Thank you so much for writing about it.*

Inquiring whether Harrington intended to attend the summer meeting of the British Anthropological Association in Toronto, Freire-Marreco regretfully had little hope of so doing, but said she would try to go to an American Anthropology Association meeting in the Hague the following September. *And if you are to be there, I shall make a great effort to go and bring some Hano vocabularies and texts for your criticism.*

*I am just re-reading your "Tewa Ethnogeography" with great admiration, and the supplementary notes in the* **American Anthropologist**. *One or two points occur to me:*

*In 1911, when the delegates from Santa Clara went to the junta general at Santo Domingo, we rode across the mesas to Cochiti. Leaving Santa Clara at 8:30, we struck up hill opposite San Ildefonso, and rode on the high ground all the forenoon, and soon after noon ate our lunch at P'eju'u. All the party agreed that the name meant a projection with trees on it, and they said there were traces of a ruin near. There is a conspicuous rock there, on the top of which rain-water lodges, and for that reason parties traveling across the hills to Cochiti usually eat and drink there as we did.*

*If you are at Santa Clara, Santiago, Victoriano Sisneros, or Pedro Cajete could certainly tell you just where it is. How I wish I had your maps in those days!* (ibid. 16 Jan. 1924)

One wonders if these thoughts led her to remember with some nostalgia and humor holidays as celebrated in the United States.

### *Super Flumins*

*I wisht I was back Over There Tonight*
*Where dey sure knows how to fix things right.*

*Turkey, cranberries 'n 'pie –*
*O my! O my!*
*Why, where I'm a living,*
*They don' <u>know</u> it's Thanksgiving!*
*(Say, can you beat it?)*
*An' turkey? Why, dey eat it*
*Jes' a month too late.*
*Well, I calkerlate*
*That, fer Fourth o' July, an' de*
*Pres'dent's birthday, an' Thanksgiving, an' all der sure-to-goodness <u>vital</u> dates,*
*There ain' nothin' der matter with stayin' <u>right home</u> in God awmight's United States!*

—Aitken, *Verses* 1924

In an attempt to protect Native people from exploitation she appealed to Harrington: *I wish most heartily that you would use your influence with the Department of Indian Affairs, whenever occasion arises, against the granting of leave to Indians to come to Europe in shows. I have been sorry to see the effect of London on the Arapaho party who came here with the "Covered Wagon" film. Their employer seems to pay them well; he certainly lodges them comfortably and feeds them regularly; and the men of the party are taken sightseeing. But what months of dreary idleness! Just two short performances a day-and they go by tube: no exercise even then—and nothing on earth to do besides. The women sit sadly at home and say they live "like prisoners;" some of the men are said to be drinking heavily and taking to other bad courses. Their children too, all these months out of school, and kept in idleness and confinement! It is no life for simple people.* (National Archives, Harrington, 16 Jan. 1924)

This event in London was remembered by Anthony Marreco, who recalled it as an exciting experience for a fourteen year old English boy. Sponsored by the British Museum in London, the spectacle featured Native American men who danced and whooped, emulating war cries, while waving tomahawks. However, his recollection of the boarding houses where the Arapahos stayed was of crowded and foul smelling dwellings with the performance costumes draped around over the furniture. It was Anthony's Aunt Barbara's responsibility to get the performers to the cinema at 2 p.m. every day and this she did by marching them single file, herself in the lead. Her participation was obviously remembered with regret.

Continuing their exchange, she wrote Harrington: *Do you happen to know Pedro Cajete of Santa Clara? I hear from his family that he has spent the last three winters at Los Angeles; and unless he goes there to work with some other ethnologist, wouldn't it be rather a good thing for you to get hold of him there next winter? He is elderly and intelligent—one of the chief men on the Winter Side (or was so in 1913) -muy catolico, but he dances k'osa (a clown) at San Juan. I think he joined the society there for his health when he was quite young. He is pretty well off, I fancy. This may be of no use to you, but I thought I had better tell you. If you don't want him, perhaps Mrs. Parsons would like to have a shot at him. I admire her very much as a sociologist, but not as a linguist.*

By now she had no hope of attending the meeting of the Americans in The Hague. *I am not going to Toronto. Are you coming to The Hague? I would be tremendously pleased to see you here on the way.*

*P. S. Judging from the letters I have had from Santa Clara, the Winter Side has been dancing a good deal. Zuni Basket Dance (as in 1911) with sun symbols; some kind of Antelope or Mountain Sheep dance (I believe the right to bring out Mountain sheep dance was in dispute between the Sides), and a rain dance of sorts. I think they have made a new Ojike or are in the process of making one. The Summer Side has made a new cacique, Jose Cleto. "Very young for the place," they say. The old cacique, Jose Maria, died little more than a year ago, so no time has been lost.*

*San Ildefonso news of course you know better than I; only Dr. Hewett told me that your friend Ignacio is cacique there now. People at Santa Clara are getting horribly American, Christening their children "Roosevelt!" and "Gladys!!"* (ibid. Mar. 20, 1924)

Another inquiry: *Can you remember and tell me the name of the man who was collecting Tewa folk-tales in 1913—was it possibly Mr. Spinden or Mr. Tozzer?*

Alfred Tozzer has been identified earlier. Herbert Joseph Spinden, 1879-1967, American archaeologist and ethnologist did his field work among the Tewa from 1909-1913 and also worked on the Yucatan Peninsula, deciphering the Mayan dating system. At various times he was with the American Museum of Natural History, was curator at the Peabody Museum, Harvard, the Buffalo Museum and the Brooklyn Museum.

*You and I and he spent an evening together, and he told two admirable stories from Tesuque, one about the little boy carried away by a Deer katsina, the other about the woman saving her babies in the great flood. I want particularly to meet with those stories again, and I should be so grateful if you could remember the man.* (ibid. 1 June 1924)

In other correspondence to Harrington a little later that year she wrote: *I don't know much news about Oxford anthropology. In London we have Bronislaw Malinowski lecturing now—good stuff, and noticeably influencing Lowie and Kroeber—so the University College people like Elliot Smith are not having things all their own way. I gave a short course in London University last year when Malinowski was ill, and another in Oxford, but hadn't much of an audience. If you come over some year, couldn't you arrange a course of lectures which would cover your loss of salary?* (ibid. 8 Dec. 1924)

The esteemed scholars she mentioned were famous in the English speaking world. Kaspar Bronislaw Malinowski, 1884-1942, was a social anthropologist and a pragmatist. He founded a functional school of anthropology bringing it from speculation to a science. An author of repute, he lectured at the University of London's School of Economics and, like Aitken, had an interest in Pueblo Indians.

Sir Grafton Elliot Smith, 1871-1919, a British anthropologist and anatomist was a Professor of Anatomy at Manchester College. Critical of the methods used by his fellow anthropologists, classical scholars and Egyptologists, it must have caused unrest among his colleagues. Barbara Freire-Marreco Aitken's letters, however, were never openly judgmental concerning the anthropological or ethnological work of others. Certainly she had strong convictions, but she always recognized and encouraged other professionals, all the while maintaining a courteous attitude.

It is regretable that none of Harrington's correspondence to Barbara in England has survived, but we do know she continued to consult him on a variety of subjects until at least 1931, including the expected ones about Native languages, mainly Tewa. Occasionally there would be an off-beat remark. In one letter she mentioned those *queer pale Indians at Oraibi*. (ibid. 25 Jan. 1925) This phrase could have been a reference to people of mixed blood, Native and White, or to the fact that there were Albinos on the Hopi Reservation.

On one occasion she congratulated him on some of his publications and urged him several times to come to England. She was willing to arrange lectures for him and even suggested ways for him to defray expenses. Perhaps the most unusual remark Aitken made to Harrington was a compliment: *American anthropologists are so kind to the stranger and so fierce to each other! But I refuse to believe that anyone can spoil the life of a worker like yourself.* (ibid. 2 Mar. 1925)

〰 〰 〰

Even though Barbara Aitken never returned to the United States, she kept abreast of what transpired by subscribing to American scientific publications. Seeing one article by Walter Fewkes, in 1923 she wrote: *I have just read with delight and wonder your second report on Mimbres Pottery.*

The Mimbres Valley in southern New Mexico had interested archaeologists since the 1880s, but not until the mid-1920s and early 1930s did extensive excavations begin. Although their origin is still in dispute, it is assumed the original inhabitants were not Pueblo people, though they lived in villages, but probably were related to nomad Apaches coming from the Mogollan area of what is now Arizona about 200 A. D. They produced some of the best pottery at that time, leaving behind very thin walled black-on-white unique bowls, not only with geometric designs, but also pictographs of animal and human figures depicting the life of the ancient people. A pioneer archaeologist in the area, Fewkes made several trips to the Mimbres site from 1914 to 1924 and produced a number of publications on the subject.

To continue with Aitken's letter: *What an astonishing collection of studies! The fish seems to me particularly successful as decoration. The ceremonial human figures are delightful. Do you think that they may represent the Little War Gods carried away by a Soyokmana in her burden basket? The female figure is in the characteristic attitude of a woman carrying a heavy load—with one hand she leans on a staff and she raises the other to her forehead to relieve the strain of the forehead strap.*

In a Tewa story, the Little War Gods are carried off by the Tsaveyo in the burden basket in which he habitually steals children: next day the Tsaveyo and his wife Suyukukwiyo go wood gathering, carrying the boys on the top of the loads of wood in their baskets. The boys smear resin on the ogre's hair, draw fire from the sun, and burn them up.

*May I trouble you with three questions?*

*1. Did the Smithsonian Institution receive safely the copy of Morgan's* **Systems of Consanguinity** *which I sent to Wesley's for return to the Smithsonian in 1916 or 1917? I never heard of its arrival.*

*2. I see in a Smithsonian Annual Report that Mrs. Stevenson, when she lived near San Ildefonso in 1912, was making a study of Tewa irrigation. Have any notes of hers on the subject been put into type, and could I be allowed to see them? My husband is making a study of methods of irrigation, primarily in Spain but also in other countries, and any account of New Mexican irrigation would be very useful to him.*

*3. A good many people in Oxford have been concerned at reading a circular about Indian Dances issued by the Commissioner for Indian Affairs which, (they think) contains a threat to put down the Snake Dance and the Sun Dance. It seems to me that it would be improper for English anthropologists to express any opinion about Indian administration in the United States—we have quite enough to concern ourselves with- in Africa, for one thing! But I thought I might ask you, personally, whether as an American anthropologist you see any cause for anxiety in the circular? Personally, I read the circular as a warning against the commercialization of Indian ceremonies, and the sentence* about snakes and "tortures" as an expression of opinion, not as a threat of action. I should be so grateful for a word or two from you that I might pass on to anxious friends of the Hopi over here. (Smithsonian Institution, National Anthropological Archives, Museum of Natural History, Walter Fewkes file, 23 July 1923)

Fewkes replied: *I was very glad to receive your letter of July 23 with valuable suggestions in the interpretation of some of the figures lately published by me on the Mimbres pictography. I was much pleased that you had found the work of interest and I hope in a few months to add another and larger article to this fascinating study.*

*While the pictures of the ancient people of the Mimbres engaged in secular work—hunting, fishing and snaring of animals—are particularly interesting, the ceremonial human figures are to me the most fascinating, and with this new material I shall be able to add several mythic animals which will shed light on the mythology of the extinct people of southern New Mexico.*

*I am, of course, quite familiar with Soyokmana when she parades through the villages on the East Mesa of the Hopi with her basket on her back and the great knife in her hand threatening to cut off the heads of naughty children, and her escapades in mythological lines were always numerous.*

*I think you are quite right in suggesting that picture six is pictorially representative of the myth of the pueblos regarding the transportation of the twin gods of war in a basket, as you have found it in Tewa variants. The interpretation is complete and if you will allow me, will have a note in my paper, which I shall presently publish, speaking of your interesting letter in regard to its interpretation.*

*We are, of course, very much hampered in the absence of linguistic, sociological and mythological lore of the ancient people of the Mimbres Valley. I find no satisfactory discussion even of this subject, but I am inclined to think from the geometrical patterns that they were aberrant pueblo people.*

*As we have a copy of Morgan's* **Systems of Consanguinity** *on our Library shelves, the book was evidently returned through Wesley.*

*In answer to your second question I regret to say that I cannot at this writing give you definite information. Mrs. Stevenson's notes were all turned* over to Mr. Harrington who is now connected with the Bureau and at present in California engaged in work among the Mission Indians of that state. He has all the Stevenson manuscript under his special care and I think it better not to disturb any arrangements that he has made regarding them. In my next letter I will ask him if he remembers any studies of Tewa irrigation. Nothing has been put in type by him on this subject from Mrs. Stevenson's notes.

I can well understand how anyone who has made a study of the Pueblo Indians may be more or less troubled when the perennial threat is made by the Commissioner of Indian Affairs to stop the Indian dances and ceremonies. Although in my connection with the Government, now about thirty years, I have repeatedly heard the threats, which were being made by the Commissioner to do this, have generally amounted to nothing. In 1891 I distinctly remember a threat was made to abolish the Snake Dance at Walpi, and an inspector was sent to investigate the subject. This gentleman promptly imbibed firewater at Holbrook and when he arrived at the dance was in no condition to make any observations worthy of note. I have never seen the subject taken up with the ardor now shown by different organizations of men in different professions—artists, scientific men, explorers, etc. Personally I do not think that the Snake Dance order will be carried out, especially this year and there is a bill now in Congress which will be reported next winter bearing on this subject which will no doubt be given world-wide publicity. In this great propaganda for startling things which seems to have submerged often times, things worthy to live, many extraordinary statements appear in print, but the sober good sense of the people of the country will not allow anything to prevent those religious ceremonies which are hereditary and are a source of pleasure and profit. So although I cannot speak ex cathedra I feel quite confident that the Snake Dance will persist for many years longer. I thought in 1894, when I published my "Snake Dance," that it would cease in a few years.

In a postscript to your letter, you make another valuable suggestion in regard to Mimbres pictures. I think you must be right that the legs represented are the hind legs of the tadpole not the forelegs, as I have stated. One or two have objected to my interpretation, considering it a mace or baton, but I think the amphibian interpretation is better. Your suggestion for figure 98 is *interesting; will look it up also with my naturalist friends.*

*I hope some day you may return to America and revisit the desert lands of our Southwest. Yearly, more and more the cry for continuation of work there is heard and the region seems inexhaustible. We have never had so many people working in the Southwest as this present summer.* (ibid. 11 Aug. 1923)

Aitken thanked Fewkes for his response and assured him she would be delighted to have him use her suggestion about the Twin War Gods. She was also grateful for his promise to ask John Harrington about Tewa irrigation as well as his reassuring words regarding Indian dances.

Before the beginning of the next year Barbara Aitken had sent one of her pictures to Fewkes, for which he was clearly grateful. *I thank you very much for your interesting picture of the trail up the mesa with the various figures in it. I have compared, as you suggest, one of the pictures on the pottery from the Mimbres which I think represents either the exit of the races through the Sipapu or the descent of the same after death into the other region through the house of the sun in the west.* A Sipapu is a hole in the floor of a kiva, the sacred meeting house of Pueblo men, considered the opening to the underworld.

*I have just finished correcting proof of another paper on the picture bowls of the Mimbres in which a variety of other customs and mythological beings are figured and interpreted, and I hope next year to secure another collection containing still more pictures. Later I will put the material altogether and write a pamphlet on the ethnology of the former inhabitants of the Mimbres Valley.*

*You may be interested to know that a week ago I received a letter from a gentleman living in St. Croix in the Virgin Islands of the West Indies, calling my attention to the figure of a woman carrying a basket on her back which contained the twins and suggesting a resemblance to the virgin birth of the two sons of the sun in Carib mythology.*

*An interesting feature in the story of these twins is the fact that the mother plucked the flowers and gave them to her sons. I am rather inclined, however, to think that the true interpretation of these objects is that these boys hold in their hands a representation of the sun—their father. I do not exactly interpret them as the Bogie woman as you have done but rather as the Sowugti old woman—their mother. That was a very interesting suggestion you made to me about them. I believe that it may be possible that the Mimbres people had some early connection with the Tewa or some folk tales; but I have not yet determined that point. I will send you a copy of the new publication on Mimbres symbolism as soon as it is published.*

*You will do me a great favor if you detect any other resemblances of a mythological character, and I hope later to myself add a few more picture bowls to the collection in the National Museum that now numbers about 300 specimens.*

*This winter I have become interested in Florida archaeology and I expect to go there this month and hope to open up a rather unknown region on that peninsula, archaeologically speaking, between Tampa Bay and Cape Sable.*

*With the Season's Greetings* (ibid. 3 Jan. 1924)

In the last found letter to Fewkes, Aitken thanked him for the Mimbres material he sent her. *I have just read with admiration and delight your latest report on pottery of the Mimbres. Interesting as the clever realistic drawings are, they don't overshadow—I think—the beauty of the geometric designs. The discussion of the relation of the Mimbres to the Pueblo culture is very instructive.*

*There is a sort of human expression about many of the Mimbres animals and birds, which almost suggests that the model in the potter's mind was not the animal itself but the animal as represented by a dancer. Probably women would not have many chances of seeing the actual wild animals alive? You will no doubt have noted at First Mesa how, after a dance or katsina performance, reminiscences of the performance are apt to appear on the women's pottery made in the course of the next two or three weeks. Just as a woman sings over the music heard at a recent dance, so she makes a spoon-handle in the shape of a clown or a corn-maiden.*

*I have not any mythological interpretations to suggest. In the way of natural history, I suggest that 57 is something of the caterpillar kind, and 56 a snail for the forefoot of which the painter has substituted four legs; but these suggestions will not be new to you.*

*I hope you have every success in Florida.* (ibid. 3 May 1924)

When this correspondence was written Barbara Aitken was teaching at both the London School of Economics and Somerville College, and was recognized as the British authority on the Tewa of New Mexico and Arizona. Unfortunately, but understandably, there is not much other correspondence with her American colleagues, perhaps because of her heavy work schedule.

🦋 🦋 🦋

In an effort to keep informed of any new developments that might benefit the Rio Grande pueblos, Freire-Marreco started writing, shortly after her return to England, to those of influence. To the Honorable Commissioner of Indian Affairs, Washington, DC: *Will you allow me to ask for information (if you can conveniently give it) about the present state of the Pueblo Indian question? I must apologize for taking up your time; my excuse is that I have lived for some months at Santa Clara, New Mexico and have come to take a deep interest in Pueblo affairs, and that officials of the Department have from time to time been kind enough to give me information on the subject.*

*Has the Supreme Court given a decision on the competence of Secretary for the Interior to accept transfer of Pueblo. . . in trust? Has any legislation been introduced into Congress to enable the Secretary to . . . ? Have any transfers. . .actually taken place and if so, on what. . .?* It is unfortunate that so much of this letter is illegible.

*I left New Mexico in June 1913 and have had no reliable information since that time, and I shall value very highly any that you think proper to give me.* The letter was signed with her signature followed by *Fellow Royal Anthropological Institute of Great Britain; Honorary Member Somerville College, Oxford, England, Member School of American Archaeology, Santa Fe, NM.* (National Archives, Hewett, 15 Apr. 1914)

Two years later in keeping with her sympathetic understanding of the Tewa people, she felt compelled to speak out for them in a letter to Edgar Hewett, reticent to send it directly to the **American Ethnologist** without his approval. *For some time I have felt that I must protest against (what seems to me) Mr. Douglass's very unfortunate, unscientific and irregular* *action in spoiling the Tewa shrine of Tsik'umu.* An article consisting of eleven printed pages accompanied by seven drawings, photographs and a map giving specific information on the locality and appearance of a sacred shrine, as well as the material it contained, is housed at the Douglas Memorial Library Denver Art Museum.

*I don't like making myself disagreeable to Mr. Douglass (whom I do not know), but his action seems to me to set up such a bad precedent—so likely to be disastrous to the work of the School of Archaeology, for instance—and so unfair to the Indians, that I must protest, if no one more important has done so. I wish I had written when his article was first published, but I did not see it then.*

*I see that you are or were on the Advisory Editorial Committee of* **Records of the Past,** *and so I don't like to send my letter to the* **American Anthropologist** *without consulting you. Would it be better if I sent it to a Southwestern journal—perhaps even to* **El Palacio** *only? My only wish is to persuade people, especially amateurs, not to let that sort of thing be done.*

*I send you a copy of what I have written and will do no more until I hear from you. I hope you will not take it as a discourteous reflection on the editing of* **Records of the Past.** *It is from yourself that I have learnt to be jealous for the good reputation of ethnology in New Mexico.*

She enclosed the following letter for Hewett to see. Addressed to the Editor, presumably of **The American Anthropologist,** it read: *Dear Sir, Will you allow me to call your attention to a matter which is of some practical importance to American science? In* **Records of the Past** *for July-August 1912 there appeared an article by Mr. William B. Douglass entitled "A World-Quarter Shrine of the Tewa Indians." I learn from this article that in September 1911, while engaged as a United States surveyor of the General Land Office in a survey of the boundaries of a private land grant in the Jemez Mountains, New Mexico, Mr. Douglass discovered an important shrine on the summit of a certain peak. Of this shrine and of the offerings found there Mr. Douglass gives photographs, drawings, and an excellent description (although I must note in passing, as an instance of methods only too common in our field, that "a saucer- like depression" which the author conjectures "may correspond to a sipapu or symbolic entrance to the underworld" is boldly marked "SIPAPU" on the plan); and by further* enquiry, with the help of a forest ranger, he gained the information that the shrine was visited and the offerings deposited by messengers from six New Mexican pueblos. "Forest Ranger L. feels certain that no white men other than himself and the writer have ever visited the shrine," and when Mr. L. used the peak as a fire-outlook in 1911, the shrine was visited by messengers from four pueblos and the Indians showed the most evident jealousy of his presence and enquiries.

Nothing could be more interesting to students of Pueblo sociology and ritual than the evidence for the existnce of this living custom at the present day. Mr. Douglass was fortunate in being able to view the shrine and he rendered a service to science by describing it and by recording the information gained through Mr. L.

But how did Mr. Douglass treat his discovery? <u>He took away the vase which was left near the shrine for ceremonial use, and all the offerings</u>. I venture to say that this action is very much to be regretted and for more than one reason.

I will take the scientific objections first. Mr. Douglass has scared the Indians out of using this shrine. For the sake of a mere collection of museum specimens, he has destroyed a living custom of great antiquity and of great social and ritual interest. He notes that on his second visit in August 1912 "no prayer-sticks, vases or other offerings were found in the shrine." (What did Mr. Douglass expect?) However, "three or four matches were found at the head of the Jemez-San Ildefonso trails" leading to it. Probably runners from those pueblos arrived, found the shrine despoiled, and passed on the news to the rest. A piece of <u>collectioneering</u> such as this does untold harm to real ethnographical research in the Southwest; the Indians must feel that their attitude of suspicion and concealment is amply justified. Further, Mr. L. (the forest ranger) obtained his information about the custom from a young native of the one of the pueblos concerned, "after much persuasion and the pledge of profound secrecy. He seemed in great fear lest it become known that he had given this information." Mr. Douglass publishes this man's name and address! Does he suppose that **Records of the Past** will never reach Santa Fe or Espanola—that he can rely on Americans who read it to be less indiscreet than himself, that none of the Indians can read English? Besides, whether expedient or inexpedient, the disclosure was a breach of faith.

And this brings me to a more serious aspect of the question. Mr. Douglass was in the Jemez country in an official capacity, as a surveyor under the United States Government. He was in a privileged position. He made use of his special opportunities to rob a shrine, which he at first suspected and afterward knew for certain to be highly valued by the Indians of the locality. He did this with the connivance of the forest ranger, who was also in a position of trust. This, (I submit) was a very regrettable irregularity—a misuse of official position. If an irresponsible tourist were to outrage the Indians' religious feelings it would be bad enough; that a responsible official should do so is far worse. Mr. Douglass had the Indians "in a cleft stick," as the saying is, for they could not resist his action or complain of him without disclosing what their religious custom obliged them to conceal. No doubt Mr. Douglass acted thoughtlessly, not maliciously; but a slight exercise of sympathetic imagination (without which no one should meddle with ethnographical work) will surely make him realize the bitter, helpless mortification which he made the Indians suffer.

The Indians are entitled to the same measure of religious liberty and toleration as the other inhabitants of the United States, in so far as their customs are harmless and do not conflict with the law; and there is absolutely no reason why a government official should collect curios at the expense of their feelings. It is not pleasant to reflect that an English official in Nigeria would incur a severe reprimand if he offended the religious sentiments of the lowest "pagan" cannibals; while in New Mexico a peaceable tribe like the pueblo Indians may be annoyed with impunity. This is not the way to help Indian administration in the Southwest.

I do not know Mr. Douglass, and I am sorry if this seems like a personal attack on him. I am concerned with the precedent which he has set. I write in the interests of religious toleration and of our science. I desire to appeal to every scientific society working in the ethnological field to maintain the standard of opinion in these matters, to protect Indian life as well as Indian antiquities, and to think very seriously before they countenance or publish work of a kind which will certainly undo what they themselves are trying to do. And I desire to appeal to a just public opinion which will restrain government employees from making improper use of their official powers and opportunities. (Museum of New Mexico, Laboratory of Anthropology, File # 89ELH.161, 16 June 1916)

Showing generosity of spirit and her willingness, as well as determination, to help those with infirmities, on the 30th of December 1927 she requested a favor from Alfred Kroeber then at the University of California, Berkeley. *Your* **Anthropology** *has been asked for by two blind students, and is to be copied in Braille accordingly, and I am trying to contrive intelligible copies of the maps for them. The best thing we have contrived so far is to make enlarged copies of the map, mount it on card, cut it out, mount it again on a sheet of card so that the continent stands up in relief, and mount the various divisions, cut out in paper stamped with Braille lettering, again upon that. After making one or two rough experimental copies, I find that they are not satisfactory unless enlarged about four times from the book illustrations: to do this by hand is difficult, and by photography costly, though I will do it one way or the other if necessary. It occurs to me as possible, though by no means to be taken for granted, that you might be willing to lend the manuscript maps from which the book illustrations were reduced and allow me to trace from them. I shouldn't venture to ask you, but for the special difficulties of blind students, and of course I shan't be at all surprised if you are unable to consent.* (University of California, Berkeley, The Bancroft Library, Records of the Department of Anthropology, Kroeber file, 30 Dec. 1927.)

Kroeber complied. *Under separate cover I am forwarding you the original drawings of my maps.*

*I am very glad to send these on. In fact, I am much pleased at your undertaking. If possible I will ask you to try to use the maps so that they can be returned to me. The book continues to be used as a text in many of our colleges so that there is a likelihood of a revised edition being called for some day. In that event some of the maps will probably have to be revised and without the originals I would be under the same difficulty as you are now, of enlarging from a small printed copy, which is never satisfactory.*

*I am not quite clear as to how the drawings would enter into the process of reproduction which you describe. If it is a matter of cutting them up you could* probably without much trouble or expense get pencil tracings made from my maps and apply the scissors to these outlines; I hope so at any rate.

I do not know what is customary in regard to Braille editions, but it occurs to me that you would probably want to write to the publishers of the book. The American copyright would probably not hold in England, but they sold five hundred copies to one of your publishers for an English edition and they may be copyrighted on your side. If I am in any way involved please quote me as being not only agreeable but desirous to have the Braille edition appear. (ibid. 13 Mar. 1928)

Because she was planning on an upcoming trip and she wanted the Braille project completed, she made arrangements to have it attended to in her absence and so informed Kroeber on The Royal Anthropological Institute's stationery. *I had your very kind letter before the Easter holiday, and your maps arrived today. Thank you very much indeed on my friend's behalf and on my own.*

*It is unfortunate that now I am just starting to Spain, and cannot make the tracings before I go. I propose, with your leave, to keep the maps carefully packed at my friend's house (Harold Lakeman, 43a Alexandra Road, Gypsy Hill, Norwood, S.E.) and to do them as soon as I return in July. If for any reason you want them before that date, Mr. Lakeman will get tracings made and return your maps; but I would rather be responsible for doing them myself.* (ibid. 13 Apr. 1928)

What became of the Braille project is not known. The last correspondence found between Kroeber and Barbara Aitken contains the first mention of Aitken's illness that plagued her for the rest of her life. *The notice of your Huxley Memorial Lecture on the 30th has just reached me. I am truly sorry not to take advantage of this chance of seeing and learning from you again, but I am only just out of hospital and not up to traveling to London. I must content myself with reading the lecture.* (ibid. 24 Apr. No Year)

🦅 🦅 🦅

As early as 1916, only three years after Freire-Marreco had returned to England, she had written to Edward Gifford, also of the University of California, Berkeley, to thank him for a paper on California Shellmounds he had sent her. Though not stated, on one of her trips to the United States, it is possible she had met him. Edward W. Gifford, 1887-1959, the American archaeologist/ethnologist, contributed much to the knowledge about the Yavapai in Arizona which was published in the American Archaeology and Ethnology publications.

No more exchanges between them were found again until 1933 when Gifford, aware of her work with the Yavapai, contacted her. *During the month of December I did field work on the Yavapai reservation at Camp McDowell, Arizona. My interpreter was Gilbert Davis, who said that he acted in similar capacity for you some years ago when you were getting ethnobotanical data from his father now deceased.*

*I have now completed field work on the three divisions of the Yavapai, Southeastern, Northeastern, and Western. The Southeastern material has been published: I am now working up the Northeastern material. This I did not obtain at Camp McDowell, but at Prescott, Mayer, Turkey, and Jerome, I obtained a considerable amount of ethnobotanical material, perhaps 100 identified plants altogether. These were collected entirely in the Prescott and Mayor regions. I am interested to know if you have published or contemplate publishing in the near future the data which you obtained at Camp McDowell? Presumably it pertained to the Southeastern Yavapai, who form the bulk of the population on that reservation. Perhaps you know these three groups by their native names: Kewekopaya for Southeastern, Yavepe for Northeastern, and Tolkepaya for Western. I employed Gilbert Davis in the obtaining of information concerning the Tolkepaya only. I obtained no ethnobotanical information from them, as at Camp McDowell they are 100 miles away from their habitat.*

*If you have not received from the University a copy of my paper on the Southeastern Yavapai, I shall be glad to send you one.* (The Bancroft Library, University of California, Berkeley, Records of the Department of Anthropology, Gifford file, 9 Feb. 1933)

Aitken replied. *Thank you very much indeed for letting me know of the progress of your work on the Yavapai. I had missed the announcement of the* book on the Northeastern Yavapai and shall look forward much to reading it now; it is very good of you to think of giving me a copy

My report on the groups at McDowell has not been published, though part of it is more or less ready. It is not a report on the ethnology of any of the three branches, but rather an imperfect study of the new society into which the three groups were merging on the reservation.

I remember Gilbert as a very good interpreter, though not as good as Nellie Davis to whom he was then married: she was the best I ever struck.

The Ethnobotany results I got were very poor: as you say, the people at McDowell are far from their old home, and low spirited, and uninterested. The flour-coffee-bacon complex was already driving out the old food stuffs. My best stuff is on the "dreamers."

I think that all my material is the property of the Bureau of American Ethnology who paid my expenses at McDowell. If you wished to make any arrangement with them to use it, I should be perfectly willing. I get hardly any time nowadays for writing. (ibid. 11 Mar. 1933)

Gifford thanked Aitken for the offer and added some news he knew would interest her. Your letter of March 11 has just been received, and I am glad to learn more about your work at McDowell. Nellie Davis is now married to a Yavapai living at San Carlos. Gilbert has another wife, a rather stout middle-aged woman, apparently somewhat his senior. They are both pillars of the Presbyterian Church at the present time. That church has a Pima pastor.

A second church on the reservation is one which I am sure would repay some study. It is called the Indian Church (Native American Church). It makes vociferous use of drums. I did not attend any of its gatherings as my interest is solely in reconstructing the past and distinguishing the elements of culture of each of the three Yavapai tribes.

Under separate cover I am sending you a copy of my Southeast Yavapai paper, and a year or two hence when the Northeastern one is published I shall be delighted to send you a copy of it.

It is nice of you to offer me access to your material. With our rather different approaches I think that it would be a mistake to merge two lots of material. I think it would be far better for each of us to publish separately.

*Work by more than one anthropologist on any given people is certainly a great desideratum. The trouble is there are so many peoples awaiting study and so few anthropologists to do the work that we usually feel thankful if a tribe gets studied by a single anthropologist.*

*I shall speak with Professor Kroeber concerning your kind offer. If he feels differently than I in regard to it, I shall then avail myself of the privilege which you offer.* (ibid. 4 Apr. 1933)

As promised, Gifford wrote a memorandum to Kroeber. *Please read the attached letter from Barbara Aitken and tell me what you think of the idea of looking over her Yavapai material. I think we might at least look it over but reserve decision as to incorporating it with mine. It is likely that the different approaches and the possibility that she did not discriminate between NE, SE, and W would render combination of the two sets of data somewhat hazardous. I assume Stirling would not hesitate to let us examine it.* Matthew W. Stirling was their superior at the Smithsonian Institution's Bureau of American Ethnology.

A hand-written reply from Kroeber is on the same page, seemingly agreeable, but concerned about protecting others material. *Sure, Stirling will let you see it, but may not want to send it out unless it has been copied. It looks as if she had made mainly an "acculturation study." If so it will have very little reference to yours.* (ibid. 5 Apr. 1933)

Correspondence addressed to colleagues in the United States is very scarce after this. England was her home and from 1913 on, her travels were confined to the European Continent.

# ✐ World War I

When Barbara Freire-Marreco had returned to England she was yet unmarred and focused on her career, but world circumstances changed her life.

Great Britain declared war against Germany in August of 1914. British citizens directed their efforts toward maintaining the Empire and restoring peace for themselves, their European neighbors, and eventually the rest of the world. Barbara Freire-Marreco was no exception; her career plans were put on hold. Evidence of her activities during the war years are almost nonexistent and her whereabouts hard to follow. In spite of international conflict and employment that did not coincide with her professional interests and training, she tried to use her abilities to further her country's cause.

There are records of three different war-related jobs she held. Oxford's **Morning Post** of June 25 1917 reported that from September 1914 to October 1915 she held the position of Secretary and Registrar to the Woking War Emergency Committee, and from October 1915 to Easter 1916 she served on the editorial staff of the War Trade Intelligence Department.

No other evidence relating to Barbara Freire-Marreco's service with the War Trade Intelligence Department of the British War Office was found. Neither the Imperial War Museum nor the National Army Museum, both in London, produced any record of her war work efforts. Considering her ability with languages, one can speculate that she may have made a contribution as a translator. The only clue to her activities was in letter a little later to John Harrington: *I feel I have been ungrateful to my friends during the War, but I think you know how engrossing that has been, and how little energy remained for private affairs. My work in the Military Intelligence Department was interesting, but very exhausting and I did little else.* (National Archives, Harrington, 2 Sept. 1920)

Details of her tenure at the Intelligence Department are not known, but it was there she met her husband-to-be.

Another wartime job she held was a post with Barnett House at Oxford University. This institution was founded in East London in 1884 in honor of Canon Barnett, a Vicar of St. Jude's, Whitechapel; its aim was to bridge the gap between social classes. Established in Oxford in 1913, it has since undergone many changes. Its legacy is the publication of many books and the promotion of library preservation. As a charitable institution, it served through two World Wars and is credited with keeping alive the intellectual life of Oxford University as well as sheltering wartime refugees. Barnett House is now the Department of Applied Social Studies and Social Research at Oxford for graduate students working for a Masters' Degrees in Applied Social Studies as well as Social Research and Social Policy for the supervision of other students with like interests.

A report from the subcommittee to consider the appointment of a Secretary at Barnett House, in which Freire-Marreco was recommended to the Council. It was unanimously decided that the report be adopted and that Freire-Marreco be asked to accept the post of "Secretary & Librarian" from October 1917.

Work there, evidently, did not satisfy her patriotic fervor. On Easter Sunday 1918 she wrote to Sidney Ball, then president of Barnett House. *I am very reluctant indeed to write this letter; but I feel bound to ask you, as Chairman, how you think the Council of Barnett House would look upon a request to release me for more immediate service to the War. This was not in my mind at the end of term: I was, and am, convinced that the work of Barnett House is important for the future of the country, and I was content to be helping in it, if I could give you satisfaction. But the losses of the past week, and the consequent need to replace men in large numbers in the auxiliary services and* in agriculture have, I think, altered the proportion of duties, so that other work less important in the long run than yours, has become very much more urgent. It seems to me that the library work might properly, in the present emergency, be postponed, and the work of correspondence, arranging meetings, and answering enquiries might be done by someone who was not free to leave Oxford.

I recognize fully that the decision rests with you and the Council of Barnett House; you engaged me for a year, and I cannot well leave unless you think it right, under present circumstances, to let me go. Also it is clear that I could not expect you to keep the place open for me, and I should very probably lose it; for which I shall be sincerely sorry.

You will believe, I hope, that I am most truly sorry to make this proposal; I think it will be annoying for you to be asked to make a change now, but also I believe you will think that the change of circumstances justifies my asking you to make it.

Should the Council decide to release me, I should venture to suggest that they should let me go by the first of May, when the term's lectures and so on would be arranged for the notices sent out. I could come to Oxford ten days before term to get well forward: or perhaps it would be more reasonable to ask for a date just after the Annual Meeting. (University of Oxford, Dept. of Social Studies and Social research, Barnett House, Easter, 1918)

Sidney Ball responded with great respect for her intentions and judged that the institution would survive. I was rather overwhelmed by your letter, but I quite appreciate your patriotic motive, though I hope only our temporary loss will be the country's gain. You have, moreover, done much for Barnett House and are leaving it in such a high state of efficiency that we ought to be able to keep it going by some temporary arrangement. We shall be quite grateful for your proposed ten day visit as this will enable you to put us in order for the term, so that we could release you by May 1st as you desire. (ibid. 3 Apr. 1918)

Freire-Marreco's response to Ball expressed her gratitude, but provided no real information as to her future: I am most grateful for your kind answer: it is very good of you to release me, and in such a generous way. I am going to London on Monday for interviews, and if possible, I will get the

*preliminaries arranged and pass the medical examination before the 18th. I wish
I had done many times more for the House, and I shall find it difficult to tell you
how sorry I shall be to leave it, and how glad I am that you give me a hope of
coming back to it afterward.*

*P.S. What about my Monday evening opening of the Library? If it can
still be done, I want to send out the notices for it now; if not, I must send excuses
to those who have accepted. Don't you think it could be managed with volunteer
or student help?* (ibid. 5 Apr. 1918)

The letter to Ball gives no clues as to what she was anticipating
and one wonders what she was planning for which she needed to take a
physical exam. It is clear, however, she was not able to devote much time to
her chosen field of work during the war years due to patriotic employment
obligations.

**Wearing a hat, an academic and business like Barbara Freire-Marreo at the
University of Oxford's Barnett House in 1918 where she worked for a short time
during World War I. Courtesy of Anthony Marreco.**

🦋 🦋 🦋

Although dated only Fourth of July and addressed to a Mr. Walter, this letter was sent to the Museum of New Mexico. It is headed Potter's Croft, Woodham Rise, Woking and was obviously written after the start of World War I. It shows Freire-Marreco's generosity and her warm feelings toward the United States.

*Allow me to send this trifling contribution to the general expenses of the Museum, to set against the postages you so kindly pay for me. The parrot feathers you were good enough to send to Santo Domingo arrived safely and gave much pleasure, but the packet to Hano was lost in the mail, sad to say.*

*The Fourth of July has been kept by us with real depth of feeling, if quietly. In this little town, where there are no U.S. soldiers, we had church services in honor of the day; but in larger centers, of course, there were more outward signs of festivity. My only Fourth of July in America was spent on the Pajarito Plateau, and was decidedly "safe and sane."*

*You will do me a real kindness if you will give my name to any soldiers of your acquaintance from Santa Fe, who are coming over, in case they should be in England. Perhaps some Mexicans who do not speak English well might be glad to have someone to correspond with in Spanish. I scarcely hope for a Pueblo Indian.*

*Please remember me to Julian and Maria Montoya, if they are still with you.*

*We are going to live in London shortly, but letters to this address will be forwarded.* (Museum of New Mexico, Hewett, ND)

ᔑ ᔑ ᔑ

Undated correspondence between Freire-Marreco and John Myres at Oxford University's Bodleian Library written during or just after World War I, mostly concerned arrangements for anthropological meetings and publication corrections. In all probability they met at these meetings and there was little spare time during the War for writing long discussions.

It is surprising that only one letter from Henry Balfour, then curator of the Pitt Rivers Museum in Oxford, could be found in view of the fact that they had been students at the same time and she donated so much of her collected Native American material to the Pitt Rivers Museum. In all probability they met now and then at events of mutual interest. From that Museum he wrote: *I am snatching the first moment I have had for answering your letter as I have been tied up with a man from the . . . Hills whose information is most valuable and I have had to get all I could of him while he is here.*

*I would very much like to have the specimens you so kindly offer as I think that they will all fit into a series here. The prisoner's camp money will be a nice addition to the series of our emergency currencies that I am getting together.* This donation is not the American Indian items she had collected when visiting the United States. The date, July 18 1918 or 1919, is later than the 1910—1913 contributions. How she had come by this German money is not known, probably from a returned war veteran.

*Where are you moving to?* he continued. *I suppose that your war-work has now come to an end. Mine practically has. It very nearly finished me last winter.*

*I am rather anxious about your last manuscript catalogue* (probably a Native American collection she was donating to the Museum) *and I hope to get it back when you have had time to go over it. It is so often wanting for reference. I don't imagine, however, that you are blessed in spare time right now, if you are migrating.*

*I hope that you are very well and that we may see you before long in Oxford. With kind regards and many thanks.* (University of Oxford, Pitt Rivers School of Anthropology and Museum Ethnography, 18 July ca. 1918)

❦ ❦ ❦

When World War I ended, Freire-Marreco was free at last to pursue her vocation. Sometime in 1920 she received her Master's Degree at Oxford; her thesis examined Pueblo Government Organization. 1920 was the first year women were granted degrees at Oxford, probably because the University finally recognized the ability and worth of women, their having proved their abilities with contributions during the recent war. That year was notable for the many women who finally were awarded their degrees, women who had already completed the required work and received diplomas.

Although she was not the first woman to set this precedent, Freire-Marreco was the <u>first woman anthropologist graduate at Oxford,</u> becoming an example to women who followed her. One such was Maria Antonina Czaplicka, 1884-1921, who also held the Mary Ewart Traveling Scholarship in 1914.having received her diploma in anthropology in 1912. Czaplicka distinguished herself as an anthropologist during a short career by lecturing, publishing and becoming an expert on Siberia. She and Freire-Marreco were not only colleagues but good friends as evidenced by a Barbara Aitken memorial fund in Czaplicka's name that was established after Czaplicka committed suicide at the age of 37.

❧ ❧ ❧

During her two trips to the United States, Freire-Marreco had used her time well, observing and experiencing Pueblo cultures and establishing a rapport with American colleagues. She was always generous with the knowledge she acquired and shared with those who sought it, demonstrating a professional attitude that earned her a fine reputation and respect from associates on both sides of the Atlantic. Her expertise and cooperation was acknowledged in numerous letters.

William Ridgeway of Cambridge University, who possibly once defeated her application for a scholarship, asked for her input on Hopi shrines for one of his projected works. Any animosity she may have felt toward Ridgeway for probably squashing her original plans to study tragedy must have been forgotten. Now <u>he</u> was consulting <u>her.</u> Obligingly she responded to his request along with a few of her photographs accounting for the fact that they are now located at the Museum of Archaeology and Anthropology, University of Cambridge Library.

She wrote: *I send you the two Hopi stories—please do me the honor of using them in any way, only leaving me the right to republish them in my book.*

*The conclusion of each story is the relevant part, but I have written out one of them in full so that you may see the general character of the stories. They are given as nearly as possible in the interpreter's own words. Some Hopi migration stories are preserved in dramatic ceremonies with regular parts, dresses and dialogue, but I have not heard of any dramas attached to the burial places of athletes.*

*The offering-places are well described in Fewkes' "Hopi Shrines near the East Mesa, Arizona," **American Anthropologist**, Vol. 8, No.2, April 1906 and a version of my second story appears on p.369 of that article. May I remind you also (in case you have not lately read them) of Fewkes' "Growth of the Hopi Ritual," **Journal of American Folklore**, Vol.XI, No. 112, 1898, and "An Interpretation of Katcina Worship," **Journal of American Folklore**, Vol.XIV, April 1901. He shows in these three papers that the beings worshipped at these offering-places are in many cases katcinas, and that the katcinas are identified with ancestors and the dead, and that the offering-places are entrances to the underworld. See particularly the last named paper, p.82. "You have become a Katcina; bring us rain," say the relatives of the deceased to the dead before they inter them.*

*Attached is a story to account for the abandonment of Payupki, a ruined village near the Second Mesa of the Hopi reservation, Arizona, told by Gunauja, a man of the Masau clan of Walpi (First Mesa). April 1913.* (Gunauja's picture is in Freire-Marreco's 1913 Album at the Pitt Rivers Museum, Neg. No. BS1.10.8.)

In the margin she added: *Fewkes says that Payupki was deserted in mid- XIII century and that the inhabitants went to Sandia in New Mexico.*

*I had been visiting the ruins, and on my return I remarked that an offering house of piled stones was clearly distinguishable in the middle of the* village. Gunauja volunteered that "once there was a race between a boy and a girl. The girl won. They dug a hole and buried her where you saw the offering-house.

"The next village" (also in ruins) "was called Pumpkin Seed Cliff. The boy and girl ran for their two villages. The boy was the Village Chief's son of one village, Payupki, and the girl was the Crier's daughter of the other.

"There was a hair-cutting katsina race, and the Village Chief's son was a fast runner, and caught many of the Pumpkin Seed Cliff runners and cut their hair. The Pumpkin Seed Cliff people got angry and planned that their girl should run. They let her practice running with her brother and then gave a challenge for another race. They dressed the girl separately in a house, not in the kiva and no one knew of it. The women made red and yellow wafers and sweet-corn dough, and carried them over to the other village. The girl was young—her breasts were only like a man's—and her father painted her yellow and dressed her in kilt and sash and fox-skin. Even the other runners (whom they were sending out from the Pumpkin Seed Cliff kiva) knew nothing of it. Her father told her to run and overtake the other runners and not to speak to them. When they spoke to her she only nodded. They wondered at her smooth skin. When the runners took their places in a row, she went and stood with them, and they were wondering who it could be, and thinking maybe a real one had come with them!

"When men are dressed as katsinas, they represent supernatural beings and must be treated as such. Only uninitiated children, and formerly women, believe that they _are_ supernatural; grown up people know them to be men in disguise; but there is always supposed to be the possibility that a 'real katsina' may appear. The others (at Payupki) were dressing in one of the chief's houses. Each side spread a blanket and laid down food for prizes. The procedure is that a runner takes a portion of food from the blanket belonging to his party and offers it to one of the other party. This is a challenge and the person challenged must race the challenger. The challenged person, if he wins, takes the food. But if the challenger is dressed as a hair-cutting katsina, when he catches his opponent he has a right to cut off a lock of his hair. In stories of the hair-cutter, if he abuses his power by cutting off the whole of his opponent's hair, this causes fatal quarrels between villages. When both sides have expended all their food the races are over.

"The girl ran fastest, and cut the hair of many runners. She gathered the hair in a bunch and came to the place where her father was waiting for her. Then her father dug a hole, arm-deep, and put the hair in it. They got happy.

"There was a girl, a fast runner, at Payupki too. Kalemsatiju (a man of Payupki) went to Pumpkin Seed Cliff and challenged them again, for four days later. The two girls were matched to run against each other. They (the people on either side) put down much turquoise and ear-pendants and beads and blue tunics and buckskins. They ran, and the Pumpkin Seed Cliff girl won by a little and they took lots of things.

"Then they planned another race, that girl against a boy. The Pumpkin Seed Cliff people were the challengers again. They were to run around a small isolated hill and come back. The girl practiced with her brother and beat him. They gave four days notice. Both sides wagered their heads. They put on their best clothes and took their tiponis with them (decorated ears of corn, the sacred insignia of chiefs), because they did not know whether they would live or die. They drew a line on the ground and the parties sat on either side of it.

"The boy was to run with a gourd-shaped cup (i.e. by the magic of it). The night before they had had a meeting and made it for him to run with, but the girl was to run with her own legs only. The night before neither side had slept, but waked, to see which side will win. On the boy's side there was an old man, the best man in the kiva because he was so old. But that night he was getting sleepy; he had never got sleepy before (at a ritual vigil), but this time he got sleepy, and the men scolded him, and he got angry and went out of the kiva. They were planning to make the cup for the boy to transform himself into it, to run; the old man went to his house and transformed himself into a very small white beetle, and came back into the kiva unseen, and went inside the cup, and cut up into small pieces the thing inside it that was meant to run fast, and came out again.

"The girl took some sweet-corn bread dough to a bird. The bird got happy. The bird told the spider too, and both of them were willing to help her. The spider sat on the top of the girl's ear. The girl put on her black woolen dress and coiled her hair up small and tight. They started to run, the girl and the boy. The grandmother (i.e. the spider) on the girl's ear was telling her what to do, and the bird too. The grandmother made a spider-string on the road, to hinder the boy who was ahead; the girl passed, the spider allowing her, while the boy was in difficulties with the web. The one that was in the cup had another plan—it had a kind of bird too; so, as it was in difficulties with the web, it came out of the cup and ran by foot a little way, and it got into the skin of another kind of bird, a kowili. It was crying, and soon it began to cry like a man, because it was a man inside. Then it came out of the bird and ran itself again.

"The girl came ahead again. The grandmother had warned her when the boy would try to shoot her, so then she flew higher." (A stock incident in race —stories.) "So she came first.

"The boy's people said, 'This is what we planned, so we are bound to have it done.' So they began to cut the heads off. Not in the middle of the village square, but out behind the houses on a flat rock; so the rock turned red, like blood.

"Afterward, the girl said to her people, 'Since they killed those people, maybe we did something wrong (maybe our causing their death was a wrong thing), so we will not stay here. Four days hence we will go away, because we had trouble here.' The girl said, 'You will not take me with you, because on account of me those people were all killed; but you will put me in the offering house in the middle of the village-square'—so they did—and from this time forward you will pray to me and ask me for rain.' So they went away; first to (where Winslow now is), and thence to some place we do not know, where all the people are dressed in white (i.e. Mexico). So now people pray to her for rain, and when it rains it always starts from that place."

She then recounted a story told by a man named Natu, of the Stick clan of Hano, the Tewa village on the First Mesa of the Hopi Reservation. The story, though told by this Tewa, is apparently a Hopi story. It is given here in outline.

"There were Hopi living on the terrace below the present site of Walpi; and other people, some Hopi, some of another tribe, lived at P'ot'ek'ege on the mesa to the east of Hano. They quarreled over races and beat each other's katsinas. The P'ot'ek'ege people sent a hair-cutting-katsina who cut off the head of a boy at Walpi. A Walpi girl, the boy's sister, dressed as a hair-cutting-katsina, went to P'ot'ek'ege, and killed the chief's daughter who was watching the races.

"Also, some people lived near the present site of Sitsomovi, at a place called Sae lae te, and the P'ot'ek'ege people treated them in the same way. They quarreled over a game of elu, which the Sae lae te people won. They challenged them to a race. The P'ot'ek'ege people persuaded the hawk to race for them, the Sae lae te people engaged the deer. Both sides bet their heads, and a knife was laid at the winning-line. The deer won by the magical help of the deer-people.

"There was a line drawn, and the deer just fell over the line and so got in first. Then they threw up the dirt, and were shouting and taking off their blankets and whipping each other with the blankets, and throwing dirt at each other.

"So they beat them again the third time. 'Well, we can't help it: this is the way we planned it, so we cannot say anything. So you can kill us all, and cut off our chief's head first.'

"The bird said, 'They will not kill his people: just kill me. I am the one that ran and did not come first, so I would rather be killed alone. When you kill me, take my heart and bury it here, and whoever walks near it can pray to me and be a fast runner and kill rabbits by running fast.'"

So he told his people they must not try to beat each other with any kind of game any more: "This is how you get angry with each other when one gets beaten." So they cut his head off, and took his heart and buried it in a hole forearm-deep, and built something like an offering-house there. And that is why the Hopi still pray there when any of them go walking early (an expression that describes athletes in training).

And round that offering-house they turn when they race (i.e. they use it as a goal). They say, "I'll be a fast runner just like you, and I'll kill a rabbit just like you;" and they sprinkle white corn-meal toward it. (Cambridge University, Museum of Archaeology and Anthropology Library, Ridgeway papers, 16 Jan. 1914)

These stories must have been exactly what he sought judging by Freire-Marreco's reply to Ridgeway's acceptance of her material: *I am delighted to know that you can make use of the stories—they will be preserved like flies in amber! Please use the illustrations too, 'though they are not as good as Fewkes' pictures—no doubt your publisher can arrange to leave me the right of reprinting them. I enclose a few more for your choice, but I think you have* the clearest ones already. They show the shrine in the plaza of Sitsomovi on the day of a dance, in preparation for which a branch of cedar has been fixed in the ground beside it. The clowns who accompany the dance make the shrine their rallying place, "their house," and collect beside it the food which is given to them; their leader sets up in the shrine the stuffed bird which at other times he carries in his belt. I *don't* seriously suggest a comparison with the satiric drama at the tomb! Except insofar that one must have a fixed spot for the performance, and the shrine is the obvious rallying-point in the plaza. But in the New Mexican pueblos, where the clowns make "their house" much more definitely with a fire, they don't make it near a shrine, (there being none visible in those New Mexican plazas, only in some of them, a stone representing the center of the world,) but against a wall.

You will see from Fewkes' papers that shrines, at which legendary athletes are commemorated, are rather exceptional. I only know the two of which you have the stories, though the conventional tone of these stories suggests that the idea is familiar to the people. Many shrines belong to the katsinas in general, and Fewkes shows that these are really ancestors; others belong to the Sun, others to Masauwu, the personified Great Dead Man.

Nor are these shrines the *only* entrances to the underworld; all springs of water are so regarded (Fewkes), and the miniature openings, *sipapu*, in the floors of the kivas (Mindelett, **8th American Report, Bureau American Ethnology**). There is also a distant, mythical sipapu where the people came up from the underworld before they began their migration to their present homes, while in one New Mexican pueblo at least there is a place at which (like the *mundus*) the dead are fed in November, with rites curiously suggestive of the Mediterranean. Fewkes and others call these erections "shrines." I do not think that he gives a general Hopi name for them: I was given tu tu' sh kya, but I see that Fewkes has astutushkia as the name of a particular shrine near Walpi. The corresponding Tewa term k a yet'ege means (at the) fetish house, (locative used as nominative as often in Tewa), kaye being a general name for queer stones, amulets, crystals, flint implements, carved figures of animals; the twisted stone which you will see in the photograph of the shrine at the Gap would be called in Tewa, a kaye. (ibid. 19 Jan. 1914) As the name indicates, the Gap was and is a break or cleave on the side of First Mesa and today remains a sacred site.

🦗 🦗 🦗

It is obvious that Freire-Marreco was devoted to her profession, so much so during the years she spent in the United States, that there are no entries in her **Verses, 1887 to 1953**. Not until she met and married Robert Aitken did she again write her personal inspirations.

### <u>Kissing Time: to an Irish air</u>

*When the gorse is out of bloom, then kissing's out of season:*
*So our mothers taught us in the old, sweet, song:*
*Now the gorse is all in bud, o surely that's the reason*
*You should kiss me ev'ry day and kiss me long!*

*Kiss me when the spring begins and when the autumn closes;*
*Kiss me for the last white frost, and through dark rain.*
*Kiss me when the heather's red, and kiss me for the roses.*
*When you've kissed the seasons out, o kiss them round again!*

*Kiss me just a little now, and twice as much tomorrow;*
*Kiss me when you think I'm right , and make me vain;*
*Kiss me once for happiness and twenty times for sorrow;*
*O, and when I'm wrong, o kiss me right again!*

*When the gorse is out of bloom, then kissing's out of season*
*So our mothers told us, and they can't be wrong.*
*When the gorse was all in bloom, o past all rhyme or reason,*
*Robert kissed me every day, and all day long.*

—Aitken, Verses 1920

## ✑ Marriage

In a 1920 letter to John Harrington, Barbara Freire-Marreco had announced her upcoming marriage and all correspondence after April 21, 1920 was signed Barbara Aitken. The marriage was solemnized at the Parish Church of Woodham, Surrey, Church of England.

On their marriage certificate her husband Robert Aitken, was declared a bachelor, age 37.He listed his profession as an Admiralty Clerk living at 25 Gower Street, London; his father was James Aitken, a draper. Barbara Whitchurch Freire-Marreco was a spinster of 40; the witnesses were W. Freire-Marreco, probably her father, and Constance Waggett from her mother's family.

The Aitkens' first home was at 11 b Belsize Square, Hampstead, a second floor flat in a still attractive and well-maintained house not far from London. Barbara Aitkens' correspondence came from this address for several years and inspired several upbeat entries in her **Verses, 1886 to 1953**. Here are two.

### Number Eleven
*To our American friends at 11 Belsize Square*

*Eleven's a good number: I thought it so, before, and since you've shared it with us I like it all the more. It hasn't Twelve's completeness—it's not mystical like Seven—there's a touch of expectation and hope about Eleven.*

*"Clear up before eleven" is the rule of the morning shower; and half the work of the world is done at the eleventh hour. Eleven thousand Virgins climbed the steep ascent of heaven, and of the twelve Apostles the true hearted were eleven.*

**Barbara and Robert Aitken at St. Valery sur Somme, France on May 31, 1924 four years after they were married. Courtesy of Anthony Marreco.**

*Eleven is the November month, when "Better Times" begin, and wrongs*
*go up in the bonfires and new magistrates come in. And November is all for*
*remembrance, with the Saints, and the Day of the Dead, and the solemn sweet*
*Thanksgiving, when your Country bows her head; and that blessed, blessed*
*November day, the best that our eyes have seen when heaven and earth were*
*joyful together—Eleven, Eleven, Eighteen.*

—Aitken, *Verses*, 1924

### Virtue

*With a cold in the head*
*Should one linger in bed*
*And allow the Aesthetic full play, Sir?*
*No, the virtuous course*
*Is to hitch the Winged Horse*
*And proceed to the tasks of the day, sir.*

*When the rest of the staff*
*Cough whenever they laugh*
*And are full of your microbes and germs, sir,*
*You may possibly find*
*They are much of my mind*
*And think <u>virtue</u> too dear on such terms, sir.*

—Aitken, *Verses*, 1920

Robert Aitken was a tall Scotch Presbyterian with a noticeable accent and engaging laugh. Their housekeeper of eighteen years described him as one of the kindest men that ever lived, a *lovely man*. Only once did she ever hear him shout at his wife followed quickly by, *My dear, I should not have raised my voice to you*. When Edward, the British king, died in 1953, Aitken's sympathetic comment was, *That poor girl*, referring to Elizabeth who was so young to have the responsibilities of a queen. Compassionate, he became upset when grocery stores were departmentalized which he considered an infringement on green grocers, butchers, etc. He was adamant in his opinion that each should be allowed to specialize.

Only one flaw was found about Robert. Always frugal after a Spartan childhood, he once embarrassed their young nephew, Anthony Marreco, by proceeding to take a sausage out of a paper bag to consume in a Stockbridge restaurant. He also complained that their house was always too warm, having endured a cold and damp climate in his youth.

Primarily a geologist, Robert had interests in other scientific fields. He was considered an authority on plows, having published in the Encyclopedia Britannica on that subject. The Aitkens made many trips to Spain in support of his work, sometimes as a surveyor and at least one concerning methods of irrigation. The province of Burgos (Old Castile) was their main destination.

These were also recreational trips and the Aitkens developed a great fondness for Spanish food and wine variously described as "plain" or "peasant food" that Barbara produced laboriously in heavy iron kettles. She was not considered a good cook.

Surprisingly they supported the Franco regime, and considered themselves politically liberal and because of their Spanish connections they were once accused of being spies which fortunately proved to be a short lived rumor. Steadfastly, they supported the British Crown and were considered conservative in most respects during their later years.

It was a well matched, successful, and loving marriage. They were of equally high intellect that was retained into old age, sometimes conversing in Latin and making a practice of always making time for reading after dinner. *Intellectual without conceit* was a term used by an acquaintance to describe them. Gifts of mutual interest were exchanged.

> *To Robert with an etching of the Bridge at Zaragoza*
> *"Every man a priest in his own house"*
> —Aitken, *Verses*, 1928

From a distance they were judged to be reserved, but they had similar senses of humor, often sharing private jokes. Robert liked to tease, claiming Barbara wrote to him when they were courting complaining that she only saw him on the Saint's Days that were holidays and she wished to remind him there were minor Saint's Days also. Demanding of herself, she expected the same of others.

The Aitkens' shared the same religious beliefs. Those who remember Barbara described her as *church minded*, also *sore on the Bible*. At the dedication of a new church, she became incensed by a man who sat on the altar. She dashed up to him, physically grabbed him and forced him down, causing quite a commotion and demonstrating her strength and determination. *Strong minded, determined and forceful* were terms also attributed to her. However she did not evangelize or *play missionary*, rather, other beliefs were tolerated. *She shared without show.* Modest, she did not discuss her personal life and kept her accomplishments confidential.

There were no progeny, not through choice. One of Barbara's endearing traits was the manner in which she treated children, *never talked down to them.* With empathy and compassion she voluntarily conducted Bible and Nature studies for neighbor children.

*The Ten Commandments Explained for Christian Children*
*(adapted from a Jesuit mission hymn)*

> *Ten great commandments God has given*
> *To those who heed his call,*
> *To guide them on the way to heaven;*
> *And I can say them all.*

> *1. The first, from which the others start*
> *Holy, just and true –*
> *Is worship God, with all your heart*
> *And mind and body too.*

2. Remember, God is King of Kings;
   He cannot share His throne
You must not worship men, or things,
   But worship God alone.

3. When you must name the Name of God,
   Say it with reverent care.
Speak truth, keep promises; and then,
   There'll be no need to swear.

4. To church on Sundays you should go
   To praise God and to pray,
And needless work you must not do
   Upon God's holy day.

5. Young scholar, do as you are told –
   The rule has always been;
Obey your parents, mind the old,
   Honour your Church and Queen.
And, when you're all grown up, rich and strong,
   Then it will be your turn
To save the weak and poor from wrong
   And help the young to learn.

6. You have not strength to wound or kill,
   Nor would you be so mad;
But cruel words and wicked will,
   Christ said, are just as bad.
Be good to people, beasts and birds
   And every living creature,
Since God has put mankind in charge
   To rule for Him in nature.

*7. One marriage bond God's law allows*
  *One husband with one wife:*
*So, if you take the marriage vows,*
  *Remember, it's for life.*
*Keep mind and body clean and straight,*
  *Fit for the years to come,*
*Then, when you reach the married state,*
  *You'll make a happy home.*

*8. You must not steal—not even a sweet,*
  *An apple, or a shilling.*
*At school and games you must not cheat;*
  *Be generous, fair, and willing.*
*Don't be like dogs about a bone,*
  *Thievish, or mean and greedy.*
*Leave other people's things alone*
  *And share yours with the needy.*

*9. A false excuse is sin and shame;*
  *All lies a sin I call:*
*But lies to get another blamed,*
  *Those are the worst of all!*

*10. How mean is he who idly stands*
  *And envies others' wealth!*
*If you have brains and feet and hands,*
  *Go, earn some for yourself!*

*Ten great commandments God has given*
  *To those who heed his call,*
*To guide them on the way to heaven;*
  *And now I've said them all.*

—Aitken, *Verses*, 1938

After marriage, and as time distanced her from her American sojourns, there was little tangible evidence of Barbara Aitken's work in the United States. Memories of her experiences with Pueblo people and her fondness for them remained with her. They were even with her in dreams.

### Indian Friends Remembered

Grey, pungent, dry
The English wood smoke blew out in a spire
To catch me walking by;
And o, I stood beside an Indian fire!

How many years?
Thirteen—no fourteen, fifteen long, full years.
A stranger I should come
To those dun roofs I once called "home"
Better, perhaps, away.
And seldom now I wander, dreaming,
Past houses somehow dim, estranged in feeling,
And wake unsatisfied to English day.

Yet, where the candles shine
Over the common Bread and Wine,
Brothers in faith, I think I see you there,
I count you one by every one . . .
The girls—dark flowers on the ground:
The men in a long line
Standing with downcast, wistful air:
The earrings, and sleek parted hair
Of the grey sacristan.

"Lift up with your hearts!"
The great earth-circling word
That moves at the sun's pace through all earth's parts
Makes here its pause; and here, as there, is heard.
"We lift them up—we lift them up unto the Lord."

See how apart, intent,
The old cacique kneels.
Like some dull cunning child
He seems, half sullen and half wild,
Yet now to reverence bent,
Kneeling as if he feels
Here in the mass some power that heals
The hurt of his long life so strangely spent.

What thoughts of an unknown God
Are yours, old foolish heathen priest?
No thoughts? But at the least
Feet that long paths have trod,
Hands beating at the unseen door;
Eyes not unused to weep nor voice untaught to groan;
Surely a humble heart, that bows before
This mystery not your own.

The picture's gone.
A dream, that has no consummation,
A mass without a consecration,
Half seen, half done.

O, just in last night's dream I walked alone,
Hurrying, till some harsh limit should expire,
Hunting through houses where I once had friends,

*And found all young, all busy, all unknown:*
*But at the ditch, where the pueblo ends,*
*I found the house at last –*
*Kind clasping arms and voices of the past –*
*And thought, Here nothing's changed, but all stands fast.*
*And there sits Filomena by the fire,*
*And in one moment now she'll turn her head –*
*But Filomena's dead*

—Aitken, *Verses,* 1926

While memories were still fresh in her mind, her American Indian collections and photographs, dated from the 1911 and 1913 U.S. trips, along with written explanations, had been deposited in Oxford's Ptt Rivers Museum. Continuing her relationship with that Museum, she helped succeeding curators without compensation. Much of her work has been continued and built upon by anthropologists and ethnologists that followed her and is now common knowledge. She was not one to ask for credit.

Robert, however, had never been to the U.S. and probably had never met a Native American. Understandably, Barbara's life took other directions. She did remain faithful to her British commitments, especially to the Royal Anthropological Society and the British Folklore Society.

Most of her correspondence survives in the Bodleian Library, Oxford University and is between her and her lifelong friend John Myres. The following letter was sent to him when he was visiting the University of California, Berkeley. *The Folklore Council goes on not very cheerfully; they are a low-spirited crowd; but the attendance at meetings is improving a little. If only we could catch up the arrears of publication!*

*I rejoice to think of you at Berkeley, and make no doubt they are enjoying you. Do you happen to see a Mr. Strong, who has done a very interesting interpretation of Southwestern social history in the January number of the* **American Anthropologist**? *The only criticisms I would make are:*

*(1) Should he not deal in some way with the question of linguistic nearness cut across by difference in social organization? Are not his Shoshonean,*

Uto-Aztecan, and _all_ the Pueblo languages, ultimately Uto-Aztecan? And within the large divisions, Hopi, Zuni, Tanoan and (Tewa and Tiwa) very close indeed?

(2) His ingenious scheme of the Eastern and Western pueblos as branching to matrilineal and patrilineal organization respectively from "early Pueblo" times is invalidated by the very grave doubt whether patrilineal descent and male house-owning in the Eastern pueblos is any older than the Spanish influence. Besides more debatable evidence in the way of kinship terms, son-in-law inheritance, and marriage customs observe the XVI century missionaries say that all house-building was done by women. House-building and ownership go together in the west now, and presumably went together in the east then. Even now in the east it is the women specialists who build chimneys; and when a man builds a house he says to his wife, "This is your house, fix it inside as you like," and the crops once inside the house are nominally his wife's property.

E. G. Torquemade, **Monarquia Indiana, 1612.** "Ellas son las que hacen y edifican las casas, asi de piedra como de adove y tierra amasada." (Loosely translated: The women are the ones that build houses, here it's like adobe bricks.) Referring apparently to the Tewa near San Gabriel. And Benavidas, 1630, to the effect that all the mission churches have been built by women, for the men do no such work, and if we force them to it, the women laugh at them and they flee from it.

No more; must write the Society's letters now. We have hopes of starting either for Majorca or for a second visit to High Castile this Saturday—or else we may not: you cannot tell certainly which!

I should like to send my kind remembrances to Dr. Kroeber, please.

We have had a jolly session under Malinowski, and a very lively Anthropological Society meeting monthly; the papers good that is, but the debating rotten. The subject has been contact between civilized and uncivilized peoples, and a subject running through the whole session's work certainly makes it more interesting. (Bodleian, Myres, ND)

🦋 🦋 🦋

Only one letter was found from Barbara to her Uncle Philip Waggett, the renowned vicar with whom she had a close relationship. The contents have little connection to her work with Native Americans and are mainly concerned with the state of religion in Spain. From the long and interesting letter written in 1928, one comparison to Catholicism as practiced in Spain to that in New Mexico is noted here. *People's behavior in church was notably quiet and reverent, and they are anxious for the credit of the town, that it should be thought so. The clergy here, and indeed in all Castile, seem to be entirely respectable and are spoken of as such. We were in no Castilian town or village where mass was not said reverently and carefully, and the cathedral clergy at Burgos* (about 25 miles north of Madrid on the main route to the French border) *and Santo Domingo de la Calzada,* (near Lograno) *celebrated with particular devoutness, I thought. But this is rather an impertinent thing for a visitor to say; and you must excuse it, please. I only mean that it felt like a nice church at home and not like Roman services in New Mexico.* (Anthony Marreco)

# ✍ The Broughton Years

The Aitkens bought a cottage in the Parish of Broughton in 1928.

### Broughton in 1937

Broughton's on the Wallop Brook
Among the grassy meadows;
There's <u>beauties</u> every way you look
(And many <u>handsome fellows</u>).
Like other villages and towns,
Broughton has its ups and downs,
And that is why, at the Julilee,
We all went up on the <u>Downs</u> to see.

North End Broughton's brick and thatch:
The houses are so pretty;
They're painted yellow, all to match!
You'd think you're in a city.
Along the street the stranger marches,
Admiring all (except "The Arches")
Until he comes quite unaware,
To Broughton's central space, the Square.

Lower End, brick, thatch and chalk,

Is a pleasant way to take a walk,
But Rookery Lane's the sweetest spot –
To live there is a happy lot!
Up Dog Lane and past the Pound
Will lead you to the rising ground
Where, turning southward, if you will,
You view the church from Broughton Hill.
Trees hide the old Church Farm mayhap,
But Broughton House shows through a gap,
And all the village like a map.
Aren't they busy down the Hollow?
Six houses built, and more to follow!
Ana, when we get the Council Scheme,
Life will be One Glorious Dream.

Let me make a second start.
You'll be tired of hearing,
But, when a subject's near my heart,
I can't help interfering:
Broughton wants—what do you think?
Broughton wants—water to drink!
More water, first of all;
Drains, if they can get a fall;
And lower prices for this Hall.
And while you're marking time on these,
Clear the ivy off the trees
And shoot the starlings, if you please.

Broughton is a pleasant place,
Especially on Sunday;
Broughton wears a smiling face
From Saturday to Monday.
Broughton church bells fill the street,

*(And ringers are so tireless),*
*And Broughton chapels sing so sweet*
*You'd think it was the wireless!*

*At two o'clock, all clean and neat*
*Twenty lads walk up the street.*
*They walk to Nine Mile, sun or rain,*
*And then, they all walk back again!*
*While lovers tell the old, old story,*
*Round and round, by Timon's Glory.*

*Broughton is a liberal place,*
*To no good cause refusing.*
*They give to all with a good grace:*
*The number is confusing.*
*On Church and Chapel I'll be mute,*
*But Legion! Union! Institute!*
*Girl Guides!*
*Mystery rides!*
*Whist Drives here and Whist Drives there –*
*Money's wanted everywhere!*
*Somehow money's always found.*
*Broughton is—Tom Tidler's Ground!*

—Aitken, *Verses,* 1937

This part of England can be dated to about 1200 B. C., by evidence of primitive earth works. Later it was inhabited by Romans and then Saxons. Today, the residents take pride, not only in preserving its history, but also in keeping it a desirable place to live. It was awarded Hampshire's "Best Kept Village" award in September 1989 by **Hampshire County Magazine,** honoring its litter-free natural environment and maintenance of its well-kept homes and gardens.

The charming village of Broughton in Hampshire has changed little since this pre 1953 picture was taken when the Aitkens lived there. Photograph by J. Blair from a postcard by Frith's BGN3, Courtesy of Pablita Velarde.

In the Aitkens' time, as today, Broughton villagers enjoy a quiet life supporting two churches, a couple of pubs, and a few clubs and societies. Broughton suited the Aitkens' lifestyle and credit must be given them for their contributions to the intellectual life there and the preservation of its history. St. Mary's Anglican Church, established about 1340 with the present structure built in 1680, was one of the Aitkens' main interests in their later years. The Baptists of Broughton remember them helping their church as well as the Anglican one.

Another postcard, this photograph of Broughton includes Kent's Close on the left.
Photograph by J. Blair from a postcard by Frith's BGN3, Courtesy of Pablita Velarde.

Originally a small one room building in the eleventh century, Saint Mary's Church in
Broughton, Hampshire was enlarged in the fifteenth century. It was supported by
the Aitkens in regular attendance as well as financially. 1989 photograph by J. Blair.

Their home, Willianmarse cottage, later renamed Kent's Close by the Aitkens, was built by a John Kent in 1787, probably as a storehouse. It has an historic listing and looks as a storybook English cottage should, even though the thatched roof has been replaced by shingles for fireproofing and to discourage rodents as well as to protect a water supply stored on the roof from nesting birds. The rooms are cozy with low ceilings, reportedly quite dark when the Aitkens lived there.

Willianmarse in Broughton was the name of the house when the Aitkens bought it. They renamed it Kent's Close after its builder and original owner. Dated 19-12-47?, the artist's signature on this pencil drawing is illegible. Courtesy of Robert Parr.

Cats named "Willian" and "Marse" are remembered by the folk in Broughton. There must have been a series of cats in the Aitkens' lives as evidenced by Barbara's poetical tribute to two.

### To Dr. Meikle's Cat Removed to Edinburgh

*Sweet Jacob! Have you learnt to purr*
*With an authentic lowland burr,*
*While broader mewings testify*
*You've changed your nature with your sky?*
*No, puss; we hardly credit that,*
*You'll live and die a Cockney Cat,*
*And over the Midlothian fells,*
*Listen for echoes of Bow Bells.*

—Aitken, Verses, 1927

### To "Mustard," killed on the road

*Goodbye, the yellow cat! Hard luck, to part*
*With one who gave you all his little heart*
*And told you frankly, with those shining eyes,*
*He found you good and funny, kind and wise.*
*On every friendly knee by turns he sat*
*(As one not proud, altho' the Rector's cat).*
*This was the sweeter side of nature's plan -*
*Eden unshattered—beast at home with man.*
*He knew no creature that was not his friend,*
*And life, if short, was merry to the end.*

—Aitken, Verses, 1929

The Aitkens lived simply, never owned an automobile and installed a telephone only in their declining years. They refused to have electricity in their home until an incident with an oil lamp almost destroyed them and their house. They were, however, generous in giving of themselves and their time, befriending many. Broughton residents today remember the books that lined the walls of their home. Though they lived frugally, they were also kind and generous, giving books to institutions and friends on both sides of the Atlantic as well as befriending those in need.

Barbara oversaw what was called a "thrift club" in Broughton to raise money for coal to benefit those who couldn't pay for heat. What was called "the foot clinic" was a result of Barbara paying a podiatrist to come to town by taxi (because there was and still is no public transportation to Broughton) to treat those in need. An obituary in the December 1967 *Parish Magazine* observed that her contributions were directed toward education and social improvement.

❦ ❦ ❦

From Broughton Robert Aitken wrote a series of letters to John Myres to discuss his aims for employment, seeking advice and aid. Finding work for which he was qualified seemed to be a problem and at one time he had a breakdown, possibly both physical and mental, but always seemed able to recover his health. He worked mainly as a geographer, making various contributions in scholarly writing and community activity. His later letters also made mention of Barbara's deteriorating health.

He performed a variety of jobs, and in spite of a World War I foot injury, he walked long distances in his spare time, covering many miles to other Hampshire towns, as well as hiking and then mapping the footpaths.

The only correspondence found from Robert to Barbara was written as he was returning from a trip to South Africa. Though his handwriting is difficult to decipher, it was an account of his activities and is the best insight we have of the man Barbara married, clearly showing love and tenderness for his wife as well as the compassion they shared for people who were misunderstood or maltreated. This letter also mentions that the militaristic intentions of Germany were growing bolder and more fearsome week by week. The stress in England was palpable.

T.S.S. *Nestor: The Blue Funnel Line.* 14 September 1938.

*Darling, it will be a comfort to me to write to you today, though it can't be posted for more than a week (at Madeira). The wireless news, to the effect that . . . has broken off negotiations, is so serious that I suppose we must now face up to dealing with the contingency thought of during the last six months. We have had long enough to brace ourselves, however, and God will help us to meet all that is coming, even personal losses and the destruction of things. . . .* (A reference to the approaching World War II)

*We have had a most fair passage of the first week of our return voyage, we pass the line (equator) tomorrow, so it is now very warm. We spent two nights on the train, very uncomfy, for Capetown. It was a very interesting time. . . .*

*The heat was terrific there, and the dust; but we had a glorious experience in driving up to a maximum height above what they call the Valley of. . . I can give you no idea of the grandeur or sense of our smallness, in view of the relics of the terrific convolutions of nature which had left them towering columns of rock and chasms, and piled boulders. A troop of baboons was also over on the hillside climbing about. The climb and the view (not the baboons) really was a "luminous experience."*

*At Capetown one night, in a comfortable hotel, which was extremely acceptable after the African Railways; while there we met . . . wife of the commissioner for Indians in South Africa. The charm and elegance (and brains probably) surpassed anything else we met, but she may not enter a public library, or do various other things in Capetown, because she is a "non-European." The plight of the Indian is very bad indeed, under all sorts of harsh restrictions, but she doesn't see much hope of its being bettered. Visited the House of Assembly and then entertained by Mr. Ballinger, one of the three members representing Native interests (the unsatisfactory exchange given them for the Cape franchise) a Somervillian . . . a Mrs. Mitchell . . . a South African, but British in breadth of idea (the Dutch are quite incredible, though she says things are improving) took us out the last day, and showed us C. Rhodes Memorial, the University, and Fort Constantia the famous Dutch Winery and dwelling—an exquisite piece, till one saw the slaves quarters underground. . . .*

Cecil John Rhodes, 1853–1902, a British financier and politician, was a controversial figure. Reputed to be a statesman or unscrupulous speculator, he promoted British domination in south Africa where he made a fortune in diamond mining.

*The attitude of many Dutch to the colored people is like that of the Germans to Jews—but they haven't yet been allowed to proceed against them on those terms and perhaps will not, so long as they need servants and farmhands. However the Cape is spending . . . and just on new housing estates, which Doctor Mitchell rightly says is a big step forward. Their daughter, an Octavia Hill trainee under an excellent person out from England, is working on one of them. It is in the country that the housing is most disgraceful: I suppose that the Dutch farmer is . . . the most backward conservative in all belonging to his entourage in the world...*

*I wrote an account of . . . at a place called Riverdale for the* **Capetown News***. . . .; if it comes out tell me. It was extraordinarily impressive.*

*I must tell you about the more inner things of the visit when we next meet. I have widened my mind considerably, I do hope, but curiously enough realize, more than when I started, that I am an old lady in the eyes of the next generation ahead. (Somebody joined in 60 the other day!)*

*How are you, darling? "In these bad days" . . . I'd scarcely have believed I would feel so inwardly calm. May all the hurtful things be kept from you, and may we have the opportunity of serving our fellows, and keep wrath from our hearts. When you get this, things may be worse—or better; but there can be no permanent improvement while their swollen armies and air forces exist; that one has always known. I will hope . . . The Nestor will reach Liverpool on the 27ᵗʰ.*

(Anthony Marreco)

# ✐ World War II

In 1939, as anticipated, Great Britain was again at war with Germany. Though the Aitkens were not in robust health, as English patriots they made contributions to the best of their abilities. Kind and generous, they proved themselves to their community by refusing to accept more than their ration of food, even if available to them. When relatives sent food from New Zealand, they shared it with their fellow villagers. Besides continuing their church functions and maintaining the foot clinic, they added other war-related activities.

They shared their home with three girls, evacuees from the heavily bombed port city of Portsmouth. Barbara is reported, by present-day Broughton residents, to have been demanding of these girls, both with household chores and academics, but she also gained their respect and gratitude. She insisted that they use proper English, and one of their activities was the production of theatrical performances. One such dramatic recitation titled *"Portsmouth by the Sea,"* composed and produced by Barbara Aitken, traced Portsmouth's connection with the Royal Navy from the time of Henry Tudor to the present. This is recorded in her **Verses, 1886 to 1953**.

Efforts to locate women in Portsmouth with maiden names of Eileen, Margaret and Jessie Simmins were not successful. In all probability they had changed names by marriage or moved to another location.

Evidence of another of Barbara's World War II activities is in a letter from Robert to John Myres. *Barbara is as well as she usually is, although a holiday we had hoped to take has not materialized. She spends much time as la patronne at the cash-box in our Canteen, where there is not much opportunity for ethnographical observations, as you will appreciate.* (Bodleian, Myres, 21 Dec. 1943)

Not only did she give of herself, to the best of her ability, to her country's cause, she also recognized the contributions and sacrifices of others.

<u>Christmas Fires</u>
*For Mrs. Burgan, mother of a P. O. W.*

When the Christmas bells are pealing
 And the Christmas fires burn bright,
There's an ache at my heart, and a grief and a smart
 For my boy far away tonight.
There's a place too much at the table.
 There's an empty seat by the fire:
Yes, there's something I lack till the boy comes back –
The boy of my heart's desire.
 Bells of the birthday of Jesus
 Ring over the land and sea!
 Ring in his heart when we're far apart,
 Speak to his heart for me!

When the Christmas star is gleaming
 In the dusk of the wintry skies,
I look and I yearn, but the shadows return,
 And the teardrops dim my eyes.
For I gaze thro' a mist of sorrow
 At the spark of the heavenly fire:
Yes, the nights will be black till the boy comes back –
The boy of my heart's desire.
 Star of the stable of Jesus,
 Shine over the land and sea!
 Shine in his heart when we're far, far apart,
 Speak to his heart for me.

*When the Christmas songs are telling*
   *How the Saviour came to earth,*
*O, my heart flies for rest to that Babe at the breast*
   *And the mother that gave Him birth.*
*For her heart with my heart are meeting,*
   *And my heart is all on fire,*
*And I plead for a share in her love and her prayer*
*To the Son of her heart's desire.*
   *Mary, Mother of Jesus,*
   *Look over land and Sea!*
   *Mother and maid, let me not be afraid –*
   *Pray for my boy and me!*

                                        —Aitken, *Verses*, 1943

Even though there is no further exchange between Barbara Aitken and her contemporary American colleagues, her zeal to preserve information that might be of interest to succeeding investigators surfaced. In 1932 she donated The William Blackmore Collection to the Historical Society of New Mexico. William Blackmore, 1827-1879, was a British entrepreneur who, according to records, "promoted British and Dutch investment in Southwestern land. He began his career as a representative of English mining interests in New Mexico after the Civil War. He developed investment ventures in Colorado and New Mexico. His ventures involved Spanish and Mexican land grants."

How she acquired these papers is not known and some of the collection is missing, perhaps lost in transfer to the Museum of New Mexico History Library and subsequently to the State of New Mexico Records Center and Archives now shelved in Box #7—18.

🪶 🪶 🪶

Only only letter from Barbara Aitken to the United States

during the World War II years was written to W.W. Hill. The American anthropologist, 1902-1975, taught at the University of New Mexico for over thirty years and was Chairman of their Anthropology Department for over twenty. Among other publications he wrote **The Agricultural and Hunting Methods of the Navaho Indians.**

At the time he contacted Aitken, he was conducting field research on the Rio Grande Pueblos, particularly Santa Clara. He requested information for a work he had in progress. The material she sent was never published by him, as he died before his book was completed and his research is now housed at the Maxwell Museum of Anthropology, University of New Mexico. They were later incorporated in **An Ethnography of Santa Clara Pueblo, New Mexico**, Edited and Annotated by Charles H. Lange, University of New Mexico Press 1992.

Hill's acknowledgment of Barbara Aitken's Santa Clara information was not found, but her response showed her willingness to cooperate. *Thank you very much for your letter of 10th April received today. What you say of Santa Clara touches me deeply: I had not heard of the "Pueblo Constitution" except by some allusion in a letter from my "father" Santiago Naranjo; is it in print? And can I procure it? And what happened about the outrageous project of flooding the Indian lands? I suppose your T.S. Dozier's sons must be grandsons of my contemporary, the American who married a daughter of Domingo Gutierrez; and it is sad to think of Victoriano Sisneros as an old man. I admired him much, and thought him unusually frank and downright. When you are in the pueblo again, .please give my love and respects to him and all who kindly remember me, especially to all connections of Santiago, Leandro, and Domingo.*

*It is very satisfactory that an anthropologist who has the people's confidence should be working up Santa Clara—not the most romantic of the pueblos by any means, but I do think the "noblest" (in the Spanish sense of the word) ever since Benevides time! I venture to hope that you speak Spanish and can use it freely with the old people of the place.*

*Now what would you like me to do? I have no prospect of getting my own stuff ready for publication, but if I can take time from other work to put some of it roughly together so as to be useful to you, I will, supposing that you would be willing to use it with acknowledgments to Somerville College, Oxford. All my negatives are already at Santa Fe or Albuquerque, in Dr. Hewett's care.* These could not be located.

*I haven't any ceremonial information: I was trying to study village government. I have a fair lot of notes on the history of the partidos and their membership in 1911; descriptions of a few public dances, and of practices for them in the Summer Estufa; the text of the formulas used by the Gobernador in council (but not of the Capitan de la Guerra—will you be getting those from Victoriano who was Capitan in my time?); and some genealogies. I think it would be a good thing for you to go through Dr. Parsons work on the Tewa and correct it where necessary: in particular, we ought to protest against her theory that the Dual Organization among the Northern Tewa and the people of Taos and Picuris is a substitute for clan organization. It isn't so: one is a kinship system; the other is a ceremonial grouping of males, which has become so strong that it has thrown the kinship grouping into the shade. Even at Taos, J.P. Harrington found remains of clan consciousness.*

*I have published nothing on the Tewa beyond what you mention. The only thing I have in preparation is a paper on the kivas at Hano. And some war dance songs nearly ready.*

*P. S. What sanitary precautions do your wife and family take in a pueblo in summer? Daily prophylactic doses of T.C.P. Emulsion? I have never quite got over the intestinal infections picked up at Santa Clara. And is it still the case that the Summer People's well is non-alkaline, but the Winter People's agonizingly alkaline?* (Maxwell, W.W. Hill papers, 28 May 1948)

☙ ☙ ☙

Dr. Robert Parr, Broughton's physician for thirty years, now retired, not only tended the Aitkens' physical needs, but also was a friend who shared their interest in local history and town preservation. He recalled making house calls to Barbara and after attending to her medical problems, there always followed a "philosophical discussion" on a variety of subjects. He collected some of her undated writing done for local consumption as well as articles about her. Her sharp wit and sense of humor as well as a continued interest in linguistics is illustrated in the following observations she made.

The pronunciation of local families, in the generation now passing away sometimes justifies English spelling. These old people do not equate <u>died</u> with <u>ride, said</u> with <u>sed,</u> maid with made. Old Miss H. (died 1951, aged 80) said di-ed, ti-ed, etcetera, in a neat precise little voice, not at all broad, at least to "the gentry." She had a rich vocabulary. But so few people now keep pigs that the rich anatomical and culinary vocabulary is disappearing.

Being blind, Miss H. had never left home. Her sister (died 1951, age 85) had adopted the less careful pronunciation of the gentry. Old Mr. Barnes (a gardener) and Mr. Ray (rich farmer, Methodist preacher) speak Hampshire in all companies and in church, they divide the syllables and broaden the pronunciation, that is, ma-id, Ra-y, Ma-y. When the a and i are rapidly spoken they might be mistaken for Cockney vowels. Barnes' daughter (about 30) uses some of his household vocabulary without his broad speech—they have been away to service and returned here to marry: thus they always say "maid," not "girl," but whereas he says, "I got three ma-id, they pronounce, I've got three mades."

A. Butcher (40-50) speaks broad Hampshire in all company; as his father did, ma-an for man, ma-em not mum or mam. His boys say mam, a for yes, ee for thee. Ee is very common for nominative, accusative and dative in all generations—tell ee fer wy, children—ee hit we, us'll hit ee. So is the conjugation—I be, you be, he be, he iddn or he iddent, we be or we iddent/iiddn, you be, they be, they be iddent/iddn.

Vocabulary: Use of "our" with relationship terms and family names. The bilingual Mrs. Butcher tells me how she bought a pig's ear to stew and her little boy, seeing it on the stove, asked where she got it, and she told him for a joke that she had cut off their own pig's ears and tail to stew. The boy, indignant: "A'll tell our dad when he comes home!" The dad comes home. G. runs to meet him and says, "Our dad! Our mum bin'n cut off our pig's ear." Dad says, "Never mind, sit down 'n eat yer tea." G can't eat nothing, sits with big tears running down his face. "Our Dad, can I go outside?" G. goes up the garden in the dark and comes back smiling. "Our mum, our pig's ears growed a'ready 'n he've got 'e li'el tail that long!"

*Of the persons who speak "good Hampshire," some have H. vocabulary and H. pronunciation, some have one or the other. Some talk nothing but their natural degree of Hampshire, others (especially women who have been in service and, of course, school-children) are bilingual, speaking book English to the gentry. It is easier to conceal a vocabulary than a pronunciation. I have been surprised to find in common use, words that I supposed to belong to other regions. Daft = foolish, not learned from the wireless—she had known it all her life. Brogue = broad pronunciation.*

*Similarly, the word bulbeggar, said to be characteristic of Yorkshire, has been used at Horsell, Surrey time out of mind as the name of the local rustic bogey, giving its name to Bulbeggar Lane where it used to appear until about 1890. Diffusion seems improbable—these things seem to be islands of a submerged sea.*

*Another Hampshire oddity is the persistence of rustic speech in urban Portsmouth. Our evacuated children* (the above mentioned Simmins girls) *conjugated—I has-he have-we has, you have, they has; and never could be got out of it; and I am told that ten years ago Hampshire vocabulary and pronunciation were strong in the teachers training college.*

There are more of Barbara's observations on the lives and habits of the Hampshire people in Dr. Parr's collection including wine, ghosts, superstitions, some with humor

*Mrs. Stone had a sweet story of a former dairyman calling to enquire for her mother in law in a serious illness. Taking an affectionate leave of the daughter: "Well, goodbye, Miss Annie, you'll let me know when the funeral is!"*

*Mr. Beauchamp: When the nurse put on his left sleeve first: "I baint no gipsy! I was never born a gipsy! Only gypsies puts their left arm first into their coat."*

*Fleas: They say if you sweep your doorway outwards on May Day, you'll have no fleas in the house. But a rush of fleas into a house is a sign of a coming death. When Bert's father was laying ill, "the house swarmed with fleas: I had more than one good cry when I couldn't get rid of them, it seemed it must be so dirty. An old gipsy woman came to the door and was asked what to do—they often have good remedies. She only said, 'Don't you know what they means?*

Ah, you'll know by and by what they mean!'" As soon as Bert's father died they went way. But Nurse M. said to me, 'Mrs. B.,' she said, 'he's swarming with fleas, poor old man; very likely you can't see them, but I can. They're WHITE fleas, and they're swarming under his skin.'" (This of a patient who was kept admirably clean.) (Robert Parr)

Humor and whimsy, also, are in some of Barbara's **Verses, 1886 to 1953**. One would like to know what inspired them.

*Nonsense Rhymes*

Pretty Pussy, kittens' mother,
   Washed one kit and combed another.
When the kits were smooth as silk
   Pussy gave them bread and milk.
Pussy, Pussy, hunt the house!
   Feed your kittens with a mouse!
When the kits were on my lap
   Pussy went and set a trap.
When the mice were in their holes
   Pussy licked my porridge bowls.
When the mice were on the shelf
   Pussy ate the cheese herself!

—Aitken, Verses, 1953

*The Little People*

I found a fairy mushroom;
   I turned it inside out.
And what d'you think I found there?
   A little fairy Scout.
His hat, it was a withered leaf,
   His pole, a leaf of grass:
And he lit a fairy camp-fire
   For a fairy Second Class.

*I found another mushroom;*
  *I thought I'd look inside.*
*And what d'you think I found there?*
  *A little fairy Guide.*
*She tied a little fairy knot;*
  *She passed a tiny test;*
*And she got a fairy badge to wear*
  *Because she'd done her best!*

*I found another mushroom;*
  *I turned it outside in.*
*I saw a fairy Brownie*
  *No bigger than a pin.*
*She cooked a tiny pudding,*
  *She made a fairy's bed;*
*But they thought it was <u>her</u> bedtime*
  *And they tucked <u>her</u> up instead.*

*I found a great big toadstool;*
  *I turned it upside down.*
*I saw a fairy circus*
  *And a little fairy clown.*
*He turned a tiny somersault,*
  *He made a tiny joke:*
*And I don't know what else he did,*
  *For, just then, I awoke.*

—Aitken, *Verses*, 1951

As early as July 1946, Barbara Aitken wrote to her friend John Myres from a nursing home in Dorset and assured him that she was fast recovering from some undisclosed ailment and not long after the end of World War II her health seriously deteriorated. She suffered intermittently from various physical ailments, including migraine headaches for the rest of her life, her ill health described as "dark periods" by those who knew her. Letters written in the 1950s from Robert Aitken to John Myres, also make mention of Barbara's health problems.

The aging Barbara and Robert Aitken with unknown guests at Kent's Close, Broughton. Barbara needed canes while Robert seemed to be tenderly holding the child's toy animal. Courtesy of Joy Yates.

When she wasn't distracted by illness, Barbara's letters to Myres continued with discussions on many and varied subjects, with some of her American experiences surfacing now and then. One such letter recalled many tidbits of language and custom. *Ana and Kata: The Tewa have a similar use—to go into a building is always to go down into and to go out is go up and out. Pi: send, come or go up as hair from the scalp, of plants from the ground, of people from a house or lodge.*

*This applies to houses with doors as well as to houses with hatchways and to lodges with ladders through the smoke hole. But in the Pueblo country this is accounted for by a long history of underground or half-sunk men's lodges; with above-ground women's houses and storerooms, at first separated, at another period connected with the lodge, at another period separated again.*

Attached to this letter on a separate sheet, she compared Pueblo architecture to a Spanish farm house: *I saw a door in the living room wall that gave access to stairs leading to the attic. These stairs, being immediately above the main stairs (the space between walls allowing for a single width of stairs only) for which head-room had to be allowed, could not start from floor level; so the doorway was cut some way up the sitting room wall, and three wooden steps led up to the door. I suppose you might say that the top tread of this short stair formed an oaken threshold to the attic stairs on the further side of the door.* (Bodeian, Myres, St. Crispin's Day)

Another letter to Myres, was dated only Innocent's Day 1951: *Correspondence in **Man** the use of "native" (which surely should be a title of honor in contrast with "stranger") reminds me of Radcliffe Brown's first course of lectures at London School of Economics in 1911. An ironically polite Indian student interrupted him with, "I beg your pardon, what please is native? Natives of England?" Poor young R. B. was taken aback et se confondait en excuses.*

She discussed a variety of subjects with Myres throughout 1951 and 1952. (ibid. 4 Dec. and 10 Dec. 1951; 4 Jan., 6 Aug., and 11 Aug. 1952) *If the ethnologists have not been present at the invention of fundamental necessities by savages, they have many interesting inventions made by cross-fertilization or by stimulation through culture contact, for example, Canadian Indian embroideries adopted from the French.*

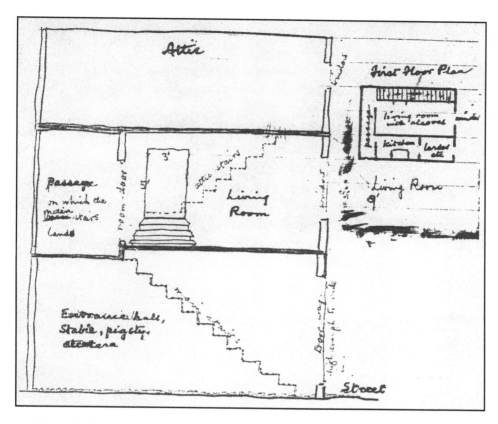

Sketch by Barbara Aitken in a letter to John Myres dated only St. Crispin's Day. This to compare the arrangement of doors and stairs in Pueblo architecture to those in a Spanish farmhouse. Courtesy of University of Oxford, Bodleian Library, Room 132 Duke Humphreys Library, Myers files.

Referring to Nampeyo, the famous Hopi-Tewa potter whose descendants carry on her tradition to this day, she said, *Nampaeju revived an extinct style of pottery from excavated fragments. Agayo, her cousin, under my eyes, adapted an embroidery pattern to a weaving pattern.*

*The Mongol Costumes book of course reminds me at once of your own work on prehistoric European costumes; trousers from leggings and trousers from breechcloths. You may see more than one process in the Pueblo-Navajo area:*

*(1) A wide soft pilch pulled up, back and front, over a string gets spread out and joined at the hips so that it looks like drawers.*

*(2) A three piece garment, of a pair of long leggings and a pilch, not sewn together but connected by the waist-string—rather like the parts of the embryo's skull.*

*Pueblo Indians who have adopted European trousers wear the Indian pilch under the trousers, some of them even in bed!*

Later in the year, Barbara's last-known letter was written to John Myres, her long time advisor, mentor, colleague and friend. She referred to her ongoing health problems.

*A week's illness has made me late in answering and thanking you. But it is now established that these affairs are not strokes but symptoms of long-standing toxemia; penicillin relieves the symptoms, and now let's hope a cure will be contrived.* (ibid. 10 Oct. 1952)

Myres died two years later, which must have been a great loss for the Aitkens, although there is no recorded evidence.

🦋 🦋 🦋

Dr. Edward P. Dozier had been a small boy when Freire-Marreco visited his home pueblo. Dozier, 1916-1971, the son of an educated father Thomas S. Dozier, was a cultural anthropologist. His contribution was in academics as he lectured, authored, and was associated at various times with the Universities of Oregon, Northwestern, Stanford, and Arizona where he established an American Indian studies program. Although Dozier was born and grew up at Santa Clara Pueblo, it was he who asked information from the British woman who had spent a comparatively short time there.

In 1954 he sent a manuscript he was writing for publication to England for Barbara Aitken's critique and she replied. The following exchange of correspondence shows that even though years and distance separated them, Aitken was informed on current happenings concerning Tewa anthropological research.

*Your manuscript and letter came this morning. I deny myself the pleasure of beginning to read this afternoon in order to get these notes finished and posted in the hope that they may be of use. Also I send some Santa Clara portraits, which you may perhaps like to use—Leandro Tafoya (mislaid: shall follow) as a young man; Francisco Naranjo as a young man; and some of the Council of 1911—Leandro (principal mayor), Santiago Naranjo (gobernador), Manuel Tafoya (a principal) and Victoriano Cisneros (capitan ala guerra). Also an attempt to photograph the gobernador in his house with the two varas hanging on the wall and some kind of sacred bundle which he hung in the corner very shortly after his appointment: I never ventured to ask what it was. (Photograph page 84)*

*Do you wish to use any of my Hano photographs? Of course they are all at your service.* (University of Arizona, Arizona State Museum, Special Collections, Edward P. Dozier papers, 19 May 1954. Hereafter cited as Arizona State Museum, Dozier)

On an attached undated sheet: *You will find my spelling very imperfect—it is a weak imitation of J.P. Harrington's. I find the loud, resonant speech of Hano easier to speak and to write down than the speech of Santa Clara. Some words baffle me entirely: I must leave it all for you to correct, and hope that you may be able to make use of it.*

These "notes" are long and detailed, and made from the ones she had made in 1910 and 1912-1913. Originally in Tewa, she had transcribed them into Spanish and then into English with a few Spanish and Tewa words remaining. They concern the organization of pueblo government including some phonetic language, and are well organized. Barbara Aitken should be credited with having made a large contribution to Dozier's work.

*Having posted a packet of notes on the consejos of Santa Clara this morning, I am able to settle down to enjoy the type-script which you are so kind as to lend me. I have also just now read the note which you sent to Dr. Leslie Spier.* Leslie Spier, 1893-1961, was an anthropologist specializing in, lecturing on, and publishing about southwest Native cultures having made numerous field trips in the United States and Mexico.

*Thank you very much for it. I am touched and happy to know that the kind people, both so kind and good in their very different ways, remember me with affection, and amused to know that they have built up a myth of my speaking Tewa well! Of course it isn't true. I could just make myself understood on simple household subjects, and understand what was said directly to me: and as for customs, well, at Santa Clara at least I was carefully guarded from knowing anything "important."*

*By this morning's post I had a kind letter from Dr. Leslie Spier proposing to send the journey-dream to* **Plateau,** *which of course I accept. May I ask Dr. Harold Colton to add what you say in your note about the two kinds of curer? I have been treated by the kind of curer who pinches out and blows away the cause of sickness.* (ibid. 22 May 1954)

Harold Sellers Colton, 1881-1970, a zoologist and archaeologist was a Professor at the University of Pennsylvania, Carnegie Institute, and later Director of the Museum of Northern Arizona where **Plateau** was published. He conducted excavations at Wupatki ruins, classified northern Arizona Native pottery types and was considered an authority on the identification of Hopi kachinas.

Aitken's next letter to Dozier recalled her happy memories of Santa Clara. *Thank you for your letter received today. How glad you and Mrs. Dozier must be to pass the summer in the clear sparkling mountain air of New Mexico, with those wonderful, transparent colored distances where clear rose color overlays clear pale blue without mingling, and the last silvery snows crown the Sangre de Cristo mountains! Would that I could see it again! But the remembrance of it is a lasting joy. Against that glorious background the slender girls in white boots, bright colored dresses and head shawls, with glossy black water pots on their heads, walking homeward from the well. The blue smoke rises from the earth colored houses. A clear orange fire shines from an oven door. I sit on the roof with Don Leandro looking down-river at the long green strip of irrigated ground. How beautiful is the view! "Yes . . . and the best of it is, it is all ours!" Or just before dawn, while the sky is still full of bright stars, a young man's strong sweet voice utters a long song from the loma on the west. Or, cantering home from Nambe, the sunrise finds us among those fantastic colored sand hills. Or the first level rays throw our long shadows ahead of us on a sea of golden rabbit-bush in Santa Clara Canyon. Or your dear grandmother sits and laughs to hear about the habits of a household at Santo Domingo and exclaims, "Esa gente de Santo Domingo son del puro cuanto-hay!"* Loosely translated: Those Santo Domingo people are really crazy.

*Enough of this.*

*I am absorbed in the Hano manuscript, and hope to return it to you soon with appreciations. Provisionally, let me say, I hope you don't accept as axiomatic Dr. Parson's hypothesis of a clanless patrilineal Rio-Arriba contaminated with matrilineal institutions from Arizona, although Dr. F. Hawley Ellis seems to endorse it (1946). I hope to knock some spots off it—with your help. I think Dr. Parsons misunderstood Hano to some extent. So did I. I was living too much in Corn-people's pocket. But one had to choose.*

Florence Hawley Ellis, 1906-1991, was an American anthropologist/ethnologist noted for encouraging female anthropologists. She taught and wrote about her field work in different areas of the Southwest United States. From 1945 to 1953 she concentrated on the Rio Grande pueblos mainly in connection with land disputes and water rights.

*You will find my spelling very imperfect, and it is too late for me to adapt to yours. Your* <u>phi</u> *is neat and convenient, but I feel a doubt. Did the Greek* <u>phi</u> *sound like a Tewa aspirated* <u>p</u>*? I still think J. P. Harrington's rough breathing after the consonant gives a fairer impression of it, but you are a better judge of this than I.*

*You need not return the notes I send you on Santa Clara, which are copies I am making for your use.* (These are now with the Dozier papers at the University of Arizona, State Museum Archives.) *You will be disappointed when you come to read them and find how carefully Santiago eliminated all that was not secular. I heard people mentioning the mountains, the trees, as well as the saints and santo rey, santo general* (holy king, holy general) *, and I suppose I ought to have demanded them from him; but he was so firm about denying me such things and I was so sleepy then because I was up every night with two pneumonia patients!*

*I will send you by ordinary post a few supplementary notes and a transcript of the principal contents of the Archive as handed over to the new governor in 1911. I found them very illuminating on the two questions running through pueblo history. As I come across additional matter I hope to send it on to you, without waiting to systematize it myself since that has been my weakness these forty years.*

*My greetings, please, to Mrs. Dozier whom I much desire to know.* (ibid. 5 July 1954)

Among other Dozier publications showing their common interest are "The Hopi-Tewa of Arizona 1954," University of California Publications in **American Archeology and Ethnology** and "Kinship and Linguistic Change among the Arizona Tewa 1955," in the **International Journal of American Linguistics**.

During the following ten years the Aitkens and Doziers became friends, involving at least one visit from the Doziers to England. One letter from Robert to Edward, mostly illegible, was written only a year before Robert's death. The salutation read, *Dear Edward: This is an honor to me, but I find it embarrassing—the Christian name business is post-World War II, you know; here, my very old friends and I never . . . Today, our young use nothing else (!) they often don't know the surnames of their friends! (There is material for the anthropologist!)* (ibid. 22 Aug. 1964)

In May 1990 Mrs. Marianne Dozier, Edward's widow, recalled a memory of the Aitkens. *My contact with Barbara and Robert Aitken was very brief since our children were very young when we visited them. I stayed with them while the Aitkens met a couple of times with Ed. Their home and guest cottage they housed us in were charming. They seemed kind—and very old. When Barbara Aitken—at that time Barbara Freire-Marreco—first went to New Mexico, Ed was 8 years old and she remembered him from that initial visit and research project. Their friendship developed through correspondence and she did send him her research materials. After Ed died, I gave all those things to the University of Arizona.*

She remembered Robert Aitken as *very tall and skinny, I believe he was a Scotsman. He greeted us most graciously.* (Personal communication)

The elderly Barbara and Robert Aitken with Elizabeth Yates who spent time when a child at Kent's Close as the daughter of a neighbor and companion/housekeeper, ca. 1950-1960. Courtesy of Joy Yates.

In 1990 Anya Enos, the Doziers' daughter who lives at Santa Clara Pueblo, answered a request for information. *I believe we (my family) visited Mrs. Aitken in England in 1960. I do know she sent presents to my brother and me at Xmas time. They were always marked with "do not open until 12th night." Until we were adults, we thought the English celebrated Christmas on January 6th. She also sent us surprise packages during the year. Once she sent us a little book about English animals. Apparently she sent us parrot feathers too—found while organizing my father's papers at U. of A. As you can tell, we developed a feeling of fondness for her even though I do not remember her.* (Personal communication)

Barbara Aitkens' fond memories of her southwest American experiences never lessened and nostalgically she recalled them from time to time, especially those with a Christian theme that composed such an important part of her life.

*"A la madrugada nacio el Nino Dios"*
*(Christmas Eve in New Mexico)*

*At dusk, little flickering fires ringed the plaza of the Indian village. Tall masked "grandfathers" stalked from house to house "to bid the children dance." But on the other side of the square a party of Mexican-Spanish boys were singing a carol in their shrill nasal voices:*

Jesus, child divine,
Came forth at the dawning.
    Mary saw Him shine
Like the sun of morning.
The poor mule shied with fright
At that beam of light;
The ox, with mild behaviour,
Breathed to warm the Saviour.

    Mary, fresh and fair,
Welcomes her sweet stranger.
    Swaddles Him with care
And lays Him in the manger.
Sleep, my little Jesus,
Sleep, my Baby precious,
Where my heart's love holds you,
Where my heart enfolds you.

Three magic kings
Come from eastern lands:
Each for Jesus brings
A present in his hands:
The three magic kings –
Each his offering brings,
Lays aside his crown,
Enters, and kneels down.

Unwrap the Babe again!
Bid him hush-a-bye!
Something gives Him pain,
Else He would not cry.
Sleep, my little Jesus,
Sleep, my Baby precious,
Where my heart's love holds you
Where my heart enfolds you.

Farewell, Mother Mary,
Mystical lily bright!
Blest was thy child-bearing
On the Holy Night.

—Aitken, *Verses* 24 Dec. 1952

# ☙ EPILOGUE ☞

In their advanced years, the couple was considered somewhat odd appearing. Both had gaunt faces and wore dark clothing. After a cane was no longer adequate, Barbara propelled around the village by means of a basket-work wheelchair, set in motion by hand-powered sticks that were pumped forward and back. A bell warned of her coming and the vehicle did well going into town, but when returning home up hill, she lacked the strength to move it, so would wait for a passer-by to help push her. Their contemporary neighbors remember Sunday School and prayer meetings Barbara continued even after she became bedridden. She relied on a hand bell for assistance from her bed.

Robert had a stroke in 1965 that left him paralyzed in both body and mind. He died soon after and Barbara paid him tribute by sending his picture to all their friends. Obviously lonely after Robert's death, Barbara appreciated the Broughton neighbors who assisted her; her employees remarking that she treated them more like friends. Only one letter recorded her feelings about his death.

To the Doziers: *Your truly kind letter came two days ago. Thank you so much for it. It does my sad heart good to read the letters of people who appreciated Robert; and he often spoke with pleasure of your visits. No, he never went to the States, but I think he would have enjoyed the Southwest and certainly he would have loved the people. Now, I believe I wrote this to you on the day that* your letter came, but I am not sure that mine was posted, it may have been lost, so I repeat today my grateful thanks.

When you think of Robert, please say for him: "Give rest, O Lord, to thy servant with thy saints, where there is no sorrow, nor sighing, but life everlasting." For he truly was God's servant from his youth onward. (Arizona State Museum, Dozier ND)

During her incapacitated later years, Barbara Aitken propelled herself around the village of Broughton by means of a unique hand-pumped tricycle. Unknown young man. Courtesy of Joy Yates.

Evidence of the Aitkens' years in Broughton still exists. When Barbara's arthritis had become so advanced, hand holds were installed in the stair well of Kent's Close cottage by which she could drag herself upstairs. They are still there. A wood box, about twelve inches long and six inches deep is labeled R. A. 1931 in which Robert kept his Book of Prayer, remains in St. Mary's Church. There are hooks on the back of a pew, in front of the one in which they sat, for holding their canes. At her request and expense, an inscribed stone lies in the church floor near their pew and reads:

Remember before God
ROBERT AITKEN
12 Oct. 1882—24 Sept. 1965
and his wife-BARBARA
11 Dec. 1897—13 Nov. 1967

Her birth year was actually 1879 and her death certificate reads 14 November 1967. Their simple grave stones stand about four feet apart in a far corner of Saint Mary's Churchyard. Robert's reads: R A 1882—1965. There is no inscription on Barbara's.

Barbara Aitken's obituary in the **Andover Advertiser** of November 17, 1967 mentioned her education at Oxford and the fact that she went to New Mexico on a scholarship, but stressed her later contributions to the community and work in connection with the welfare of the elderly and finding foster homes for children. A fine tribute was paid to her by John Harrington many years before, when he wrote in the **American Anthropologist**, Vol. 14, No.3, July-Sept. 1912: *The writer acknowledges his deep indebtedness to Miss B. W. Freire-Marreco, whose study of the social & governmental organization of the Tewa has given her a rare insight into the Tewa customs of expressing relationships and the like.*

As can be seen by her last publication printed at her own expense, *Morning, Noon, and Night with the Light of Life*, Barbara Aitken embraced her religion, which always gave her great comfort. Her mind remained lucid in spite of some depressed days.

The Aitkens' gravestones in St. Mary's churchyard. 1989 photograph by J. Blair

A stained glass window in St. Mary's Church. 1989 photograph by J. Blair

With no children to mourn her passing, her nephew Anthony, her sole surviving relative, inherited the home at Broughton. Her will also mentioned the treasured silver tea set left to her by her uncle: *To the said George Arthur Jonas the silver teapot and stand which belonged to my great uncle Marriott Whitchurch and dated 1780-1781 and 1802-3.* Mr. Jonas had been a family friend and was one of the barristers who acted as a trustee and co-executor of her estate.

Her parting must have been peaceful with the moment of her death marked by Dr. Parr, who recalled her request of him to cut an artery when he thought she was dead. He honored her desire and proved his supposition correct—she was indeed gone. Barbara Freire-Marreco Aitken now belonged to the past.

Her heritage has lived on in her professional words on record, laying a foundation for succeeding anthropologists and her incisive analysis of Pueblo government and relationships was an example for all Pueblo people. Remembered by her many professional and personal colleagues and friends, her deepest imprint may be embedded in the tribal memory of the people of Santa Clara Pueblo and Hopi's First Mesa.

Perhaps, if there is a spirit that guides us to our best-loved earthly places, Barbara's hovers where her heart returned in the years after her stay at Santa Clara Pueblo. In her own words: *In the clear sparkling mountain air of New Mexico, with those wonderful, transparent colored distances where clear rose color overlays clear pale blue without mingling, and the last silvery snows crown the Sangre de Cristo Mountains!* (Arizona State Museum, Dozier 5 July 1954)

### Last Rites

> *Treading on slippery sand,*
> > *Finding the stream run deep,*
> *As I faint away into sleep,*
> > *Give me hold of your hand.*
> *Say, say again the words*
> > *I may partly understand:*
> *Hold me fast with your hand*
> > *Till you lay my hand in the Lord's.*
> > > —Aitken, *Verses*, ND

# ✒ REFERENCES ✒

Aitken, Barbara Whitchurch. *Verses, 1886 to 1953*. Blair Collection, Unpublished.
*Administrative Report*. School of American Archaeology, Santa Fe, 1911, p.111.

Babcock, Barbara A. and Parezo, Nancy J. *Daughters of the Desert*. University of New Mexico Press, Albuquerque, 1988.
*Barnett House Index*. Easter 1918. Private Circulation.
Boulton, Peter. *The Parish of Broughton*. Feb. 1989. Private Circulation.
Bowden, Mark. *General Pitt Rivers, Father of Scientific Archaeology*. Salisbury-Wiltshire Museum, 1984.
Brew, J. O. *One Hundred Years of Anthropology*. Harvard University Press, Boston, 1968.
Butler, C. V. *Barnett House 1914-1964, a Record for its Friends*. University of Oxford, 1964. Private Circulation.

Cattell, J. McKeen and Jaques, Editors. *American Men of Science*. The Science Press, NY, 1933, p.939.
Cave, Paul and Joan. "Broughton's Best!" *Hampshire, the Country Magazine*. Southhampton, Vol. 29, No. 11, pp. 44, 45.
Chapman, Kenneth M. *The Pottery of Santo Domingo Pueblo*. School of American Research, University of New Mexico Press, Albuquerque, 1977, p.19.
Chauvenet, Beatrice. *Hewett and Friends, A Biography of Santa Fe's Vibrant Era*. Museum of New Mexico Press, Santa Fe, 1983.

Deacon, Desley. *Elsie Clews Parsons, Inventing Modern Life*. University of Chicago Press, Chicago, 1977.

*Dictionary of National Biography.* University of Oxford Press, London, 1912-1921, 1931-1940, 1951-1960.

Dockstader, Frederick J. *Great North American Indians: Profiles in Life and Leadership.* Van Nostrand Reinhold Co., NY, 1977, pp. 78, 79.

Douglas, William B. "A World-Quarter Shrine of the Tewa Indians," *Records of the Past.* July-Aug. 1912, Vol. XI, Part IV, pp. 159-173.

Dunn, Dorothy. "Pablita Velarde: Painter of Peublo Life," *El Palacio Magazine.* Museum of New Mexico, Santa Fe, Vol. 59, No. 11, pp.335-341.

Evans-Pritchard, Sir Edward. *A History of Anthropological Thought.* Basic Books, Inc., NY, 1981.

Gacs, Ute; Khan, Aisha; McIntyre, Jerrie and Weinberg, Ruth. *Women Anthropologists.* Greenwood Press, Westport, CN, 1988.

Hall, D. J. *Enchanted Sand: A New Mexico Pilgrimage.* William Morrow and Co., NY, 1933.

Harrington, John. "Tewa Relationship Terms," *American Anthropologist.* American Anthropological Society, Washington, July-Sept. 1912, Vol. 14, No. 3.

Harrington, John. 'The Ethnogeography of the Tewa Indians". *Twenty-ninth Annual Report of the Bureau of American Ethnology.* Smithsonian Institution, Washington 1916.

*International Directory of Anthropologists.* National Research Council, Washington, 1940.

James, Harry C. *Pages from Hopi History.* University of Arizona Press, Tucson, 1974.

Johnson, Eleanor H. "The New School of American Archaeology," *School of American Research Records.* Santa Fe, Folder No. 4, Ca. 1910.

Judd, Neil M. "1910 in el Rito de los Frijoles," *El Palacio Magazine.* Museum of New Mexico, Santa Fe, Fall 1962, pp.139-141.

Kroeber, A. L. "Frederick Ward Putnam," *American Anthropologist.* American Anthropological Society, Washington, Vol. 17, pp.712-718.

Kuper, Adam. *Anthropologists and Anthropology, The British School.* Penguin Books, London, 1973.

Leblanc, Steven A. *The Mimbres People: Ancient Pueblo Painters of the American Southwest.* Thames and Hudson, Ltd., London, 1983.

Lothrop, S. K. "Alfred Marsden Tozzer, 1876-1954", *American Anthropologist*. American Anthropological Society, Washington, Vol. 57, pp.614-617.

*Morning Post*. Oxford. 25 June 1917.

Nestor, Sarah, Editor. "Window on the West": *Collector's El Palacio*. Museum of New Mexico Foundation, Santa Fe, 1989.

Parezo, Nancy J. and Babcock, Barbara. *Women Who Have Worked and Published on Southwest Native Americans*. University of Arizona Press, Tucson, 1985.
Parezo, Nancy J., Editor. *Hidden Scholars*. University of New Mexico Press, Albuquerque, 1993.
Penniman, T. K. "The Pitt Rivers Museum," *The Pitt Rivers Museum Journal*. Oxford. Vol. 52, No.10, pp.243-245.
*Prospectus*. University of Oxford, Department of Applied Social Studies and Social Research, Oxford, 1990-1991.

Schroeder, Albert H. "Pueblos Abandoned in Historic Times," *Handbook of North American Indians*. Smithsonian Institution, Washington, Vol. 9, 1979.
Steward, Julian H. *Alfred Kroeber*. Columbia University Press, NY, 1973.

Walter, Paul A. F. "A Summer in the Pajarito," *Denver and Rio Grande Publication*, after 1910. School of American Research, Santa Fe, Folder No. 6.
Winters, Christopher, Editor. *International Dictionary of Anthropologists*. Garland Publishing, NY & London, 1991.
Woodbury, Richard B. *Alfred Kidder*. Columbia University Press, NY, 1973.

## CORRESPONDENCE OF, TO, FROM AND RELATED TO BARBARA FREIRE-MARRECO AITKEN

Cambridge University: Museum of Archaeology and Anthropology Library:
Barbara Freire Marreco to William Ridgeway, 16 and 19 Jan. 1914

London School of Political and Economic Science:
Barbara Aitken to Bronislaw Malinowski, 22 July 1926, one undated

Museum of New Mexico: Palace of the Governors, Fray Angelico Chavez History Library, Edgar L. Hewett Collection (AC 105):
Barbara Freire-Marreco to Edgar Hewett: 8 Dec.1909, 13 Sept. 1910, 9 Oct. 1910, 2 undated probably late 1910, 25 Nov.1910, 5 Jan. 1911, Report of New Mexico Pueblos' meeting 5 Jan. 1911, 18 Jan. 1911, 2 May 1911, 9 May 1911,

5 Nov. 1911, Petition in Spanish ND 13 June 1913, 16 June 1916

Barbara Freire-Marreco to Helen Darbishire: 27 Apr. 1911
Barbara Freire-Marreco to Commissioner of Indian Affairs: 28 Apr. 1911
Barbara Freire-Marreco to Secretary School of Archaeology: 8 Dec. 1913
Barbara Freire-Marreco to Mr. Walter, Museum of New Mexico: Fourth of July

Edgar Hewett to Robert Marett: 16 Dec. 1911
Edgar Hewett to Barbara Freire-Marreco: 21 Dec. 1911
Edgar Hewett to Lorenzo Hubbell: 15 Nov. 1912
Edgar Hewett to John Harrington: 11 Dec. 1912, 19 Dec. 1912
Edgar Hewett to Santiago Naranjo: 16 Jan. 1913

President of Somerville College to Edgar Hewett: 3 May 1910
Thomas Dozier to Edgar Hewett: 16 Aug. 1910
Alice Fletcher to Edgar Hewett: 18 Feb. 1911, 4 Mar.1911
Robert Marett to Edgar Hewett: 21 Nov. 1911
D. Abram to Edgar Hewett: 5 Jan. 1912
Clara True to Edgar Hewett: 13 May 1912, ND in 1912 file, 13 Aug.1912
William Johnson to Edgar Hewett: 25 Nov. 1912
John Myers to Edgar Hewett: 26 Dec. 1913

Smithsonian Institution, National Anthropological Archives including the
former Bureau of American Ethnology and the Bureau of Indian Affairs:
(Fewkes, Freire-Marreco Aitken, Harrington, Hewett, Hodge, and Valentine
files):
Barbara Freire-Marreco to Frederick Hodge: 24 Sept. 1910, 8 Dec. 1910, 17
Dec. 1910, 22-23 Dec. 1910, 20 Feb. 1911, 27 May 1911, 11 June 1911, 18
June 1911, 4 July 1911, 30 Aug. 1911, 11 Sept. 1911, 1 Nov. 1911, 12 Apr.
1912, 28 June 1912, early Sept. 1912, early Jan. 1913, 25 Feb. 1913, 27 Feb.
1913, 26 Apr. 1913, 9 May 1913, 19 June 1913, 11 Aug. 1913, 11 Nov. 1913,
9 Dec. 1913, 2 Feb. 1914, 3 Feb. 1914, 3 Mar. 1914, 10 Mar. 1914, 27 Mar.
1914, 3 Apr. 1914, 4 June 1914, 9 July 1914, 4 Aug. 1914

Frederick Hodge to Barbara Freire-Marreco: Dec. 1910, 9 June 1911, 26 June
1911, 30 June 1911, 11 Oct. 1911, 7 Dec. 1911, 20 Apr. 1912, 9 July 1912,
19 Sept. 1912, 25 Nov. 1912, 24 Jan. 1913, 27 Feb. 1913, Undated telegram,
30 Sept. 1913, Feb. 1914, 20 Feb. 1914, 17 Mar. 1914, 23 Mar. 1914, 15 Apr.
1914, 28 Apr. 1914, 13 June 1914, 20 July 1914, 19 Aug. 1914, 23 Oct. 1914

Frederick Hodge to Robert Valentine: 11 Nov. 1910, 14 Dec. 1910, 17 Dec.
1910.

Frederick Hodge to C. F. Hauke: 28 Nov. 1910
Frederick Hodge to Clark Wissler and George Gordon: Identical 31 July 1912
Frederick Hodge to John Harrington: 11 Dec. 1912, 19 Dec. 1912

Memos to Frederick Hodge from H. W. Dorsey, J. G. Gurley, W. J. Gill, C. T.
Hauke and Miss Clark, dated 19 Sept. 1911 to 17 Aug. 1914
C. F. Hauke to Frederick Hodge: 22 Nov. 1910
D. Abram to Frederick Hodge: 5 Jan. 1912
M. W. Modey to Frederick Hodge: 23 Jan. 1913

Barbara Freire-Marreco Aitken to John Harrington: 9 Oct. 1910, 10 Oct.
1910, 20 Oct. 1910, 4 Nov. 1910, before 25 Nov. 1910, Jan. 1911?, 18 Feb.
1911, 19 June 1911, Feb. 1912, Dec. 1912 (probably should be 1910), 8 Jan.
1913, after 8 Jan. 1913, Jan. 1913, 28 Jan. 1913, 4 Feb. 1913, 5 Feb. 1913,
before 10 Feb. 1913, 10 Feb. 1913, after 26 Feb. 1913, 19 Nov. 1913, 5 Feb.
1914, 26 May 1914, 26 June 1914, 13 Dec. 1919?, 2 Sept. 1920, 16 Mar. 1921,
16 Jan. 1924, 20 Mar. 1924, 1 June 1924, 23 Oct. 1924, 8 Dec. 1924, 5 Jan.
1925, 28 Jan. 1925, 2 Mar. 1925, 25 Apr. 1931

Barbara Freire-Marreco Aitken to Edgar Hewett: 24 Nov. 1910, 3 Jan. 1911,
28 Jan. 1911
Barbara Freire-Marreco to Robert Valentine: 28 Apr. 1911
Barbara Freire-Marreco to Commissioner of Indian Affairs: 29 Apr. 1911,
Sept. 1911, 15 Apr. 1914
Barbara Freire-Marreco to J. G. Gurley: 9 July 1914
Barbara Aitken to Walter Fewkes: 23 July 1923, 27 Aug. 1923, 3 May 1924

Robert Valentine to Frederick Hodge: 16 Dec. 1910
Robert Valentine to Shelby Singleton: 5 May 1911
Robert Valentine to Barbara Freire-Marreco: 6 May 1911

Edgar Hewett to Alice Fletcher: 9 Jan. 1911
Report of New Mexico Pueblos Council Meeting: 20 Jan. 1911
Petition to Commissioner of Indian Affairs from New Mexico Pueblos: 26 May
1911
Shelby Singleton to Barbara Freire-Marreco: 25 July 1911
Herbert Smith to Barbara Freire-Marreco: 4 Feb. 1913
Walter Fewkes to Barbara Aitken: 11 Aug. 1923, 3 Jan. 1924
J. D. DeHuff to Clara True: 29 May 1925

University of Arizona, Arizona State Museum Archives:
Edward P. Dozier Papers, MS23, Sg4, S1, F149

Barbara Aitken to Edward Dozier: 19 May 1954, 22 May 1954, 5 July 1954, ?1965
Robert Aitken to Edward Dozier: 10 Sept. 1964

University of California, Berkely, Bancroft Library,
Records of the Department of Anthropology (CU-23, box23):
  Barbara Freire-Marreco Aitken to Edward Gifford: 6 May 1916, 11 Mar. 1933
  Edward Gifford to Barbara Aitken: 9 Feb. 1933, 4 Apr. 1933
  Barbara Aitken to Alfred Kroeber: 30 Dec. 1927, 13 Apr. 1928, 24 Apr. after 1928
  Alfred Kroeber to Barbara Aitken: 13 Mar. 1928
  Edward Gifford to Alfred Kroeber Memo: 5 Apr. 1933

University of New Mexico, Maxwell Museum of Anthropology:
W. W. Hill Collection:
  Barbara Aitken to W.W. Hill, 28 May 1943

University of Oxford, Bodleian Library: Room 132, Duke Humphries Library,
MS. Myres 1, fols.54-110, 10, 24, 57, 59, 61, 82-83, 84, 85-86, MS. Myres 16,
120 General Correspondence:
  Barbara Freire-Marreco Aitken to John Myres: 30 Apr. 1906, 10 May 1906,
  11 May 1906, 16 May 1906, Two - 19 May 1906, 21 May 1906, 14 June 1906,
  11 July 1906, 9 Aug. 1906, 9 Sept. 1907, 16 Sept. 1907, 24 Nov. 1907, 6 Dec.
  1907, 18 Feb. 1908, 28 Mar. 1908, 29 Aug. 1908, 2 Sept. 1908, 7 Sept. 1908,
  10 Dec. 1908, 1 May 1909, 16 June 1909, 1 July 1909, 5 July 1909, 14 July
  1909, 3 Nov. 1910, 15 June 1910, 31 Aug. 1910, 6 Oct. 1910, 13 Oct. 1910,
  27 Mar. 1911, 27 Aug. 1911, 31 Aug. 1911, 10 Jan. 1913, 22 Mar.1913, Whit
  Sunday 1913, 5 July 1913, Undated 1919?, Undated after 1920, 20 July 1924,
  22 July 1924, 21 July 1927, 22 Feb. 1934, 7 July 1935, 22 Jan. 1936, 15 Aug.
  1943, 22 July 1946, 16 Aug. 1948 or 1949, St. Crispin's Day 1949, 12 Oct.
  1949, 12 Oct. 1951, 4 Dec. 1951, 11 Jan. 1952, 13 Mar. 1952, 6 Aug. 1952?,
  11 Aug. 1952, 25 Mar. 1953

  John Myres to Barbara Freire-Marreco: 10 May 1906, 18 May 1906, 21 May
  1906, 12 Feb 1908, 27 Mar. 1908, 12 May 1909, 17 June 1909, 21 June 1909,
  ND 1909, 18 July 1909, 5 Oct. 1909, 24 Oct. 1910, 24 Apr. 1911, 30 Aug.
  1911, 29 Dec. 1911
  John Myres to ? 6 May 1906
  John Myres to Selection Committee, Somerville Research Fellowship: 20 May
  1909, 27 May 1909
  John Myres to Alice Fletcher: 16 July 1909
  John Myres to Mrs. Gertrude Freire-Marreco: 14 Oct. 1910

Robert Aitken to John Myres: 27 Apr. 1924, 20 July 1924, 25 Jan. 1927, 10 Dec. 1943, 6 July 1950, 25 Oct. 1950, 8 Aug. 1952, ? 12 1953

Barnett House, Department of Applied Social Studies and Social Research:
Barbara Freire-Marreco to Sidney Ball: Easter Sunday 1918, 5 Apr. 1918.
Sidney Ball to Barbara Freire-Marreco: 3 Apr. 1918.
Anne Thackery to Barbara Freire-Marreco: 3 Apr. 1918

Pitt Rivers School of Anthropology and Museum Ethnogrphy:
Barbara Freire-Marreco's Albums: New Mexico and Arizona 1911. No.34,
New Mexico and Arizona 1913
Barbara Freire-Marreco's Collections: Yavapai or Mohave-Apache
Reservation. McDowell, AZ, Dec. 1910
New Mexico and Arizona 1911, No.1911.86.1.12F
New Mexico and Arizona 1912 – 1913, No. 1913.87.1-136
Barbara Aitken: "Difficulty of Identifying Kachina Masks."(Attached to Beatrice
Blackwood's undated collection of Hopi Kachina paintings)

Balfour Library:
Henry Balfour to Barbara Freire-Marreco: 18 July 1918.
Barbara Aitken to Henry Balfour: 29 May 1936

Somerville College:
Barbara Freire-Marreco to Helen Darbishire: 13 Sept. 1909, 16 Sept. 1909, 18 Sept. 1909, 13 Dec. 1909, 19 Aug. 1910, 26 June 1910, 17 Feb. 1911, 27 Apr. 1911
Barbara Freire-Marreco to Anthropological Society: Oct. ?
Frederick Hodge to John Harrington: 17 Feb. 1911

Unpublished Personal Correspondence:
Barbara Aitken to Philip Waggett: 1928
Robert Aitken to Barbara Aitken: 14 Sept. 1938
Barbara Aitken to Beatrice Blackwood: 1948, 26 June 1959, 13 Aug. 1962, others undated
Barbara Aitken to Pablita Velarde: Our old lady's day
Barbara Aitken to Robert Parr: Undated notes
Beatrice Chauvenet to Blairs: 29 Mar. 1989
Anya Dozier Enos to Blairs: 21 Feb. 1990
Marianne Dozier to Blairs 1 May 1990